Divided
Passions

NORTHEASTERN UNIVERSITY 1898–1998

THE NORTHEASTERN SERIES ON GENDER, CRIME, AND LAW

Edited by Claire Renzetti, St. Joseph's University

Kimberly J. Cook

Divided
Passions

Public Opinions

on Abortion and

the Death Penalty

NORTHEASTERN UNIVERSITY PRESS *Boston*

Northeastern University Press

Library of Congress Cataloging-in-Publication Data

Cook, Kimberly J., 1961–
    Divided passions : public opinions on abortion and the death
penalty / Kimberly J. Cook.
        p.   cm. — (The Northeastern series on gender, crime, and law)
    Includes bibliographical references and index.
    ISBN 1-55553-330-2 (cloth : alk. paper)
    1. Abortions—United States.   2. Capital punishment—United States.
3. Abortion—United States—Public opinion.   4. Capital punishment—
United States—Public opinion.   5. United States—Public opinion.
HQ767.5.U5C666   1998
363.46'0973—dc21   97-20960

Designed by Diane Gleba Hall

Composed in Caslon by G&S Typesetters, Austin, Texas. Printed and bound by Maple Press, York, Pennsylvania. The paper is Sebago Antique, an acid-free sheet.

MANUFACTURED IN THE UNITED STATES OF AMERICA

02   01   00   99   98   5   4   3   2   1

For Greg

Contents

Acknowledgments

This book would not exist without the support of many friends and colleagues. I am very grateful for the assistance and support of many people: my Ph.D. dissertation committee at the University of New Hampshire; Murray A. Straus, Sally K. Ward, Michael Donnelly, Kristine Baber, and Michael Radelet (University of Florida), who guided me through many of the early conceptual issues with my dissertation (which this study extends). Also, my graduate school professors to whom I owe a debt of gratitude are: Larry Hamilton, Bud Khleif, David Finkelhor, and Arnold Linsky. Colleagues at Mississippi State University during my first year as a faculty member: Karin Mack, Xiaohe Xu, Barbara Costello, Greg Dunaway, Phyllis Gray-Ray, Ralph Brown, Christopher Duncan (who really encouraged me to send this to the publisher), and Brad Anderson. Colleagues at the University of Southern Maine: Piers Beirne, Jim Messerschmidt, Barbara Perry, and Wendy Chapkis. I am grateful to Dean Richard Stebbins and Provost Mark Lapping for their support. Also, the University of Southern Maine Faculty Senate Research Fund partially subsidized this project and I am deeply grateful for their support. And to Joe R. Feagin, whose advice and moral support have been invaluable: Thanks! Other people along the way have been there to provide moral support and practical support in the process of writing this book: Deena Peschke, Teresita Camacho, Judith Jackson Pomeroy, Earle and Judith Custer, Barbara Johnson (who transcribed all the taped interviews), Nick Leonard, Bill and Joan Humphrey, George, Gloria and Lisa Perrine, Alan Cameron, Hazel Ferland, Denise Donnelly, Debi Van Ausdale, Phoebe Stambaugh, Mona Danner, Walter DeKeseredy, Michael Mello, Liesel Miller Ritchie, Scott Brassart and Bill Frohlich at Northeastern University Press, and my work-study student Melissa Gower.

I am not a writer by trade, as copy editor Susan Cassidy knows so well. She persevered through the manuscript with an incredibly keen eye, integrity, and respect for the material. To Susan goes much credit, and I also thank Yvonne Ramsey for her post-edit review of the manuscript; any mistakes that remain are my own. I appreciate Claire Renzetti's support for getting this book into production. And to Ann Twombly at Northeastern University Press, thanks for the support and guidance through this process. You have helped to make my first book a really fun and interesting experience!

My deepest appreciation is reserved for my family. Deanna and Kenny Gallant have "adopted" my son and me as their own and their unconditional love is a miracle. My oldest best friend, Rhonda Pratte, has been a steady and loving friend since we were six years old. My parents, Everett and Freda Cook, who taught me how to work hard and persevere through all the bumpy roads. My sister and brother-in-law, Carolee and Mike White and children; Meghan, Andrea, Jessica, and Jay, who always shared their home with my son and me (and Jessica still remembers to say "I'm a feminist!" when she stands up for herself). My brother Rick Cook and his family. For the many gifts from Bob Whitcomb, I am deeply thankful. Finally, to my son, Greg, who has been the greatest joy, inspiration, and challenge I've ever known. Now that the book is done, I owe him a terrific vacation. This book is dedicated to him with all my love.

Introduction

Upon his return from the nascent United States of America, Alexis de Tocqueville observed, "The taste for well-being is the prominent and indelible feature of democratic ages" (Tocqueville 1899, 27). Tocqueville referred to this as a "deep seated passion" in the American people, stemming from their blind quest for equality. In many respects this book examines "the taste for well-being" in modern society: the interviewees are sharing with me and with the reader their notions of how to advance the well-being of people in the United States today. These are indeed "deep seated passions," for few have been complacent about the issues of abortion and capital punishment. The bitter passions that these issues elicit are flamed by religious beliefs, political persuasions, and personal experiences; those who shared their time and opinions with me have expressively articulated these passions. The title of this book, *Divided Passions*, is intended to capture both the spirit and the divisiveness of these controversial social issues.

This is a study of the cultural forces that contribute to the formation of personal opinions on moral issues. What a person thinks about abortion is largely influenced by what he or she *believes* is the answer to the question "When does life begin?" Likewise, what a person thinks about the death penalty is largely influenced by what he or she *believes* about its deterrent value, its cost effectiveness, and its retributive value. What people believe to be real will be real in its consequences, as W. I. Thomas has reminded us. Attitudes people hold also play an important role in shaping personal opinions on these social issues. Respondents shared with me their attitudes toward women and the women's movement, as well as their attitudes toward ethnic minorities, who are believed by many death penalty supporters to be largely responsible for the crime problem. One respondent, Warren, believes that pregnant women are not capable of thinking rationally, and that in African-American cultures there is a tendency toward "fornication" and "out of wedlock births" as well as reliance on criminal activity to gain material possessions. Another respondent, Mildred, expressed her positive attitude toward the women's movement, based on her experience as a "founding mother," as well as her conviction that "it takes a village" to ensure the well-being of all children. Mildred is an African American who values what she calls this "Black idea" of community responsibility.

Regardless of the diversity of opinions on abortion and capital punishment, there is a common foundation among the respondents; they all place a high value on quality of life. For some that value is expressed by promoting an anti-abortion agenda because they feel that to deny the unborn their "inherent" right to life destroys the quality of life for all in modern society. For others, that value is expressed by promoting a pro-choice agenda because they believe that children who are truly wanted are more likely to be provided for effectively by their parents than are unwanted children forced upon their parents. The high value placed on quality of life is also expressed in opinions on capital punishment. Some support the death penalty because they believe it is the ultimate expression of how much society values innocent human life, while others oppose the death penalty because they feel that legal executions are barbaric and undermine quality of life by promoting brutality.

This study proceeds in three parts. First, the histories and theories of abortion and capital punishment are reviewed, and these issues are examined in the context of recent presidential elections. Second, the bulk of the study is an analysis of four groups of respondents: a) pro-choice, anti–death penalty; b) pro-choice, pro–death penalty; c) pro-life, anti–death penalty; and d) pro-life and pro–death penalty. Third, interpretations and conclusions are presented.

Data and Methods

This book employs two methods of data gathering and analysis. First, public opinion polls are examined to demonstrate the frequency of four sets of opinions on abortion and capital punishment in the United States. Public opinion data used are from the General Social Surveys (GSS) from 1977 through 1994. The surveys are suitable for exploring the overall contours of American opinion over those seventeen years, which were selected because of the increasing attention abortion and capital punishment have been given in national elections since 1976. The GSS is a full probability, nationally representative sample of English-speaking adults in the United States (Davis and Smith 1992). The surveys are conducted in the spring of each year, through personal interviews. Because of the size, cost, and complexity of the surveys, the designs used have included different survey forms and rotations, split samples, and split ballots. Over the years, compromises have been made in order to allow inclusion of as many questions as possible, within a reasonable cost range. These compromises mean that not all questions are repeated every year, and with split ballots not all respondents are asked the same questions. The trade-off is seen in the fact that diminished numbers of respondents have answered key questions.

Second, qualitative methods were used to gather interview data on people's opinions of abortion and the death penalty. In the tradition of "grounded theory" (Glaser and Strauss 1967), which "depends on methods that take the researcher into and close to the real world so that the results and findings are 'grounded' in the empirical world" (Patton 1990, 67), I employ qualitative methods to discover the context of the interviewees' opinions. To this end, the qualitative research in this book delves into the texture and complexities of these opinions. The data were obtained through in-depth interviews with volunteers for the study, what Patton refers to as "conversations with a purpose." The interviews began in June 1995 while I was employed in Mississippi (although I had already made plans to begin a new position in Maine later that year). Initially, I intended to use snowball sampling by relying on the "information rich" extreme cases (Patton 1990, 169). I spoke with Carolyn, the director of the local Crisis Pregnancy Center in rural Mississippi. Upon describing my research project I asked if I could interview her. She agreed, and when I conducted the interview, I asked Carolyn if she knew of others who might be interested in this research and willing to participate. She hesitated to give me people's names without their consent, so this snowball strategy did not work well. Since the first problem faced by qualitative researchers is that of access, I was back to the drawing board.

I then relied on "purposeful sampling" and recruitment of interviewees through an advertisement in a local newspaper. My ad[1] ran for three days, in which time twelve people volunteered to be interviewed. The first person with whom I had an appointment failed to show up. Another caller decided not to participate after I described the project to her. The ad yielded ten more respondents with whom I had conversations: four pro-life and pro–death penalty, three pro-choice and anti–death penalty, one pro-life and anti–death penalty, and two pro-choice and pro–death penalty. Upon meeting these volunteers at a place convenient to them, I introduced myself and briefly described the research again, asked for their consent to tape-record the conversation, and began by discussing abortion. The interviews were later transcribed.

When I resumed the research (February 1996) in Maine, I placed an advertisement in a local paper with the same solicitation I had used in Mississippi. This ad also ran for three days, during which time I was inundated with responses. A total of eighty-seven callers volunteered to be interviewed. I asked callers into which categories they would put themselves regarding abortion and the death penalty, "pro" or "con." Based on their responses, and my need for adequate diversity in opinion sets, I chose those who called first. Having budgeted money to interview approximately twenty people, I could not have provided financial compensation for all those expressing their willingness to participate. Twenty-one appointments were made. Two people canceled their appointments, which left me with nineteen interviewees: five pro-choice and anti–death penalty, three pro-choice and pro–death penalty, five pro-life and anti–death penalty, and six pro-life and pro–death penalty. Courtney requested her geographical location remain confidential.

Upon interviewing a few of the volunteers, I was faced with the dilemma of re-categorizing them. In the case of Johann, for instance, it became increasingly obvious that while he described himself as tolerant of legal abortion his overwhelming objections to abortion were far more abundant. Therefore, since most of our conversation revolved around his anti-abortion feelings and opinions, I have placed him in the appropriate group of anti-abortion and pro–death penalty. Similarly, with respect to some death penalty opinions, Felicia and Leigh

Table 1 Interviewees by Group

ONE pro-choice anti–death penalty	TWO pro-choice pro–death penalty	THREE pro-life anti–death penalty	FOUR pro-life pro–death penalty
Emma	Autumn	Bob	Harold
Madeline	Johnnie*	Connor	Harry
Felicia	Maria	Glenn	Johann
Mildred	Rick*	Louise	Leo
Leigh*	Olivia	Marcia	Suzanne
Sara*	Courtney**	Jeanie*	Warren
Sonny*			Carolyn*
Wayne			Enoch*
			Rebel*
			Dave*

Mississippi interviews; others are Maine
**Geographical location undisclosed*

expressed a low level of tolerance for capital punishment, and the majority of our conversations hinged on their deep objections to the death penalty. Therefore, I have placed them in the appropriate groups also.

Either at the beginning or at the end of the interviews, I asked interviewees to select their own pseudonym. Some people chose the name of a loved one, one man chose a character from the Bible, and another chose "Rebel" because of his love for the South and the memorabilia associated with the "War of Northern Aggression." The sampling yielded a good mixture of opinions central to my research. This method allowed for an examination of the "internal homogeneity" among like-minded interviewees, as well as the "external heterogeneity" of those with differing sets of opinions (Patton 1990, 403).

After each conversation, I recorded my notes and wrote summaries of the perspectives shared with me. A professional transcriptionist was hired to transfer the data to computer disk, verbatim. I then proofread each transcript with the tape recording of the conversation, to fill in any gaps within the transcript (I often could decipher difficult passages on the tape since I was the one who conducted the interviews) so that the exact wording was preserved. The tapes were then destroyed to ensure the anonymity of the interviewees. I printed and coded the transcribed conversations using a list of concepts and themes that emerged from the data. Separate files were constructed based on each of the major themes of the conversations, within each set of opinions. This yielded 160 pages of single-spaced data output for each of the first three sets of opinions. The last set of opinions, pro-life and pro–death penalty, resulted in 325 pages of coded data. All the data were then analyzed using a cross-case analysis (Patton 1990, 376), which appears in subsequent chapters of this book. In the chapters that follow, I have chosen to let the interviewees' voices dominate and to save my analytical and interpretive comments for the end of the book. The advantages of this method of reporting the findings are that the words of the interviewees are uncluttered by my own (as much as possible) and that the reader can hear the interviewees more authentically. The disadvantage is that I sacrifice some of the analytical points that could be made within each chapter.

I made several assumptions before I began the interviews. First, I assumed the interviewees were reasonably up to date on current events with respect to abortion and capital punishment. I assumed they were regular readers of a newspaper (or they would not have responded to my advertisement), and therefore were generally aware of the state of the laws on abortion and capital punishment. Second, I assumed that each person would be influenced by religious convictions. This proved to be a valid assumption in most cases, but there were some interviewees who described themselves as either "atheist" or "anti-religious" and for whom religion played no role in the formation of their opinions. Third, I assumed that interviewees would be sufficiently aware of local and national politics to answer some basic questions related to abortion and death penalty politics, and I assumed that they voted in national and local elections. This assumption proved valid in all but two cases.

Since the group of interviewees comprises people from both Mississippi and Maine, one might expect regional distinctions to become apparent. On the whole this was not the case. The people interviewed in Mississippi were a bit more likely to discuss their religious convictions than those interviewed in Maine, but this may have been due to "Yankee individualism" and the private nature of religious convictions in the Northeast. Or it may have resulted from the pervasive influence of Christian churches as centers for community activity and social life in the Deep South. On the other hand, several of those interviewed in Mississippi were not native southerners. Some discussed their opinions as "southern," but this was not a prominent theme. With the exception of Rebel, southernness was not a salient identity the members of this group claimed or denied. Among those interviewed in Maine, most were Roman Catholic natives of New England. However, none in this group discussed their opinions as "Yankee" opinions. I come from Maine, but this fact was discussed only with Rebel, who defined for me the difference between a Yankee and a Damn Yankee.

REBEL There's a difference between a Yankee and a Damn Yankee.
  KC What's the difference?
REBEL You know the difference?
  KC No, I don't know the difference.
REBEL A Yankee comes down to Mississippi to visit. A Damn Yankee comes down here to live.
  KC Well, I came down here to live.
REBEL Well, you're going back, you said.
  KC Right.
REBEL You're just a Yankee, not a Damn Yankee. But that's the difference between them.

Throughout these conversations, I was asked questions by the person I was interviewing. When that occurred I answered her or him honestly or tried to hedge the question as best I could without disrupting the progress of the conversation. Among feminist researchers this is seen as a difficult area for the qualitative interviewer (Oakley 1981; Finch 1984; Haney 1996). In some cases answering personal questions with complete honesty would have run the risk of ending the conversation. In other cases, answering the questions factually helped the conversation to flow. Therefore, I did not apply a strict rule of what I should do under these circumstances, but rather followed my own intuition as to what was best for keeping the conversation on course.

I did some "paced" self-disclosure when that assisted in establishing rapport (Reinharz 1992, 32). For instance, in a number of conversations the topics of single parenting and welfare recipiency were broached by the interviewee. Regardless of their opinions about abortion, interviewees considered single parenting as less desirable for children. Because I am a single parent, Olivia said to me, "Of course, you know what I mean because you've been there." Or, as Bob put it, "You said you had a son, but I don't see any marital jewelry, so . . . whatever, the point remains that children do better when they have a mother and a father in the house." I did not dispute such opinions in the conversations.

Despite my attempts to adhere to my interview guide, many conversations ended up being guided by the interviewee (Reinharz 1992, 23–24). Often interviewees would say, "And I'll tell you another thing about that . . ." and move on to the next issue that was important to them. This helped me to move through the conversation in a more natural fashion, as they were comfortable enough to control the direction of the conversation. Interestingly, some of the most useful data emerged from those moments when the interviewee felt compelled to say whatever was on her or his mind. Common themes that emerged in this way are welfare dependency, "proper" roles for women, ethnic tensions, and interviewees' "real" feelings about politics.

I have chosen to use the categories "pro-choice" and "pro-life" (rather than pro-abortion or anti-choice) because these are the labels the interviewees used to describe themselves. Chapters 3 through 7 move from "left" to "right"—that is, from political liberals to political conservatives.

A note on generalizability is in order. The qualitative data presented in this book should not be viewed as generalizable to the general population, but rather should be seen as in-depth explorations of the opinions of the people who volunteered to be interviewed. The extent to which these qualitative data are representative of the general public cannot be measured. Therefore, I caution the reader not to make broad generalizations from these qualitative data to the entire population.

Abortion and Capital Punishment in the United States

Scholars who are concerned with abortion and capital punishment have been curious about the seemingly inconsistent views of those who oppose legal abortion and also support the government's use of legal executions (Luker 1984; Blanchard 1994; Blanchard and Prewitt 1993; Johnson and Tamney 1988; Claggett and Shafer 1991). This study is an empirical exploration of abortion and capital punishment opinions in four broad categories: pro-choice and anti–death penalty, pro-choice and pro–death penalty, pro-life and anti–death penalty, and pro-life and pro–death penalty.

The law, and therefore politics, plays a critical role in these points of view. In most states and under federal statute, the death penalty is a legally permissible punishment for those who are convicted of specific forms of first-degree murder in which the aggravating circumstances outweigh the mitigating circumstances. For the death penalty to be used, a series of legal procedures must be followed. The prosecutors must prove beyond a reasonable doubt that the defendant committed the murder with the deliberate intention of killing the victim. Upon conviction, the prosecutor must demonstrate (to a jury and/or to a judge) that there are sufficiently heinous aspects to the murder that outweigh any other elements that could mitigate the culpability of the convicted murderer. Once the convicted murderer is sentenced to death, the long process of legal appeals begins, which is designed to guard the due process rights of the condemned. Throughout this process the prosecutor acts on behalf of the state (and the citizens of that state) to secure an execution of the defendant. Prosecutors often rely on general public support for capital punishment to advance the slow journey toward death (Von Drehle 1995). With executions through 1996 included, there have been 358 legal executions in the United States since the Supreme Court reauthorized capital punishment in 1976. Problems with racial disproportionality persist: of those 358, 135 (37.7 percent) were African American and 201 (56.1 percent) were white, with other ethnic minorities accounting for the remainder.[1] Race of the victim is another important variable in detecting racial discrimination in death sentences (Baldus, Woodworth, and Pulaski 1990; Gross and Mauro 1989). Baldus et al. report that "the average defendant with a white victim faced a statistically significant 7- to 9-percentage-point higher risk of a death sentence than did a similarly situated defendant whose victim was black." More advanced analysis confirmed this, indicating that when the victim is white, the defendant faces "average odds of receiving a death sentence that are 4.3 times larger" than when the victim is African American (Baldus et al. 1990, 401).

The law is also an important element in the abortion process. A woman considering abortion must know the laws of her state when seeking to legally terminate her pregnancy. States vary with regard to the legal restrictions on abortion services. The Pennsylvania Abortion Control Act, for example, requires that a woman wait for a period of time, notify her parents or seek judicial bypass if she is underage, and read material designed to discourage her from having an abortion. After meeting these requirements, she may then follow through on her decision to have the abortion performed legally. However, if she has no medical insurance or is a Medicaid recipient, she must pay in cash for the procedure.

There are approximately 1.5 million legal abortions performed annually in the United States (Henshaw 1990). Of women who have abortions in the United States, the vast majority are over eighteen years old, 64.4 percent have never married, 45.4 percent have never had a live birth, and 42.5 percent had one or two live births prior to their abortions. A slight majority report that they were using contraceptives at the time they became pregnant (Henshaw and Kost 1996). The majority of abortions occur within the first twelve weeks of pregnancy, with only 1.5 percent of all abortions being performed after the twentieth week of gestation.

The legal processes of capital punishment and abortion are necessarily quite different, but the role of the state is the same: to ensure that the laws are followed. The paradox is that these are legal procedures to prevent, or safeguard, an action in one situation (abortion) and to produce an action, under due process, in another (execution). When considering the legal security of these state-controlled activities, it is not uncommon for legislatures to rely on public opinion research as a barometer for their constituents' views on these matters. Abortion opponents and death penalty supporters argue that public opinion clearly demonstrates a desire to limit legal access to abortion and to increase or preserve the use of legal executions.

Furthermore, reliance on state and federal law to preserve the death penalty and restrict abortion implies that when departures from the legal prescriptions occur, the state may use its authority to punish those who have violated the laws. The death penalty is the ultimate punishment for those who are convicted of capital murder and appears to be safe from abolition for the time being. Death penalty retentionists want to preserve or augment the punitive authority of states to execute convicted murderers, while death penalty opponents want to abolish or limit the state's authority to carry out executions. Abortion opponents want to extend the punitive authority of the state to criminalize abortion and punish those who have or perform abortions, while abortion rights advocates want the procedure to remain a safe and legal option for women in the United States.

Since the middle of this century Americans have debated the issue of abortion (Luker 1984), while there has been a concurrent increase in public support for death sentencing (Fox, Radelet, and Bonsteel 1990). Public opinion research reveals that Americans are ambivalent about legalized abortion; 75 percent support abortion in the cases of fetal detect, health risk to the pregnant woman, and rape or incest resulting in conception, while approximately 50 percent support various restrictions on access to abortion (parental consent or judicial bypass, husband notification, mandatory waiting periods, and informed consent regulations). Nearly 10 percent of the general public between 1987 and 1991 opposed abortion under all circumstances (Cook, Jelen, and Wilcox 1992).

Public opinion research on capital punishment reveals that the vast majority of Americans support the death penalty, which reflects an increase in support over the last thirty years. Gallup polls show that in 1966 public support for the death penalty had reached a low of 42 percent, but by 1989 support had climbed to 80 percent (Gallup 1986, 1989). This increase has been attributed to greater fear of crime (Bohm 1991). However, Fox, Radelet, and Bonsteel (1990) reveal that when people are asked whether they prefer the death penalty or life without parole, preference for the death penalty drops to 43 percent.

Abortion

In direct response to these opinions, some special interest groups have become active in seeking to recriminalize abortion, while others have pushed to preserve legal abortion choice (Luker 1984; Ginsburg 1989; Petchesky 1990). It is necessary to place the current issues in their historical and social contexts as well as to examine both the efforts of anti-abortion groups and the struggles of their foes.

Abortion Legislation since the Victorian Era

The history of abortion and abortion policy in the United States is long and complex. Religious, medical, and ethnic groups have influenced evolving standards of social decency and propriety and have played important roles in shaping public opinion on abortion (Davis 1985). Before the late nineteenth century, within the confines of Victorian morality legislation, deliberate termination of a pregnancy was regarded primarily as a means of fertility control (Gordon 1976). Because women often relied on various forms of self-induced abortion, both the decision and the act of abortion were widely considered a domestic matter. Social perception of terminating an unwanted pregnancy served not to proscribe abortion by political interference, but to place abortion within the sphere of domestic privacy. However, this social approval of deliberate termination was not absolute throughout the pregnancy; abortion was popularly proscribed after "quickening" of the fetus (Luker 1984; Davis 1985; Gordon 1976; Petchesky 1990).

As medical knowledge expanded into obstetrics and gynecology, professional men became increasingly involved in the termination procedure and in the abortion debate that later developed (Luker 1984; Davis 1985; Gordon 1976). In 1847, the establishment of the American Medical Association served as a vehicle that allowed physicians to lobby and exert political pressure on policy makers to increase control over reproductive health matters; the formerly private issues of pregnancy and abortion quickly became subject to regulation and control by the field of scientific medicine (Luker 1984). Davis (1985) discusses many of the interest groups that influenced the movement toward criminalization of abortion in the late nineteenth century, specifically those religious groups that opposed abortion on moral grounds. Eventually, according to Gordon (1976), women lost their original right to self-defined fertility control and were forced to succumb to the power of the male-controlled medical profession. Through the Comstock Laws, procuring contraceptive and birth control information and devices became illegal (Davis 1985). There are no systematic data available to inform us how the general population regarded these new laws at the time.

In the middle of the twentieth century these laws began to change through Supreme Court decisions and legislative measures at the state level (Epstein and Kobylka 1992). In 1965 the U.S. Supreme Court decided that it was a violation of marital privacy (extended to single people because of the Fourteenth Amendment's "equal protection" clause) to prohibit access to contraceptives (*Griswold v. Connecticut*). In 1973 the Supreme Court, basing its rulings on the privacy doctrine in legal theory, handed down companion decisions regarding birth control and abortion in *Doe v. Bolton* and *Roe v. Wade*, thereby overturning state laws that prohibited abortion in the first trimester. The prohibitive and restrictive abortion laws then in place were invalidated by the Supreme Court. But the right to privacy was not absolute under *Roe* (Davis 1985; Epstein and Kobylka 1992; Luker 1984). The states were allowed to restrict access to abortion in the second trimester of pregnancy and to pass prohibitions on third trimester abortions. Further legal battles have been waged at the Supreme Court since the 1973 decisions, and Congress has passed restrictions on funding for poor women to use Medicaid coverage to pay for abortions. Through the Casey decision in 1992 and Webster in 1989, the Supreme Court has allowed restrictions on access to abortion, provided those restrictions do not place an "undue burden" on the woman seeking to terminate her pregnancy (Epstein and Kobylka 1992).

The general population is aware of these legal changes and may well be one of the forces driving such changes. Therefore, the use of public opinion research becomes increasingly important in an advanced democratic society. Politicians and other policy makers refer to this research when determining the mood of their constituents. Likewise, public opinion can be used as a barometer of the evolving standards of decency in society. The level of popular support for restrictions on abortion has resulted in state regulations on access to legal abortion services (Epstein and Kobylka 1992).

Contemporary Special Interest Groups

In an attempt to further shape public opinion and legal change regarding access to abortion, many special interest groups, ranging from the mainstream to the radical, have developed. Luker's (1984) research on abortion activists provides substantial information about the motivations of individuals involved in these organizations. For this discussion it is necessary to outline what these organizations are and how they have tried to affect public policy. I will discuss first the pro-choice and then the pro-life activist organizations. This is not an exhaustive list of activist groups, but rather an exemplary list of the more prominent groups.

THE NATIONAL ABORTION RIGHTS ACTION LEAGUE (NARAL) is a vocal pro-choice organization. Prior to the U.S. Supreme Court decision in *Roe v. Wade*, NARAL[2] pursued judicial repeal of the criminal abortion laws existing at the time. When the Supreme Court announced its decision in January 1973, NARAL issued a prophetic statement: "The fight is not over; it has just begun. Before the decision, it was waged in some individual states. The battleground has now widened to include all fifty states and the Congress of the United States" (quoted in Epstein and Kobylka 1992, 200). Despite this warning, however, NARAL's involvement in legislative activism was dormant for some time. NARAL reemerged as an important advocate for pro-choice legislation during the late 1980s, when anti-abortion legislation was being debated throughout the states and within the U.S. Congress. NARAL launched their "Silent No More" campaign to voice the concerns of women who had had abortions. Another major initiative by the organization was writing "friend of the court" briefs to the Supreme Court, dealing with specific cases being brought before the Court during the 1980s; these briefs sometimes included excerpts from the "Silent No More" campaign (Epstein and Kobylka 1992).

Currently, NARAL's efforts are divided into three arenas: the nonprofit organization, the political action committee, and a charitable foundation. The nonprofit organization monitors the status of abortion rights throughout the United States and publishes an annual survey entitled "Who Decides? A State-by-State Review of Abortion and Reproductive Rights." Boasting thirty-five state affiliates, NARAL has been important in preserving legal access to abortion in various states where that access is threatened. In addition, NARAL's president is one of the most prominent and vocal advocates for abortion rights. Kate Michelman has been on the front lines of congressional action on abortion rights, always supporting a woman's right to privacy and choice. Michelman cites her own experience with abortion prior to *Roe* as one foundation of her activism. When testifying before the Senate Judiciary Committee's confirmation hearings for Justice Clarence Thomas in September 1991, Michelman related this abortion experience and told the committee that "this right is absolutely fundamental: Fundamental to our dignity, to our power to shape our own lives, to our ability to act in the best interests of our families. No issue has a greater impact on the lives and futures of American women and their families."[3]

PLANNED PARENTHOOD FEDERATION OF AMERICA is a government-funded agency charged with distributing birth control devices and information. Having operated through most of the twentieth century, Planned Parenthood has provided contraceptives and abortion services within the boundaries of the law (McKeegan 1992). With Margaret Sanger as the "birth mother" of the concept of planned parenthood, the first clinic opened its doors in 1916 in Brooklyn, New York. Planned Parenthood was very influential in the court cases that set the stage for the *Roe v. Wade* decision and eventually joined the fray, advocating abortion rights, after which "progress accelerated" (McKeegan 1992, 41). Because Planned Parenthood receives funding from the federal government, the organization has been targeted for destruction by anti-abortion groups. One anti-abortion activist called Planned Parenthood "the most evil institution in this nation . . . [out to] undermine all parental authority . . . subvert all Christian morality . . . [the organization] encourages abortion whenever possible" (McKeegan 1992, 41). During the first Reagan administration, Planned Parenthood suffered bruising reductions in their federal funding because of the controversies surrounding contraception and abortion services.

THE NATIONAL ORGANIZATION FOR WOMEN (NOW) was established in 1969, during the "second wave" of the modern women's movement in the United States. NOW is vocal in its concern for many issues related to women's well-being, including (but not limited to) abortion rights. Early in the battle for legal rights to abortion, NOW was among the feminist groups that "invaded the [1969 American Medical Association] meeting, as well as courtrooms, legislative hearing rooms, district attorneys' offices, and the streets—no bastion of patriarchy was sacrosanct—and provided the most visible external pressure for change in the abortion laws" (Petchesky 1990, 129). Since those early days, NOW has remained active in the abortion-rights movement. The organization's activities have ranged from testifying in congressional hearings against Supreme Court nominees who oppose abortion rights to organizing grassroots action in local abortion battles and providing counterprotests to anti-abortion demonstrations (Epstein and Kobylka 1992; McKeegan 1992).

THE NATIONAL RIGHT TO LIFE COMMITTEE (NRLC) is one of the oldest and most powerful anti-abortion organizations. The NRLC evolved after the Supreme Court legalized abortion in the United States. Serving primarily as a national center for smaller, local anti-abortion organizations, the NRLC boasted more than eighteen hundred affiliates and eleven million members by 1979, with an annual budget in the millions of dollars. Bolstered by the 1978 electoral successes of conservative candidates, the NRLC continued its fund-raising for anti-abortion candidates. The NRLC focused its energies largely on mainstream political action and legislative and judicial change, in conjunction with other "pro-family" organizations. The NRLC political action committee funds were important sources of campaign support in Reagan's 1980 election (McKeegan 1992).

Primarily concerned with political change, the National Right to Life Committee has supported a number of legislative agendas at the local, state, and national level. Endorsement of the Human Life Amendment, one of their earlier lobbying efforts, was an attempt to grant personhood to the fetus and thereby ensure it constitutional protection equal to that of adult citizens of the United States. The NRLC used graphic images of late-term abortions to build public outrage and raise money for the organization. Initially opposed to abortion in most circumstances, the exception being to save the life of the pregnant woman, their platform changed over time. By breaking down the legislative agenda into smaller, manageable initiatives, the NRLC successfully lobbied Congress to discontinue funding of abortions provided by the Planned Parenthood Federation of America as well as the worldwide United Nations Fund for Population Activities, since both provided those services to their underprivileged clients (McKeegan 1992).

In 1984, the NRLC's top priority became reelection of Ronald Reagan. With his continued promise to appoint abortion opponents to the federal benches and to cabinet positions, Reagan was the pro-life movement's greatest hope for federal legal change. Formerly pro-choice, both Reagan and Bush supported the NRLC's legislative agenda in return for its endorsement and financial support and in an effort to shore up socially conservative support. By the late 1980s the NRLC tempered its agenda by reluctantly supporting access to abortion in cases of pregnancy resulting from rape or incest, or when medical evidence indicated that the fetus would have serious birth defects. The NRLC became increasingly involved in lobbying for restrictions on access to abortion for teens, supporting parental consent; restrictions for married women, supporting husband consent and notification; informed consent, mandating that women seeking abortions be told of the fetus's development; and withdrawal of all public funds that support facilities providing abortion services, such as family planning clinics. With their emphasis on legislative change, the NRLC was vocal in its condemnation of violence at abortion protests (McKeegan 1992). Currently the National Right to Life Committee boasts three thousand chapters nationwide and remains active in its political efforts.

THE AMERICAN LIFE LEAGUE (ALL) was founded by Judie Brown after she left the National Right to Life Committee. Brown was dissatisfied with what she viewed as the NRLC's capitulation to the moderates and she advocated a more conservative approach. The American Life League became known as the "Marine Corps of the anti-abortion movement" (McKeegan 1992, 25). By using mailing lists from other sympathetic organizations, such as the Eagle Forum, the NRLC, and other "pro-family" groups, ALL became a moderately powerful and vocal anti-abortion force. The American Life League lobbied for total restrictions on abortion and removal of funding for all publicly supported Planned Parenthood and family planning facilities, opposed sex education in schools, and urged powerful pro-life congressional representatives to block testimony of pro-choice organizations and individuals at key hearings. ALL extended its activities to legislative opposition of other forms of birth control as well, calling the IUD and the Pill abortifacients (McKeegan 1992). Judie Brown and her colleagues were relatively tolerant of forceful resistance to abortion, stating that jailed anti-abortion protestors, including convicted arsonists, were also victims of abortion and that they were "well-meaning" in their actions (McKeegan 1992, 113). The American Life League claims to be the largest pro-life educational organization in the country and has a large number of speakers, including Brown, in its anti-abortion speaker's bureau. Currently, ALL's mailing list includes 300,000 people and organizations around the United States. The American Life League jealously guards its "no exceptions, no compromises" position on abortion, promoting its belief that every unborn human life is sacred and worthy of governmental protections.

THE MORAL MAJORITY, formed in 1980 by evangelist Jerry Falwell, marked the Religious Right's involvement in anti-abortion politics. The Moral Majority not only was concerned about abortion, but also desired to restore traditional patriarchal morality to American society by restricting access to abortion, re-establishing prayer in schools, and opposing sex education. The organization began its successful fund-raising using mailing lists from ALL and the NRLC, among other "pro-family" groups. In addition, the Moral Majority made their mailing lists available to politicians who supported their political plans. Viewing abortion rights, gay rights, sex education, and pornography as Satan's agenda, the Moral Majority launched a fervent campaign based on fear and moral outrage—calling their agenda God's agenda (McKeegan 1992, 22). They urged husbands to restore wifely submission, argued against funding for battered women's shelters, and railed against civil rights for homosexuals. The Moral Majority gained considerable local support for their positions, couching issues in terms of the forces of Good (the religious conservatives) against the forces of Evil (the religious and secular liberals, whose lifestyles were sinful), while "advocating the penalty of death for transgressors" (McKeegan 1992, 39). The group has since disbanded, but many of its members have found a new home in the Christian Coalition.

THE CHRISTIAN COALITION is a conservative religious organization founded by television evangelist Pat Robertson in 1989. The group claims a membership of nearly three million people throughout the United States, state affiliates throughout the country, and a budget of more than $10 million annually (Gregg 1994). The coalition's former executive director, thirty-five-year-old Ralph Reed, has been a lightning rod for criticism as well as a young and rising star of the conservative religious movement. The official concerns of the Christian Coalition are "choice in education, reforming school curricula (e.g., opposing sex education), opposing abortion, supporting tax cuts, and getting tough on crime" (Penning 1994, 337). The first major victory for the organization was the defeat of a gay-rights initiative in Broward County, Florida, in 1990. The first national agenda in which the coalition participated was the 1992 presidential election (see chapter 2). The group's tactics include using "stealth" campaigns that consciously avoid publicity, advertising, and the traditional methods used in elections (Penning 1994). The coalition distributes "voter guides" and "in pew" voter registration cards in churches prior to elections. The guides do not specifically endorse candidates, since the organization is officially nonpartisan. Reed declared 1992 a victorious year for the Christian Coalition's political activism, which helped elect conservative candidates in about 40 percent of the five hundred contests that year.

> We focused on where the real power is: in the states and in the precincts and in the neighborhoods where people live and work. . . . On the one hand, George Bush was going down to ignominious defeat in a landslide. On the other hand, the anecdotal evidence is that at school boards and at the state legislative level we had big, tremendous victories. (cited in Penning 1994, 339)

OPERATION RESCUE (OR), established in 1988 by Randall Terry, is one of the more radical anti-abortion organizations. OR is a fundamentalist Christian group devoted to the issue of ending abortion altogether. In addition, Operation Rescue is opposed to most forms of birth control, sex education, the ERA and feminism, and women's equality in general. Characterized primarily by their grassroots activism, rather than the political efforts of their allies, "rescuers" blockade clinic entrances, conduct "sidewalk counseling," track license plates with DMV searches, and harass clinic patients, workers, and doctors. Using civil disobedience, rescuers chain themselves together, under cars, and to clinic equipment and use other intrusive measures in efforts to stop abortion. Claiming to have found the "weak link" in abortion access, rescuers attempt to harass doctors who perform abortions out of practice. Operation Rescue is a proudly militant group that believes in defending fetuses from abortionists. The organization has incurred hundreds of thousands of dollars in fines and generated significant costs to public coffers by way of their blockades (McKeegan 1992). Operation Rescue leaders have encouraged and advised the formation of local anti-abortion groups around the United States, such as the Lambs of Christ in the Midwest and Rescue America in the Southeast.

However, this militant activism has eroded some public support for the anti-abortion agenda. The reaction to OR was overwhelmingly negative in Wichita, Kansas, after a summer 1991 "rescue." Operation Rescue staged two months of protests during that summer that included "protestors and their children [who] badgered patients, lay down under vehicles to prevent them from moving, and resisted arrest" (McKeegan 1992, 164). Seventy-eight percent of local residents reportedly disagreed with the tactics of Operation Rescue and 23 percent reported that the incident affected their personal views; more than half said the incident strengthened their pro-choice positions (McKeegan 1992, 165).

Violent Protests Against Abortion

Studies of the religious roots of violent anti-abortion protest show that the perception of the Judeo-Christian God as punitive and judgmental becomes a justification for extreme anti-abortion sentiments (Blanchard and Prewitt 1993; Blanchard 1994). Furthermore, the belief in traditional sexual division of labor and traditional concepts of femininity impel some people to oppose abortion because they view it as a wholesale rejection of the proper, religiously mandated domestic role of women (Luker 1984; Blanchard and Prewitt 1993). Luker argues that abortion has become a "referendum on the place and meaning of motherhood" (1984, 193). Blanchard and Prewitt demonstrate that violent protest against abortion is an attempt to enforce the belief that "God's law supersedes man's" (1993, 268).

Criminal violence at anti-abortion protests fluctuated in the years between 1980 and 1992 (Blanchard and Prewitt 1993; Blanchard 1994). For example, the occurrence of anti-abortion bombings and arson went from 0 in 1980 to 30 in 1984 and 22 in 1985, decreased to 12 in 1987 (Blanchard 1994, 55), and rose to 17 again in 1992. The National Abortion Federation reports that 1992 and 1993 were the most dangerous in recent years at abortion clinics. When charged with their crimes, violent protestors make claims such as that "blowing up the clinic was necessary to prevent the larger crime of abortion" (Blanchard and Prewitt 1993, 206). Violent anti-abortion activists try to shape public opinion through their

Table 2   Criminal Behavior in Anti-Abortion Protesting

	1992	1993	1994	1995	1996*
Murder	0	1	4	0	0
Attempted murder	0	1	8	1	0
Bombing/arson	17	10	9	14	3
Attempted bombing/arson	13	7	4	1	0
Invasions	26	24	2	4	0
Vandalism	116	113	42	31	10
Death threats	8	78	22	61	6
Assault & battery	9	9	7	2	0

*As of August 1, 1996. Source: National Abortion Federation, August 1, 1996.

Abortion and Capital Punishment in the United States

acts: "Immediately following his conviction [for criminal mischief and assault, an activist] told a group of about thirty supporters, 'We got our word out . . . and we're going to do better'" (Blanchard and Prewitt 1993, 192).

Other forms of violent protest are waged against abortion providers and patients. Doctors who perform abortions have faced death threats and other terroristic activity. The most severe examples are the murders of abortion providers and clinic workers in 1993 and 1994. The first victim was Dr. David Gunn, killed on March 10, 1993, in Pensacola, Florida. Gunn, who had performed abortions in three states, was shot by Michael Griffin, an anti-abortion protestor and new member of Rescue America. During pre-trial hearings, Griffin requested a continuance "until after material witnesses could be born." This request was denied by the judge.[4] Griffin was convicted of the murder of Gunn and is now serving a life sentence in Florida.

Immediately following Gunn's murder, John Burt of Rescue America (a high profile anti-abortion protestor in Pensacola with ties to the Ku Klux Klan)[5] was interviewed on an ABC television news program and stated, "The real violence occurs everyday in America when thousands of babies are killed by abortionists. This event will save at least a dozen babies' lives" (*Good Morning America*, March 11, 1993).[6]

On August 20, 1993, another abortion provider was shot. Dr. George Tiller, one of the few physicians in the United States who performs third trimester abortions, was shot in the arms. Tiller survived and was back to work the next day. His assailant, Rachelle Shannon, had written numerous supportive letters to Michael Griffin after the murder of Gunn and had contributed money toward Griffin's defense. The *New York Times* reported that in one of her letters to Griffin, Shannon wrote that "if there was ever a justifiable homicide, this [Gunn's murder] would have been it."[7]

These cases of bombing, arson, murder, and attempted murder indicate the punitive nature of extreme anti-abortion activism. Some of the newsletters distributed by anti-abortion activists contain numerous justifications for these shootings and other attacks and include calls for further violence. For instance, activist Paul de Parrie writes that "even when a pro-lifer hates Griffin's method, there is a sense of relief that the 12 condemned babies in their death row wombs still live. It is very hard to avoid the mental calculation, 'Twelve for one? Not bad.'" He concludes his commentary with this tally:

"Dead Babies (since 1973)   30,000,000
Dead Abortionists   1"

(de Parrie 1993)

In an article entitled "Griffin is a hero!" activist Gary McCullough compares abortion to shooting children in an elementary school:

> David [Gunn] has a machine gun. Every day David visits a grade school classroom and murders 11 or 12 second graders. David has "diplomatic immunity" and the police will not stop him.
>
> Michael has a pistol and is waiting for David outside a classroom full of children. When David arrives, Michael asks him to stop killing children. David refuses and begins to enter the classroom. Michael shoots and kills David. (McCullough 1993)

Finally, McCullough argues that while the first option is nonviolent protest against abortion, when that fails the "violent solution is the only one left" to end "child-killing."

Paul Hill, founder of the radical group Defensive Action, who encouraged the use of violence in protesting abortion, offered a lengthy defense of Michael Griffin's actions while appearing on the *Phil Donahue Show* on March 15, 1993. After the show, Hill (1993) wrote a detailed essay outlining his defense of Michael Griffin. "If next to Dr. Gunn's dead body were to be spread the gruesome remains of the thousands he killed, the mere space needed would be staggering," began Hill's defense of Griffin and of anti-abortion violence. The essay contains Hill's biblical and ethical justifications for murdering Gunn, arguing in the words of John Calvin that "if a person is led to inflict punishment by a just and well-regulated zeal toward God, it is not his own cause, but that of God which he undertakes." Hill further maintains that his views are the "commonly accepted truths" of Christianity.

Casting Gunn in the role of a "paid killer," Hill attempts to incite the moral outrage of his readers and fellow activists, reduce Griffin's culpability, and place all blame at the feet of Gunn. Hill challenges the Sixth Commandment against killing by claiming that "Christian soldier[s] may, therefore, with love and humility, take guilty life to defend innocent life from unjust harm." He concludes that not only is this action justified, but also it is a God-given responsibility to take defensive action to stop abortion. Anti-abortion protests throughout the 1980s had proved less effective than Hill had hoped, and he believed that the time had come for direct and even violent action. He saw little hope for legislative efforts after the election of President Clinton and states that rather than wait until six million more unborn babies are slaughtered, it is "our duty . . . to pursue a defensive war if possible." Referencing the Second Amendment to the United

States Constitution, Hill argues that "one of the reasons we have the responsibility to keep and bear arms is so we may individually and corporately take all just action necessary to protect innocent life."

When the ultimate victory comes, according to Hill, those who laid down their lives (such as Griffin, and eventually himself) to stop abortion will be venerated: "Never before will so few have the opportunity to accomplish so much for so many." Challenging readers that it is their Christian responsibility to take defensive action against abortion, Hill promises that they will live in eternal glory in heaven with God for helping stop the slaughter of innocent children by taking violent action against those who have abortions or perform them.

On July 29, 1994, Paul Hill was arrested for murdering two men outside the Ladies Center in Pensacola, Florida. Hill shot and killed Dr. John B. Britton, an abortion provider, and the man escorting Britton to the center, retired Lt. Col. James Barrett. Barrett's wife, June, was also shot but survived the attack. When arrested, Hill said, "I know one thing. No innocent babies are going to be killed in that clinic today."[8] At trial, Hill was not permitted to use the "justifiable homicide" defense and was convicted. He was sentenced to death in Florida and is currently on death row. The Florida Supreme Court has upheld Hill's conviction and sentencing on direct appeal.

On December 30, 1994, John Salvi went on a shooting spree in two Boston-area abortion clinics. Salvi, a devout Catholic with notions that a worldwide conspiracy existed to eliminate Catholicism, killed Shannon Lowney and Lee Ann Nichols, who worked at different clinics in Brookline, Massachusetts. He also seriously injured many other people who were at the clinics that day. Eluding police for one day, Salvi drove to Norfolk, Virginia, where he shot at the outside of another abortion clinic. He was arrested in Virginia and extradicted to Massachusetts, where he was convicted and sentenced to life in prison without parole, despite his expressed desire to be sentenced to death. (Massachusetts does not have a death penalty option for first-degree murder.) On November 29, 1996, Salvi was found dead of asphyxiation in his prison cell—an apparent suicide.[9]

Salvi appeared to have been mentally unbalanced, and his lawyers used an insanity defense for his trial. The jury, however, was unconvinced that Salvi suffered from paranoid schizophrenia and convicted him of first-degree murder.[10] While in prison, Salvi wrote letters to a man he had wounded on his shooting spree. The *Boston Globe* reported that Salvi's "plan for America" included racial protection for white Christians because "he saw abortion as a form of genocide for whites, particularly Catholic whites." Most of these letters ended with a postscript that read "pro-life, pro–welfare state, pro–Catholic labor union, pro–family values."[11]

Capital Punishment

As with anti-abortion activists, death penalty proponents argue that the general public is behind them and wants capital punishment not just retained, but used more frequently. Capital punishment has a long history in the United States, and public opinion analysis requires some historical context.

Use of Legal Executions in the United States

Between 18,000 and 20,000 executions have been carried out under state or federal jurisdiction in the United States and American colonies since European settlement (Espy 1980, 1988). More than 7,000 people have been executed in the United States since 1900 (Bowers 1974). Between 1930 and 1967, there were 3,859 executions of people convicted of various crimes, including homicide, treason, rape, and kidnapping (Radelet 1989).

Until 1967 the death penalty was permitted for rape and first-degree murder. Since 1976, the only capital crimes in the United States have been first-degree murder and felony murder (homicide that occurs during the commission of another felony, such as robbery, kidnapping, or rape). The five leading execution states are Texas, Florida, Virginia, Louisiana, and Georgia. Since the Supreme Court ruled in 1972 in *Furman v. Georgia* that, as administered, the death penalty violated the Eighth and Fourteenth Amendments to the Constitution, there have been more than three hundred executions. Currently, more than three thousand people are on death rows in the United States.

Until the 1950s the popular wisdom about the death penalty was that it had a deterrent effect on criminal activity. However, this untested assumption had been theoretically challenged as early as 1764 by Cesare di Beccaria in his influential book *Dei Delliti e delle Pene* (On Crimes and Punishments). Beccaria wrote that the "certainty of a small punishment will make a stronger impression than the fear of one more severe, if attended with the hope of escaping" (cited in Cooper 1974, 29).[12] Criminal justice reformers in England and the American colonies used Beccaria's book as a guide for advocating reform. Jeremy Bentham and John Howard in England (Ignatieff 1978) and William Penn in America were influenced by Beccaria's arguments for relatively humane reforms and for limiting the use of public executions.

Sutherland (1925) examined the deterrent effect of the death penalty and found that in states where the death penalty is used, murder rates are higher. Following Sutherland's lead, Thorsten Sellin (1959) looked at homicide rates in states that use the death penalty and in those that do not. Using cross-sectional data, Sellin found that states without the death penalty did not have significantly higher homicide rates than states with the death penalty, as the deterrence hypothesis would predict. He concluded that the death penalty had no effect on homicide. Given the simplicity of this research and the unpopular conclusions to be drawn from it, state legislators and prosecutors dismissed this work and social scientists criticized it. Further studies have also examined the effect of capital punishment (Erlich 1975; Passell 1976; Klein et al. 1978). There is currently no valid scientific evidence of the deterrent effect of the death penalty (Radelet 1989; Peterson and Bailey 1991; Cochran, Chamlin, and Seth 1994).

Other evidence has suggested a brutalizing relationship between the death penalty and homicide in the United States. Bowers and Pierce (1980) found that within several months after an execution, homicide rates increased for a short time and then declined to their normal levels. While there is some question as to the consistency of this relationship (Peterson and Bailey 1991), most social scientists agree that there is more evidence of a brutalization effect (albeit weak) than of a deterrent effect.

Higher levels of public support for capital punishment in recent years have been attributed to the growing "law and order" political agendas of recent elections (Rankin 1979; Bohm 1991). Supporters of the death penalty are generally more politically conservative, punitive, and authoritarian than opponents of the death penalty (Rankin 1979). Political conservatives, from Nixon in the 1970s to Reagan and Bush in the 1980s and 1990s, have claimed to be "tough on crime." This "law and order" agenda includes harsh penal policies, such as capital punishment, which are supported by many prominent political leaders (Rothman 1995).

Common Themes

Legal Rational Authority of the State

What, from a legal standpoint, do abortion and capital punishment have in common? Both involve the use of state authority to transform a specific version of authority into political and legal power. By passing legal restrictions on access to abortion or further expanding access to abortion, and by stepping up the pace of executions or advocating their abolition, government becomes the domain in which special interest groups battle over their agendas.

Passage and enforcement of abortion and capital punishment laws serve to legitimate the beliefs of the proponents of specific political agendas. Conservatives in the United States enjoyed a groundswell of support throughout the 1980s and into the 1990s, due in part to the successful coalition of organizations devoted to sculpting a New Right in American politics. With the promised loyalties of powerful politicians, the New Right raised considerable money for candidates and demanded specific legislation. After the 1988 presidential election, Democrats faced this challenge by constructing the New Democrat, a centrist, as opposed to the demonized "tax and spend" liberal. The New Democrat is pro-choice, pro–death penalty, tough on crime, and in favor of programs that prevent crime.

The New Right was quite successful in advancing "tough on crime" policies throughout the 1980s. Post-*Furman* executions were stepped up (Radelet 1989). Incarceration rates substantially increased from 100 per 100,000 people in 1975 to 150 in 1980, doubling to 300 in 1990, and rising to 387 in 1995 (Cole 1995; Samaha 1997). The War on Drugs has spurred an increasingly punitive response from the federal government (Reuter 1992; Rothman 1995), exemplified by a Bush presidential campaign promise in 1988 to expand the use of the death penalty to "drug king-pins." The criminal justice system is overburdened because of increasing punitiveness, even though crime rates remained fairly stable throughout the 1980s. President Clinton and the New Democrats have unreservedly endorsed the trend of punitiveness and have called for more sanctions for domestic violence and "sexual predators" (Sheingold, Olson, and Pershing 1994).

With regard to abortion laws, the New Right has been fairly successful at passing state-level restrictions on access to abortion (Cook 1993). Beginning with the Hyde Amendment, which restricts use of government money to provide abortion services, anti-abortion activism demonstrated its muscle in state legislatures, Congress, and the federal courts. Activists and constituents in various states have persuaded legislators to pass husband consent/notification laws for married women, parental consent or judicial bypass laws for teens, and informed consent laws, as well as to institute waiting periods for obtaining an abortion. These restrictions were tested for constitutionality under *Roe v. Wade* and were upheld in most cases. The ultimate victory for anti-abortion advocates remains elusive, however. Attempts at overturning *Roe v. Wade* have not been successful at the Supreme Court and the Human Life Amendment has not been passed into law anywhere in the United States.

The New Democrats have largely endorsed pro-choice legislation, indicating that their general support for women's rights requires support of legal abortion. On the other hand, they have supported restrictions on federal funding for abortion in order to appease pro-life constituents, and most New Democrats supported the ban on dilation and extraction abortion procedures (referred to by anti-abortion activists as "partial-birth abortion").

Traditional Morality and Moral Outrage

In 1835 Alexis de Tocqueville wrote:

> No free communities ever existed without morals; and . . . morals are the work of women. Consequently, whatever affects the condition of women, their habits and their opinions, has great political importance. (quoted in Heffner 1984, 233)

Under this code of morality, women were viewed as the guardians of moral behavior. The traditional roles within which women were considered moral were domestic. Traditional morality required a woman to remain virginal until marriage to ensure certainty of paternity when she gave birth. Having children was not simply another choice women made—it was the duty of Christian wives to give their husbands sons and daughters. Motherhood, though not revered as many in the New Right would have us believe, was certainly the most respected role many women could have within the confines of marriage (Solinger 1992). The abortion debate in contemporary society is a critical element in the struggle over whose definition of morality will serve as the cornerstone for legislation. The moral outrage expressed by those who advocate legal abortion reflects their concern for the quality of life of unwanted children, and of women who suffer the consequences of giving birth to unwanted children (Luker 1984).

Regarding capital punishment, traditional morality also includes retributive justice, though this has been primarily a part of the masculine domain. Men are urged to seek "an eye for an eye" in settling personal disputes or to defend The Good (Katz 1989). Retributivists' sense of morality is based on the traditional notion of "just desert" in punishment (Austin 1979; von Hirsch 1995). An offender deserves to be punished, for punishment's sake. Anyone who takes a life deserves to pay with his or her own life, and it is the moral obligation of the state to see that justice is served in this sense.

Defenders of capital punishment also rely on the Bible to support the execution of criminals.

> The Bible quotes the Lord declaring: "Vengeance is mine" (Romans 12: 19). He thus legitimized vengeance and reserved it to Himself. However, the Bible also enjoins, "the murderer shall surely be put to death" (Numbers 35:16–18), recognizing that the death penalty can be warranted—whatever the motive. Religious tradition certainly suggests no less. (Van den Haag 1982, 330)

Thus, moral precepts can be drawn from social sources external to the individual—in this case, religious tradition. In these terms it is justifiable that society as a whole, and the state in particular, express righteous indignation toward those who violate society's moral order. Walter Berns expands on this theme, applying it specifically to capital punishment by arguing that it "serves to remind us of the majesty of the moral order that is embodied in our law, and of the terrible consequences of its breach" (1982, 339).

Death penalty opponents likewise agree on moral grounds that executions are barbaric penal rituals that should be abolished in all civilized societies. They point to many problems with the imposition of the sentence, such as racial bias, arbitrariness, failure as a deterrent, and costliness (see Bedau 1982). Some opponents of the death penalty also use the Bible to uphold the morality of their opinions, specifically references to "turn the other cheek" and "let anyone who is without sin throw the first stone." [13] It would be inaccurate, however, to presume that death penalty opponents are opposed to punishment qua punishment. Most support life sentences for convicted murderers and other terms of incarceration as a mechanism for punishing convicted felons.

It is clear that views of state authority to punish offenders underlie abortion and capital punishment opinions. Punishment arises out of a demand for justice. Opponents of abortion argue for justice on behalf of unborn fetuses and death penalty supporters argue for justice on behalf of victims and society in general. The common foundation upon which those who support the death penalty and oppose abortion stand is the traditional moral order, within which people protest what they consider injustices and call on the state to remedy the situation. The common foundation for supporting legal abortion and opposing the death penalty is a progressive moral order in which the injustices are seen differently—the government is called upon to remedy injustices to women, ethnic minorities, and the poor, rather than expand punishment under state authority.

Understanding Abortion and Capital Punishment

Social theory has grappled with gender and state authority as two of the key components of social organization. What follows is a discussion of relevant theoretical frameworks regarding the sociology of punishment. Theories in the sociology of punishment have been primarily concerned with public and legal punishment of criminals (Garland 1990; Ignatieff 1978).

Punishment Theory

The power to punish is one of the most influential social forces in human societies. Americans believe in the use of punishment. In a national survey, 90 percent of American parents agreed that physical punishment of children was "normal, necessary and good" (Straus, Gelles, and Steinmetz 1980). Approval of corporal punishment remains high in the United States (Straus 1994). One of the primary motivations of incarceration is to punish those who breach the social and moral contract (Foucault 1979; Garland 1985, 1990; Ignatieff 1978; von Hirsch 1995). The major incentive to promote capital punishment is that of punitive vengeance (Ellsworth and Ross 1983). Garland writes that punishment "rests, at least in part, upon a shared emotional reaction caused by the criminal's desecration of the sacred things" (1990, 30). He goes on to argue that despite the veneer of utilitarian motivations of punishment there is an underlying "vengeful, motivating passion which guides punishment and supplies its force" (1990, 31). Therefore, to look at punishment as a simple social interaction between those with the power to punish and those who receive the punishment is inadequate. What is needed is a closer and more deliberate examination of the cultural forces (specifically beliefs, attitudes, and values) giving rise to the institution of punishment.

Nietzsche argued that viewing punishment brings pleasure to people, that it reaffirms their sense of justice, "to cause another to suffer affords even greater pleasure; [t]his severe statement expresses an old, powerful, human, all too human sentiment" (cited in Garland 1990, 63). An act of punishment is an appeal to the popular sovereignty of society—it establishes the status of one person over another (or one group over another), keeps the punished subjugated, and finds its justification and motivation in the legal and moral authority of society. This serves to reinforce group solidarity and the definition of propriety. According to Mead (1918), punitive sentiments gain energy and emotional strength through the exemplary use and threat of punishment.

These punitive sentiments become formalized into laws designed to regulate human behavior, legitimating the moral outrage upon which punishment is based. Garland offers an understanding of punishment based on two levels of analysis—mentalities and sensibilities. In this framework *mentalities* refers to scientific and rational objectivity in the use and understanding of punishment, while *sensibilities* refers to the emotional forces that affect the visceral nature of human interaction. Therefore, evolving standards of civilized punishment are dependent on the overall cultural sensibilities of propriety and impropriety. These sensibilities are grounded in the beliefs, values, and attitudes people hold about offending behavior and offenders. Throughout the historical evolution of punishment, the sensibilities may have become progressively more compassionate (Foucault 1979), and the replacement of torturous executions with the guillotine can be seen as a step in the direction of "quick and painless" death. Marquart, Ekland-Olson, and Sorensen (1994) suggest that one of the reasons that methods of execution evolved from hanging or electrocution to lethal injection is the overall public distaste for inhumane punishment.

The vast majority of death penalties have been carried out on men, but women have been subjected to the sentence of death in a gender-specific fashion (Rapoport 1991). Some feminist scholars argue that because women face a different set of cultural expectations, they provoke social condemnation that is an outgrowth of societal views of womanhood (Rhode 1989; MacKinnon 1989). During the eighteenth and nineteenth centuries women were incarcerated and otherwise punished for giving birth to "bastard" children (Ignatieff 1978; Bynum 1992). The punishment of these mothers (not the fathers) was based on the cultural condemnation of inappropriate pregnancy, defined as pregnancy outside the marital union, a circumstance seen as a threat to the moral authority of paternity and patriarchal society (Messerschmidt 1987, 1993).

Women are punished within the traditional cultural framework of femininity: "Cultural understandings of what women are like, and how they ought to behave, operate to define the appropriate response to their misconduct and to structure the punishment of women" (Garland 1990, 202). Garland makes a similar argument with respect to ethnic minorities and charges that evidence of the deep-seated nature of these cultural forces is found in the slow pace of reform, even after discrimination is officially eradicated. Karlene Faith (1993) argues that women are punished largely because of cultural views of what is appropriately feminine—when women violate that code of prescribed behavior they are punished for their offense and also for being "unwomanly."

Page and Clelland (1978) argue that protests to preserve traditional institutions are an attempt to maintain a lifestyle based on traditional morality and social order. Anti-abortion legislation is an attempt to preserve a particular lifestyle through political means—criminalizing abortion and punishing "abortion criminals." This "cultural fundamentalism" (Blanchard 1994) is seen in the political right in the United States, where maintaining the status quo is of paramount concern.

There appears to be an identifiable punitive element to the restrictive abortion legislation passed in recent years. Women have been targets of punitive control by the traditional patriarchal social order for hundreds of years, but there have been cultural shifts toward redefining what deserves punishment and what does not.

CHAPTER TWO

Abortion and Death Penalty Politics

This chapter examines abortion and capital punishment in light of recent presidential elections and summarizes the current literature on public sentiments about abortion and capital punishment in the United States. An examination of abortion and death penalty politics in the 1988, 1992, and 1996 presidential elections illuminates some important themes to be explored further in chapters 3 through 6. I will also summarize findings on demographic differences in public opinion and the common justifications for these differences. Finally, research that examines both abortion and death penalty opinions will be closely reviewed.

Presidential Politics, Abortion, and the Death Penalty

Since the middle of the 1970s, abortion has been an increasingly divisive political issue (McKeegan 1992). Simultaneously, "law and order" election campaigns have increased in popularity. In 1988 the abortion issue collided with the "law and order" campaign style. The presidential election campaign of 1984, a contest between Republican incumbent Ronald Reagan and Democratic challenger Walter Mondale, foreshadowed this collision: Roman Catholic bishops stated that abortion would be "the critical issue" of that election,[1] and Cardinal Bernardin publicly promoted the "seamless garment" philosophy,[2] which is wholly pro-life (i.e., opposed to abortion, capital punishment, nuclear war, extreme defense expenditures, etc.).

The appearance of abortion as a significant issue in 1984 was spurred by the Democratic party's endorsement of the first woman vice presidential candidate. Until the 1984 election, Geraldine Ferraro had been a relatively unknown congressional representative from Queens, New York.[3] Mondale and Democratic strategists attempted to secure the "women's vote" by placing Ferraro on the ticket. Ferraro, a Roman Catholic from a heavily Catholic district who publicly supported legal abortion, was in a difficult position. She announced, "I would never have an abortion if I became pregnant because, quite frankly, that would be a child that would be conceived in love. The choice has to be the choice of the woman." However, she also said that if she became pregnant as a result of rape, she was unsure "whether [she'd] be as self-righteous on the issue."[4] The press gave extensive coverage to the abortion issue, documenting the views of clerics, political writers, and the candidates themselves; however, the voting public seemed relatively unconcerned about it. Only a "tiny fraction" of potential voters said they would base their decisions "solely on the candidates' positions on abortion."[5] In a *New York Times/CBS News* poll conducted in the fall of 1984, 64 percent of respondents opposed a constitutional ban on abortion, while 27 percent supported such a ban. As usual, economic issues were the central consideration for voters.[6]

Reagan and his running mate, George Bush, were reelected with the largest electoral college victory in the history of the American presidency. One political columnist, Bruce S. Ledewitz, indirectly blamed the abortion issue for the Mondale/Ferraro defeat. Ledewitz listed his "four nominees for those most responsible" for the defeat "party professionals, big labor, feminists, and Gary Hart and the Yuppies." He suggested that the Democratic party was too eager to court the vote of feminists, which forced the party to sacrifice the pro-life Democrats to the Republicans. Ledewitz claimed that feminists in the party "destroyed the Democrats' opportunity to build a liberal 'pro-life' political movement," suggesting that the Democratic party ought to be a place where "people of good faith can disagree" about abortion. He ended the essay by stating that "Despite the debacle, the Democrats seem strangely unwilling to clean out those responsible. But, unless we do, I am afraid we shall witness yet another defeat in 1988."[7] This opinion piece proved prophetic in more than one sense: the Democrats experienced another stinging defeat in 1988, and Ledewitz's vision of a New Democrat, based on the principles of "prosperity, justice and peace," would lead the way to electoral success for Democrats in 1992.

In 1984, George Bush began to position himself as the Republican presidential nominee for 1988, despite his testy relationships with the media and with members of his own party. Bush made several embarrassing blunders during the 1984 campaign. He "forgot" his congressional voting record on abortion and his previous support for abortion under some circumstances.[8] Despite these blunders, Bush prepared for 1988 by demonstrating his loyalty to Reagan and his steadfast support of the Reagan administration's foreign and domestic policies.

The daily protests over abortion in 1984 demonstrated the effectiveness of this emotional issue in galvanizing voters. Although most exit polls showed that people based their votes primarily on economic issues,[9] abortion remained in the forefront of the political news for several months. New grassroots organizations were formed[10] and in 1984 "opponents of abortion boast[ed] eight times the number of political action committees" as their pro-choice counterparts. The 1984 presidential election forecasted some of the most divisive campaign rhetoric of the 1988 election, rhetoric that addressed the death penalty as well as abortion.

1988

In the summer of 1987, the National Abortion Rights Action League and Voters for Choice released the abortion rights records of the possible presidential candidates for 1988.[11] They reported that among Democrats, Senator Paul Simon, Reverend Jesse Jackson, and Governor Mario Cuomo were steady supporters of the legal right to choose abortion, while Senator Albert Gore of Tennessee "opposed federal financing of abortions except when life was endangered." Vice President George Bush was reported to have an unclear record on abortion (stemming from his equivocations on the topic in 1984). Potential Republican candidates Senator Robert Dole and Representative Jack Kemp supported a constitutional amendment "that would give states the option to make abortion illegal" and also opposed federal financing for abortion services. Tangled up with the abortion issue was the nomination of Judge Robert Bork to the United States Supreme Court. With the announcement that Supreme Court Justice Lewis Powell would resign at the end of the 1987 term, Reagan was presented with another opportunity to fill a vacancy on the Supreme Court. He nominated former U.S. Solicitor General Robert Bork whose positions on many controversial issues were well-known, including his declaration that *Roe v. Wade* was "itself an unconstitutional decision." Activists on all sides of the issues rallied to gain support among the general public to phone their senators urging action on the Bork nomination. By September a poll showed that a majority of Americans were opposed to Bork's nomination, and "only 29 percent supported it." Central to the public opposition to this nomination was Bork's early rulings that the U.S. Constitution does not guarantee privacy to married couples who sought contraceptives (Epstein and Kobylka 1992).

In September 1987, Kemp enthusiastically predicted that Bork would be confirmed to the Supreme Court, and that the confirmation would signal the beginning of the end of legal abortion. While courting the endorsement of Iowans for Life, Kemp won 37 percent of their straw vote; Pat Robertson, a television evangelist and vocal anti-abortion candidate, received 31 percent; and Bob Dole earned 17 percent. Bush received less than 1 percent because he did not make an appearance at Iowans for Life meetings.[12] A month after the Caucus, Bush was called upon to clarify his position on abortion while making a campaign visit to Iowa. Bush remarked, "There's been 15 million abortions since 1973, and I don't take that lightly. There's been a million and half this year. . . . I'd like to see the American who, faced with [these numbers of] abortions, isn't rethinking his or her position."[13]

Early in the primary season, Bush was in a tight contest in Iowa with Dole and Kemp. The vice president's position on abortion was questioned in a campaign flier "paid for and authorized by Jack Kemp for President," which stated that Bush had "changed his position on abortion three times and promoted abortion while serving as U.N. ambassador." Bush responded that he did "not promote abortion as U.N. ambassador."[14] The Iowa Caucus presented the Republican candidates with their first major opportunity to state their positions on abortion and other issues in the 1988 race. Abortion was a decisive factor for the Republican candidates.[15] Kemp, Dole, Bush, and conservative Christian Pat Buchanan advocated recriminalizing abortion, with various provisions. Dole prevailed in the Iowa Caucus, Pat Buchanan finished second, and Bush had "a disappointing third place showing."[16]

For the Democrats in Iowa, abortion was not a central concern. Representative Richard Gephardt from Missouri, Senator Paul Simon from Illinois, and Governor Michael Dukakis from Massachusetts finished in that order. Their platforms focused on economic issues; they advocated "sacrifice" and alerted the country to the need for moderate reductions in defense spending in order to balance the budget.[17]

In the New Hampshire primary, the economy was the central issue for both Republican and Democratic candidates. However, after Bush's victory in New Hampshire, the death penalty became an increasingly volatile issue. Calling for the "swift application of the death penalty to criminals convicted of drug-related murders," Bush sought to demonstrate his "toughness" on crime in general and drug-related crime in particular. While campaigning in New York state,

Bush referred to a recent case of a police officer who had been shot and killed in a drug bust:

> We have to go after them in any way we can, we have been too tolerant. . . . we've got to find a way to speed [the death penalty] up. . . . I favor the death penalty for drug kingpins. That penalty should be available for those who commit drug-related murders, like the guy who pulled the trigger on Eddie Byrne [the slain police officer]. These people are dealing in death and that's what they should get. And frankly, I'd like to find a way, I don't know how this could be done, to make it swift. Only a swift penalty could deter the kind of crimes we are seeing in this country.[18]

Continuing on this theme of drug-related crime and the death penalty, the Republicans dared the Democrats to "be very assertive" on the crime issue, knowing that the G.O.P. would probably win on "the toughness quotient" because Governor Dukakis and other Democrats had publicly declared their opposition to capital punishment.[19]

Vice President George Bush was the 1988 Republican presidential nominee, enjoying some benefits of having been a member of the popular Reagan administration. Governor Michael Dukakis was nominated by the Democratic party. The candidates' choices of running mates became critical decisions in this election. Bush selected a young Republican "family man"—Dan Quayle was revered by the conservative right, which still had an instinctive dislike for Bush's "blueblood" lineage. Dukakis selected a Southern Democrat from Texas, Lloyd Bentsen, who was widely respected in the Democratic party as a moderate-to-conservative politician with friends in both parties.

The 1988 Republican convention showcased the party's anti-abortion and pro−death penalty positions in the nominating speeches and in the candidates' acceptance speeches. In New Orleans, Governor Kay Orr of Nebraska, chairwoman of the platform committee, announced that the 1988 platform would not be a "major departure" from the 1984 platform. Republicans would continue to support the Human Life Amendment to the U.S. Constitution, call for a complete ban on all federal money used for abortion services, and appoint to the federal benches judges who "respect the sanctity of innocent human life."[20] Despite some efforts by moderate and liberal-leaning Republicans to soften the party's platform on abortion, the platform remained pro-life[21] and reaffirmed the "bedrock principles in Ronald Reagan's presidency—opposition to abortion . . . and support for the death penalty."[22]

The Democratic convention, in contrast, was marked by an absence of discussion about abortion and capital punishment. Perhaps this indicates the

Democratic party's failure to read "the tea leaves"[23] in terms of how the Republicans could exploit these divisive issues for political gain. At the Democratic convention, Dukakis declared in his acceptance speech that the campaign would not be about "meaningless labels" but "about American values. Old fashioned values like accountability and responsibility and respect for truth."[24] He was correct, but those "old fashioned values" worked against Dukakis as abortion and the death penalty became politicized.

After the conventions, Dukakis and Bush campaigned on typically Democratic and Republican themes. Dukakis shored up support among women voters by promising to keep abortion legal, while Bush gained support among the Religious Right by promising to work toward overturning *Roe v. Wade.*

In September, anti-abortion protestors interrupted a Dukakis campaign speech in Illinois, shouting "What about abortion? Abortion is murder!" and displaying photographs of fetuses. Dukakis asked the protestors to respect his right to speak to the gathering, and Democratic supporters began yelling back at the protestors. Eventually, the protestors were removed from the audience. This was not an isolated incident in the Dukakis campaign; it was the second such protest in as many days. Joseph Scheidler, a well-known anti-abortion activist and author of a book on how to stop abortion through activism, was among the protesters at the Illinois rally and promised that similar protests would be common. Scheidler said, "We're trying to bring out the fact that Mike Dukakis is the abortion candidate . . . and if the American people don't know he's the pro-abortion candidate, we want to inform them and the way to do it is to go to his appearances and protest."[25]

In October, Dukakis faced problems from within his own party, primarily because of his opposition to capital punishment. Powerful Southern Democrats openly stated that they did not support the national ticket. In Georgia, Democratic Speaker of the House Tom Murphy said that he was unsure how he would vote in the fall election, while in North Carolina a 1984 gubernatorial candidate, Rufus Edmisten, blamed the Democratic party for his defeat. Edmisten felt that close ties with the 1988 ticket would be damaging for Southern Democrats because of the candidates' "unacceptably liberal leanings." Bush was able to transfer the support of white southerners from the popular Reagan to his own campaign, largely because of "southern values" such as opposition to abortion and support for capital punishment.[26]

Continuing the pro–death penalty campaign, Bush once again addressed the emotional issue of police officers murdered in the line of duty.[27] This time, however, he introduced the electorate to convicted murderer "Willie" Horton. William Horton was nicknamed "Willie" by the people sponsoring this advertisement (Feagin and Vera 1995; Abramowitz 1994; and Jamieson 1992). At campaign speeches, Bush repeatedly referred to the case of Horton, an African American.[28] Incarcerated in Massachusetts, Horton was released on a weekend furlough program and fled to Maryland, where he was convicted of raping a white woman and stabbing her fiancé. In their research on this case, Feagin and Vera (1995) reveal that one of Horton's accomplices may in fact have been the killer. "The police never determined who actually did the stabbing. According to a law-enforcement source, one of Horton's co-defendants allegedly confessed to the murder, but the confession was not admissible in court because the police officers had not read the suspect his rights" (Feagin and Vera 1995, 120). The case was featured in a television advertisement supporting the Bush/Quayle campaign that was produced and paid for by an independent organization. Entitled "Weekend Passes," the advertisement compares the positions of Bush and Dukakis on crime. First, an image of Bush appears and the narrator says, "Bush supports the death penalty for first-degree murder." The next image is Dukakis, and the narrator continues, "Dukakis not only opposes the death penalty, he allowed first-degree murderers to have weekend passes from prison." Then the faces of "Willie" Horton and another black man appear, while the narrator reports, "Horton fled, kidnapped a young couple, stabbing the man and repeatedly raping his girlfriend"—the words "kidnapping," "stabbing," and "raping" flash on the screen. The final image is a photograph of Dukakis. The narrator concludes, "Weekend prison passes: Dukakis on crime."[29]

This advertisement was criticized by many Democrats, who argued that the Bush campaign was using images of a black murderer/rapist and white victims in order to inflame racial tensions. Susan Estrich, campaign manager for Dukakis,[30] said that "if you're going to run a campaign of fear and smear and appeal to racial hatred, you could not have picked a better case to use than this one." The Bush campaign spokesman responded, "My advice to them is 'grow up.' The whole idea is childish to say there is some sort of racial overtone in the Horton case. The issue isn't Willie Horton, the issue is why did he get out and why didn't Michael Dukakis stop it."[31]

The Bush campaign officially disavowed the Horton ad, which was produced by Elizabeth Fediay for the National Security Political Action Committee. Fediay commented, "Officially, the campaign has to disavow themselves from me. Unofficially, I hear that they're thrilled about what we're doing."[32] According to news reports, Fediay had alerted the Bush campaign that she would air the advertisement for twenty-eight days and asked if they objected. She received no objection until the twenty-fifth day of the ad's being aired.

Dukakis's campaign was badly damaged by this development, and in the last days of the election season, he returned to his support of abortion rights as a means of "proudly defin[ing] himself as a liberal" in the tradition of John F. Kennedy,

Harry Truman, and Franklin Roosevelt. Dukakis boldly declared, "I believe that a choice that personal must be made by the woman in the exercise of her own conscience and religious beliefs. And that's one of the reasons why we don't want George Bush and Dan Quayle appointing new Justices to the Supreme Court of the United States." He went on to say that the Republicans are "on the wrong side of every issue of special importance to American women."[33]

The presidential debates were another venue where the candidates were asked about their views on abortion and the death penalty. The first debate of the 1988 election was held on September 25. Dukakis was asked a question regarding "a conflict between [his] opposition to the death penalty and support for abortion on demand." He responded that he saw no conflict between these positions and that "they've got to be dealt with separately." Dukakis continued, "I am opposed to the death penalty. . . . I don't favor abortion. I don't think it's a good thing. . . . The question is, who makes the decision. And I think it has to be the woman in the exercise of her own conscience and religious beliefs that makes that decision."

When Bush had the opportunity to respond, he was relatively brief, stating, "I favor the death penalty . . . and I think most people know my position on the sanctity of life. I favor adoption; I do not favor abortion."[34] He was asked what penalties he would support for abortion should it become illegal, as he advocated. He stumbled around the issue by answering that he had not thought that through yet. The next day, James Baker III, Bush's campaign manager, tried to answer the question by declaring that Bush had thought about it overnight and felt that women who have abortions should not be punished, because, like unborn babies, they are "victims," but that doctors who perform abortions should be punished.[35] The specific punishment recommended by Bush was not stipulated.

During the second presidential debate, on October 13, CNN journalist Bernard Shaw began the questioning with "Governor, if [your wife] Kitty Dukakis were raped and murdered, would you favor an irrevocable death penalty for the killer?" This moment has been recalled as one of the most poorly handled in presidential debating history. Dukakis dispassionately declared, "No, I don't, Bernard, and I think you know that I've opposed the death penalty during all of my life. I don't see any evidence that it's a deterrent and I think there are better and more effective ways to deal with violent crime." Bush's one-minute rebuttal included the statement "I think it is a deterrent and I believe we need it."

Questions about abortion became even more personal. When asked if he would tolerate abortion in the case of severe fetal defect, Bush replied, "I don't think that you can make an exception based on medical knowledge at the time. I think every human life is very, very precious." Bush related a personal experience of having lost a child. The child was given "a few weeks to live" because she had "acute leukemia," but "thanks to the miraculous sacrifice of doctors and nurses, the child stayed alive for six months and then died. If that child were here today and I was told the same thing . . . that child could stay alive for 10 or 15 years or maybe for the rest of her life." Next, Dukakis recounted his experience of fathering a child who had lived for "about twenty minutes after it was born. But isn't the real question . . . who makes this very difficult, very wrenching decision? . . . I would hope that we would give the women in this country the right to make that decision." [36] These emotional issues characterized the 1988 presidential campaign. [37]

The election results demonstrated the power of emotional campaigning. In what was then the lowest voter turnout since 1924, [38] (approximately half of all eligible voters) the pro-life and pro–death penalty Republicans were elected by 54 percent. The South was solidly behind the Republican ticket, with more than two thirds of white southern voters favoring Bush. [39] Sixty percent of Alabama voters supported Bush/Quayle; Arkansas favored Bush 57–43 percent, despite then-Governor Bill Clinton's nomination of Dukakis at the national convention. [40] While the majority of exit polls showed that the economy and Bush's "no new taxes" pledge were the most important issues of the campaign, capital punishment and abortion were clearly on people's minds. The "Willie" Horton ads had fueled a deeper division between whites and blacks. In all regions of the country, the vast majority of black voters supported Dukakis (between 83 and 91 percent), while a majority of white voters supported Bush (between 54 and 67 percent). The "gender gap" was not detectable—women split their votes evenly between the two parties. [41] According to a Southern Democrat, "The cultural issues and Dukakis not responding to them put a wall up between Dukakis and voters he could have gotten. The wall got so thick that people forgot about the economic issues." [42]

Two days after the election, President Reagan initiated a legal assault on reproductive rights, requesting that the Supreme Court consider the constitutionality of Missouri's abortion regulations. This case, *Webster v. Reproductive Health Services,* presented "an appropriate opportunity for overruling *Roe v. Wade.*" [43] It was some time before the case was heard and decided by the Supreme Court (Epstein and Kobylka 1992), but Reagan's pushing the issue forward so soon after a highly charged presidential election indicated to many on both sides of the abortion issue that Reagan and Bush intended to follow through on their pro-life promises. Referring to the election as a "feather in the pro-life cap," Joseph Scheidler predicted that the new president would nominate justices to the Supreme Court "who will overturn *Roe v. Wade.*" [44] With three justices approaching retirement, this was a very realistic scenario. A sense of foreboding crept through the pro-choice ranks. While anti-abortion activists were hailing the progress made during the Reagan years, pro-choice activists were growing weary of the repeated assaults on reproductive liberties. David Andrews, president of the Planned Parenthood Federation of America, commented, "From our point of view, it certainly has been a very long eight years . . . the Reagan Administration has tried every trick in the book."[45]

In 1989, the Supreme Court ruled in *Webster* that restrictions on access to legal abortion were not unconstitutional. At the same time, governors around the country, including Bill Clinton, were speeding up the execution process. Clinton signed more than sixty death warrants between 1988 and 1991, presided over one execution before announcing his intention to seek the Democratic presidential nomination in 1992, and presided over two more executions while campaigning.

1992

After what appeared to have been a successful war in the Persian Gulf, President George Bush was generally considered certain to win in the 1992 elections. However, there were a few problems facing him: the economy and the perception that he was out of touch with "common folks." In December 1991, Governor Bill Clinton appeared in New Hampshire in preparation for the 1992 primaries. Clinton quickly gained the attention of the media and was dubbed the front-runner early in the primary season, despite allegations of personal indiscretion. Within days of the New Hampshire primary, Bill Clinton and his wife, Hillary Rodham Clinton, appeared on the CBS television news program *60 Minutes* to answer questions about the stability of their marriage. This was the first time Clinton had the attention of a national prime-time audience, and he impressed many viewers.

Despite Senator Tom Harkin's hometown win in the Iowa Caucus,[46] presidential aspirants continued to pursue voters in the Democratic primaries throughout the winter of 1992. An important issue in the Democratic primaries was capital punishment. Only one candidate, Clinton, had personal experience using the death penalty. In late January, Clinton left the campaign trail in New Hampshire, returning to Arkansas to preside over the execution of Rickey Ray Rector. Rector, an African American, had been convicted of killing a police officer. After the killing, Rector had shot himself in the head; he survived, but suffered severe brain damage and, according to his lawyer, was left "a zombie." (Rector was unable to finish his last meal and wrapped up the dessert to save for when he was hungry again.) Clinton offered no public statement on the case and has never given an interview about his use of the death penalty in Arkansas.[47] Because of the issue of racial bias in capital punishment, Clinton had to be careful not to be seen as a racist. Rector was the second man to be executed in Arkansas while Clinton was governor. The first was a white man, John Swindler, also convicted of killing a police officer.[48] Later in the campaign, Clinton returned again to Arkansas to preside over the execution of a white man convicted of killing a state trooper.

Senator Paul Tsongas of Massachusetts won the Democratic primary in New Hampshire. Clinton took second place, and declared himself the "Comeback Kid,"[49] having weathered bruising accusations of marital infidelity. Clinton's showing in New Hampshire strengthened his position in the Super Tuesday primaries, held throughout the Northeast and the South.

Meanwhile, President Bush was facing a primary challenge from the right. Pat Buchanan campaigned in the New Hampshire Republican contest, focusing much of his energy on the abortion issue, as well as attacking Bush for breaking his pledge of "no new taxes." The margin of victory for Bush was "smaller than the Bush campaign had hoped, [which] left the impression that Mr. Bush had barely defeated his rival."[50] Buchanan took 37 percent of the Republican vote in New Hampshire and "drew blood" from his opponent. This contest was a struggle between conservative and moderate Republicans over which faction would control the party's agenda.[51] Bush was seen as weak on the "right flank," while Buchanan was a standard bearer for the conservative right. This internal upheaval demonstrated to the Democratic candidates the vulnerabilities of the Republican party.

Pro-choice activists, spurred by the *Webster* decision, were determined to have a greater voice in the 1992 election than they had had in 1988. The National Abortion Rights Action League organized a pro-choice demonstration in Washington, D.C. Clinton attended the march and declared his allegiance to abortion rights.[52] Some of the pro-choice activists were Republican women who were trying to encourage their party to abandon its anti-abortion plank. Ann E. Stone of Republicans for Choice wrote a commentary in the *New York Times* in which she chastized the G.O.P. for using the abortion issue as a "litmus test" in selecting nominees to the Supreme Court and other top government posts. She argued that it was a "grave miscalculation" to assume that all Republicans would prefer pro-life nominees.[53] According to a poll released in June 1992 by the Voter Research and Surveys organization, a majority in both parties favored legal abortion rights.[54] (The same poll demonstrated that the majority in both parties supported the death penalty.)

Anti-abortion groups were active as well. Operation Rescue prepared to protest in New York City at the Democratic National Convention. Anticipating physical confrontation with abortion rights protestors, some anti-abortion groups planned to practice self-control by taunting their fellow protesters. One anti-abortion activist elaborated: "We will likely walk through the room and shove them to the ground. We may apply a certain amount of pain. We also will likely throw things at them as they kneel in the room." This guerrilla training was intended to prepare pro-life activists for counterprotests by pro-choice activists. However, pro-choice activists were preparing for "completely non-violent" protests.[55]

Pro-life activists were also trying to influence voters. One pro-life leader said, "President Bush has done everything he could for the babies. Now the message of Right to Life to the Republican Party and the pro-life voters is that we should help him. . . . Stopping abortion is such a big part of my life that nothing else is important." Another activist proudly declared herself a "single issue voter."[56] This passion for voting pro-life has led to a consistently high voter turnout among pro-life activists.

In June 1992, Vice President Quayle gave a "family values" speech in which he called the creators of the television character Murphy Brown, a single mother, "cultural elites" who consider single parenting "just another lifestyle choice." Quayle reiterated this message for several weeks. When addressing the Southern Baptist Convention, he declared that people who are pro-choice "treat God's greatest gift, new life, as an inconvenience to be discarded." He continued:

> They believe that moral truths are relative and all "lifestyles" are equal. They seem to think the family is an arbitrary arrangement of people who decide to live under the same roof, that fathers are dispensable and that parents need not be married or even of opposite sexes. They are wrong. . . . But, we have the power of ideas, the power of our convictions and the power of our beliefs. And we shall carry the day.[57]

Later in the election season, Quayle appeared on the CNN interview program *Larry King Live.* The host asked Quayle what he, as a father, would do if his thirteen-year-old daughter became pregnant. Quayle responded that he would support her "on whatever decision she made," even if she decided to have an abortion. Issuing a press release the next day, Quayle and his wife, Marilyn, clarified the statement by claiming that "under the current situation, she would have the child. . . . We are pro-life and we are opposed to abortion."[58] Pro-life activists rallied beside the Quayles, stating that they viewed Quayle's comments as "consistent" with his pro-life position. The same question was then posed to President Bush. If one of his granddaughters wanted an abortion, Bush said, "Of course I'd stand by my child. I'd love her and help her, lift her up, wipe the tears away and we'd get back in the game." In the final analysis, he said, the decision should be left up to the woman in cases of rape, incest, and maternal health threat—"Who else's could it be?"[59] This inspired pro-choice activists, both Republican and Democrat, to criticize Bush and Quayle for having two standards of tolerance for abortion: a liberal standard for their own family members and a restrictive one for the general public.

A few weeks later, Quayle lashed out at Clinton for being "soft on capital punishment." Clinton had announced that, if elected, he would consider well-known death penalty opponent Mario Cuomo, former governor of New York, for a cabinet post. Quayle stated:

> [Clinton's] party is divided on this issue, so Bill Clinton says, "Well, I'm for capital punishment but, by the way, those of you who oppose capital punishment be reminded that one of my first appointments would be somebody like Mario Cuomo, if not Mario Cuomo, and of course you all know that he's an outright opponent of the death penalty." It's having it both ways. That's why he has the name Slick Willie.[60]

At the 1992 Democratic National Convention, the major concerns were to harness the energy from the primaries, rally around nominee Bill Clinton, and learn from the mistakes of 1988.[61] Abortion and capital punishment were not as divisive to the Democratic party as they might have been. With the realization that independent candidate Ross Perot would likely draw the pro-choice Republicans in the electorate away from Bush, the Democrats were happy with their position. Therefore, very little argument was offered on either abortion or capital punishment at the convention. One notable gaffe, however, was the decision to exclude Pennsylvania Governor Robert P. Casey from speaking at the convention. A pro-life Democrat, Casey supported Pennsylvania state laws restricting access to abortion. Activists on both sides of the abortion issue felt the decision to exclude Casey was "outrageous and indefensible."[62]

The abortion issue was more divisive at the Republican National Convention. Shortly before the convention, First Lady Barbara Bush announced that she felt the abortion issue would be better left out of the platform altogether.[63] The Republican platform called for a total ban on legal abortion, even in cases of rape and incest, which was more restrictive than President Bush's position on abortion. The party platform declared its allegiance to a "Judeo-Christian tradition" that requires the promotion of "faith in God, hard work, service to others and limited Government." In the preamble to the Republican platform, the party declared itself "the last best hope for man on earth." Some women delegates unsuccessfully challenged the gender-specific language of that declaration. Others challenged the phrase because it implied that Jesus Christ was not the "last best hope for man on earth."[64] In the end, the conservative wing of the party prevailed in maintaining conservative anti-abortion language[65] and at the same time avoided a floor fight over abortion at the convention.[66] Two main themes united the Republicans: disdain for the Democratic nominee and his wife, and "family values," which included an ideal of parents as heterosexual, married, and working hard to earn a living. These unifying themes converged in the Republican criticism of Hillary Clinton, and many conservatives labeled her an "unwifely feminist." Contrasting Hillary Clinton with Barbara Bush and Marilyn Quayle, both of whom rejected a professional career in order to stay home to raise their children, the Republican party identified what they considered to be a flaw among liberals: women didn't know "their place." Marilyn Quayle's speech at the Republican convention was widely hailed as an attack on feminism. She declared that "most women do not wish to be liberated from their essential natures as women."[67] The Republican convention inspired *New York Times* columnist Anthony Lewis to label the Republicans "merchants of hate." Lewis wrote:

> If the official Republican platform is carried out, a 13-year-old girl who becomes pregnant as a result of being raped by her father and has an abortion could end in the gas chamber. The platform says that every abortion, whatever the reason, however early in the pregnancy, is the unjustified killing of a human being. For the woman and the doctor, no mercy.[68]

Following the convention, the Bush/Quayle ticket enjoyed an upsurge in the public opinion polls, but a widening in the "gender gap" was noticeable. The margin of support for Clinton was 45 percent to Bush's 42 percent. Among women, support for Clinton had grown significantly (49 percent of women supported Clinton and 37 percent favored Bush), while among men support for Bush had expanded (47 percent of men supported Bush and 40 percent backed Clinton).[69]

The presidential and vice presidential debates of 1992 proved instructive for understanding the politics of abortion and capital punishment. Neither issue was mentioned in the initial debate between Bush and Clinton on October 11.[70] In the vice presidential debates two days later, Gore, Quayle, and Perot's running mate, Admiral James B. Stockdale, each offered their positions on abortion, but the topic of capital punishment was not raised. Gore responded to a question regarding the "bitter controversy" of abortion rights:

> Bill Clinton and I support the right of a woman to choose. That doesn't mean we're pro-abortion; in fact, we believe there are way too many abortions in this country, and the way to reduce them is by reducing the number of unwanted preg-

nancies, not vetoing family planning legislation the way George Bush has consistently done. The reason we are pro-choice and in favor of a woman's right to privacy is because we believe that during the early stages of a pregnancy, the Government has no business coming in and ordering a woman to do what the Government thinks is best.

Quayle responded:

This is an issue that divides Americans deeply. I happen to be pro-life. I have been pro-life for my 16 years in public life. My objective and the President's objective is to try to reduce abortions in this country. We have 1.6 million abortions. We have more abortions in Washington, D.C., than we do live births. Why shouldn't we have more reflection upon the issue before abortion—the decision of abortion is made? I would hope that we would agree upon that, something like a 24-hour waiting period, parental notification. . . . Let's not forget that every abortion stops a beating heart.

Stockdale, who began the debate by asking, "Who am I? Why am I here? I'm not a politician," offered his opinion: "I believe that a woman owns her body and what she does with it is her own business—period. Period."[71] The final debate between Bush, Clinton, and Perot did not cover the issues of abortion or capital punishment.[72]

After the debates, abortion and capital punishment faded from prominence in public dialogue. Clinton defeated Bush with 43 percent of the popular vote. Bush took 38 percent and Perot earned 19 percent. Again, exit polls revealed that the economy was the most important issue for voters. The death penalty was not cited by voters as an important issue, perhaps because all three candidates supported it. For approximately 10 percent of respondents in the exit polls, abortion was the key issue. The majority of those respondents indicated that they favored the anti-abortion position of the Bush campaign.

Subsequent research demonstrates that, in fact, abortion may have been a key issue in deciding the 1992 election. A study shows that "attitudes towards abortion had a strong influence on candidate choice in the overall electorate" (Abramowitz 1995, 185) over and above other political issues including the economy, defense spending, party identification, and the death penalty.

1996

The *New York Times*, on the Sunday before the election, declared the entire 1996 election year "the year of the yawn."[73] Abortion, however, remained a key issue for Republican contenders and was a threat to the congenial convention Republican leaders were trying to orchestrate in San Diego. In the Republican primaries, Bob Dole experienced a bumpy ride to the nomination, having been challenged by Pat Buchanan. A significant theme in Buchanan's campaign was his abortion position. When campaigning in the Southwest, Buchanan was asked about his opposition to abortion in the case of rape. His response was that the rapist should be executed, not the baby. Buchanan opposed abortion in all cases except to save the life of the "mother," while Dole opposed abortion in general but favored exceptions for women who are pregnant as the result of rape or incest, or when the fetus has severe defects. Consequently, the anti-abortion forces within the Republican party viewed Dole with suspicion because his views were not only more liberal than what the orthodox anti-abortion factions were willing to tolerate, but also more liberal than the party platform.

Buchanan gave the Dole campaign "the willies" after finishing first in the New Hampshire primary and holding his own in later primaries. In addition to their divergent views on abortion, there was a difference in the two candidates' economic messages. Buchanan utilized the traditionally Democratic populist economic strategy, appealing to the general population rather than the economic elite. Dole seemed unsure how to handle the Buchanan challenge; his future running mate Jack Kemp offered this advice: "I don't think we should turn our backs on the many fine people who have been supporting Buchanan."[74]

In late April, as the Republicans organized their convention, moderates within the party were planning on challenging the anti-abortion plank in the platform. The Voters News Service, a polling organization, reported that nearly 60 percent of Republicans voting in the twenty-eight state primaries in late March opposed the Republican abortion plank.[75] The abortion rights battle was waged by California Governor Pete Wilson, New Jersey Governor Christine Todd Whitman, Massachusetts Governor (and U.S. Senate candidate) William Weld, and Senator Olympia Snowe of Maine. This formidable team of moderate Republicans with national stature expressed the desire of the Republican majority that the pro-life plank be removed. A powerful special interest group, the conservative Family Research Council warned of a Republican rebellion if these individuals persisted in pressing the abortion rights issue at the convention. Council president Gary Bauer warned, "This is a prescription for disaster for Bob Dole and the Republican Party. These Governors are on this issue on the fringe. By pushing a fight, they're running the risk of blowing up the Republican Party." The Buchanan campaign also issued a statement: "If the Republican Party chooses to abandon the unborn, politically, it will be absolutely foolhardy." In light of this deep factionalism, Dole announced that he would appoint Representative Henry Hyde, a well-known abortion foe, to chair the Republican Platform Committee.[76]

At the Texas Republican Convention, pro-choice Senator Kay Bailey Hutchison's status as a delegate to the national convention was challenged by pro-life advocates. Dozens of Dole's Texas delegates were barred from the national convention because of their pro-choice or moderate pro-life positions. The *New York Times* reported that "most of the battles were not between abortion rights supporters and their opponents, but among anti-abortion factions over whether delegate candidates were sufficiently hard-line on the issue." A delegate from Texas said, "We wanted people who were pro-life before pro-life was cool." And the executive director of Texans United for Life addressed the convention: "When it comes to killing unborn children, there is really no room for tolerance. This convention has decided to say, 'we're not sending pro-aborts to San Diego to try to change our party platform.'"[77]

By July, Dole was in the unenviable position of having to appease two factions of his party who were bitterly divided over abortion. The polls indicated he was far behind President Clinton and he realized that he needed to do something remarkable to gain positive press coverage and the attention of the electorate. Dole's first move was to announce his support for tolerant language in the national abortion plank. Another strategy was to pepper the convention speakers with pro-choice moderate Republicans. Dole chose Representative Susan Molinari of New York, a well-known pro-choice Republican, to deliver the keynote address. Retired General Colin Powell, also an advocate of legal abortion, was selected to give a prime-time address on the opening night of the convention. The challenger who had gained a significant number of delegates during the primaries, Pat Buchanan, was eliminated from the list of speakers. Later in the campaign, Dole's daughter Robin announced her support of abortion rights and stated that the issue "belongs outside of politics."[78] These strategies were intended to send a message of inclusion to the national electorate.[79] Even with these movements toward compromise, Dole remained far behind Clinton in the public opinion polls, even in conservative strongholds.[80]

Meanwhile, the pro-life convention delegates were preparing for "war." Using top-of-the-line technology, the delegates were prepared to react within seconds should the whole convention be required to vote on the anti-abortion plank. Ralph Reed, executive director of the non-partisan Christian Coalition and a delegate to the convention, said, "Our goal was to have the largest number of religious conservatives on the floor of a national convention, and to have those delegates linked in a sophisticated high-tech communication system that would be real time and instantaneous."[81] Tactics included a "war room" in an undisclosed location, where the central computer was located, and small "personal communication services," which were available to every pro-life delegate on the floor, as well as to the whips, who were additionally armed with "personal digital assistants." The Christian Coalition spent $750,000 on these and other convention efforts. In the end, the Republican platform stated that "the unborn child has a fundamental individual right to life, which cannot be infringed," endorsed a Constitutional amendment to overturn *Roe v. Wade,* opposed the use of federal funds to pay for abortions in the United States or around the world, and opposed the contribution of money to organizations that advocate abortion rights, notably Planned Parenthood.

The Republican Convention was devoid of the conflict anticipated by abortion foes. The abortion plank issue was settled with a compromise that allowed a tolerance statement in the platform appendix. In fact, the convention as a whole was so well-scripted and congenial that Ted Koppel, the ABC television reporter and host of the late night show *Nightline,* left the convention early and hung a sign on his door: "gone fishin'." Koppel publicly announced that no news was being made in San Diego and it was not worth his time to stay. The convention was a nod to "inclusion" within the Republican party. Despite the vast majority of conservatives in attendance, most convention speakers were moderates, and their speeches addressed issues related to ethnic minorities and women.

The Democratic Convention was also relatively uneventful. Meeting in Chicago for the first time since 1968, the Democrats presented an image of inclusion and moderation as well. Abortion was not a contentious issue for the Democrats in 1996; the majority of the delegates were pro-choice and opposed Republican efforts to restrict and criminalize abortion. However, the label "liberal," successfully hung on Mondale in 1984 and Dukakis in 1988, was avoided at all costs. Clinton attempted to present an image of moderation to the general public.[82] The Democratic platform was not characterized by bitter disagreements over abortion; the Democrats stated:

[The] Democratic Party stands behind the right of every woman to choose, consistent with *Roe v. Wade,* and regardless of ability to pay. President Clinton took executive action to make sure that the right to make such decisions is protected for all Americans. Over the last four years, we have taken action to end the gag rule and insure safety at family planning and women's health clinics. We believe it is a fundamental constitutional liberty that individual Americans—not government—can best take responsibility for making the most difficult and intensely personal decisions regarding reproduction.[83]

Complicating abortion politics in 1996 was President Clinton's veto of the "partial-birth abortion" ban. The political debates about this procedure began during the summer of 1995, when the bill was introduced in Congress. The procedure, technically called "dilation and extraction" or "intact dilation and evacuation," is used in late-term abortions. It is an abortion procedure that requires the fetus to be partially extracted from the uterus through the birth canal, whereupon the cranial fluid and tissue is evacuated so that the fetus can be removed easily. Sponsors and supporters of the "partial-birth abortion" ban used graphic images of the procedure to sway public opinion and legislative votes. Furthermore, supporters of the ban argued that thousands of late-term abortions are performed in this manner. Opponents of the ban argued that the procedure is used in extreme and rare cases when continuing a pregnancy clearly poses a lethal threat to the pregnant woman or when a fetus is fatally deformed. They stated that the procedure is performed about 450 to 500 times per year in the United States, and that it is not an "elective" procedure.

The legislation called for punishing abortion providers with two years in prison for performing the procedure.[84] Editorial writers shared their opinions of the procedure and the legislation, giving both mixed reviews.[85] Abortion opponents hailed the legislation as one step in the right direction toward elimination of abortion, and, by focusing on a rare form of pregnancy termination, gained the support of many formerly inactive members of the "right to life" movement.[86] The bill passed in the fall of 1995 in the House of Representatives (288–139) and in the Senate (54–44).

Exploiting the presidential veto, Bob Dole attended a Christian Coalition rally and declared, "When I get the partial-birth abortion bill, I won't veto it, I'll sign it!" At the same rally, Pat Robertson, the coalition's founder, said that it would take a "miracle from God Almighty" for Dole to win the presidency, to which he added the following advice for Dole: "It's not the economy, stupid— it's morality, stupid and that's where the issue's going to be decided in this campaign." Dole left it up to his running mate to offer the crowd what they most wanted to hear:

> It is impossible to speak credibly about compassion for the weak while allowing the tragedy of partial-birth abortion. These children, just moments away from their first breath, must be allowed to live. Our nation must be humane enough and inclusive enough to welcome them into life. . . . And Bob Dole would never veto any attempt to save these precious lives.[87]

The Christian Coalition expressed concern over what they perceived as the moral vacuum evident in the Dole campaign. In order for Dole to win the election, they believed, it was crucial for him to emphasize the moral conservatism they advocated, which would then mobilize the coalition's dedicated activists to volunteer for local Dole/Kemp campaigns.[88]

The Christian Coalition was joined by many Roman Catholics, who sent approximately eight million postcards to their congressional representatives, urging an override of the veto. In September, the House of Representatives voted 285–137 to override the veto.[89] Shortly after the House vote, former Surgeon General C. Everett Koop wrote an opinion piece in which he urged the Senate to join the House in voting to override the veto. Koop wrote:

> In their strident efforts to protect partial-birth abortion, the pro-choice people remind me of the gun lobby. The gun lobby is so afraid of any effort to limit any guns that it opposes even a ban on assault weapons, though most gun owners think such a ban is justified. . . . Neither AK-47's nor partial birth abortion have a place in civil society. . . . The current and necessarily graphic debate about partial-birth abortion should remind all of us that what some call a choice, others call a child.[90]

On the day that the Koop piece was printed, *New York Times* editorial writers urged the Senate to uphold the abortion veto.

> Reliable statistics are difficult to come by, but the Alan Guttmacher Institute, which has long tracked abortion issues, reports that only some 15,000 of the estimated 1.5 million abortions each year take place after 20 weeks and only about 600 of those take place after 26 weeks or during the third trimester. A minority of these third-trimester abortions use the procedure that has stirred Congress's ire.[91]

The Senate voted on the override on September 27 and failed to gain the two-thirds majority needed, although a majority supported the override (57–41). Before the vote, Pennsylvania Senator Rick Santorum shouted, "My God, this is not an appendix. It's not a blob of tissue. It's a baby! It's a baby!!" Washington Senator Patty Murray commented, "It's really difficult for me as a woman to hear those men describing a procedure they've never gone through that has never affected their family with such arrogance. And I really find it objectionable to see pictures of women's body parts on the Senate floor." Ralph Reed predicted that the "second vote"—the presidential election—would go his way. National Abortion Federation director Vicki Saporta remarked, "I don't think [the abortion issue] will ever be over, [anti-abortion activists] think they're onto something."[92]

The Clinton campaign remained steady and emerged from the controversy relatively unscathed. Within two weeks of this bitter debate in Congress, new statistics were released indicating a drop in teen pregnancy and a drop in the number of abortions performed in the United States. President Clinton quickly claimed credit for this positive turn of events, stating that "the American family is getting stronger and we are making responsibility a way of life, our economy and our society are on the right track."[93]

Republicans' strict opposition to abortion was partially responsible for creating a "gender gap" among the electorate. Women voters favored Clinton by 10 percentage points, while men favored Dole by 16 percentage points. Likewise, 48 percent of women viewed Clinton favorably, while 44 percent of men viewed him favorably; 23 percent of women and 37 percent of men viewed Dole favorably.[94] Throughout the campaign, Dole trailed Clinton in the polls.

The death penalty was a minor issue in 1996. Early in the fall, Clinton won the endorsement of the Fraternal Order of Police (FOP), the largest police union in the country.[95] The FOP had endorsed Republican candidates for the previous two decades, and this Democratic endorsement marked an important departure from their traditional support of "law and order" Republicans. In an attempt to distinguish themselves in the war on crime, both Dole and Clinton went on the offensive. Dole cited statistics that teen drug use had doubled since Clinton took office and pointed to Clinton's own drug use. Meanwhile, Clinton cited the one hundred thousand new police officers he had put on the street and his support and use of the death penalty as reasons for the overall drop in crime rates.[96] Clinton continued trying to shed the label "liberal."[97] When Dole accused him of being a liberal, he responded, "There's a real problem with that, one is my record, my record as Governor, my record as President," pointing to his use of the death penalty while governor of Arkansas.[98]

Dole countered by visiting a tent jail while on a campaign swing through Arizona. The candidate praised Sheriff Joseph M. Arpaio for making incarceration as unpleasant as possible for the inmates. Maricopa County Jail inmates live in tent cities without air-conditioning in the Arizona desert, are served bologna sandwiches in paper bags for lunch, and are required to wear pink underwear. Inmates also work on a chain gang. Dole said he "talked to one of the inmates, who said: 'I don't want to come back here. I learned my lesson. I don't want to come back.' And I hope he never comes back."[99]

Late in September, Richard Allen Davis was sentenced to death in California for the well-publicized rape and murder of 12-year-old Polly Klaas, kidnapped from her bedroom during a slumber party.[100] A few months earlier, the jury had recommended the death sentence; Davis responded with an obscene gesture to the family members of his victim. At the final sentencing hearing, Joe Klaas, the victim's grandfather, gave a statement in which he said, "Mr. Davis, when you get to where you're going, say hello to Hitler, say hello to Dahmer and say hello to Bundy." Afterwards, Davis had a chance to address the court. He outlined possible areas of appeal for his case (ineffective assistance of counsel and procedural errors in collecting evidence) and went on to make a personal statement about his actions with the victim: "The main reason why I know I did not attempt any lewd act that night was because of a statement the young girl made to me while walking up the embankment: 'just don't do me like my dad.'" This case can be seen as an archetypal situation that justifies the death penalty in the United States; it is the type of case most often used by public officials to explain their support of the death penalty. Such a case can easily inflame public outrage and influence the electorate. After Davis's sentencing, Republicans running for Congress in California began to air television advertisements linking their Democratic opponents with Davis because of the Democrats' opposition to capital punishment.[101] However, these ads did not receive the national attention that the "Willie" Horton case did in 1988.

Bob Dole's performance in the presidential debates was a critical element of his campaign. A Dole adviser reported that "all strategic decisions have been put on hold . . . until after the debate."[102] Clinton was reportedly confident in his ability to perform well in the debates. Ignoring Pat Robertson's advice, Dole did not make morality a major issue in the debates. The first debate focused on economic issues, tax cuts, budget deficits, and foreign policy issues. Neither abortion nor the death penalty was discussed.[103] A well-known Republican strategist, William Kristol, implied that the debate was a missed opportunity for Dole: "The whole medley of social and cultural issues utterly disappeared Sunday night, and what's ironic are that those are the issues on which you could make a real case that Clinton is a liberal—and stayed to the left."[104]

Before the second presidential debate, Dole promised to "get tougher" on Clinton's character and liberalism.[105] Although he was more forceful in this debate, Dole missed several opportunities to attack Clinton on moral issues, as many of his advisors had suggested.[106] Dole's language often seemed more conciliatory to the moderates in the Republican party than to the conservatives. The second debate left many Republicans scrambling to secure their own congressional races by distancing themselves from their "lame-duck" candidate.[107] The debates did not significantly shift the public opinion polls or strengthen Bob Dole's stand in his challenge to Clinton.

Abortion was addressed in the vice presidential debate. Kemp was asked what, if anything, the Dole/Kemp administration would do to change the legal status of abortion. Kemp replied:

We should recognize that every human life is precious, and there should be all of the protection that we can give for an unborn human being. And to think that in this country, for every three births there is one abortion. But even worse than that, as ugly as that might be—and I know it's a tragedy to many people both on the pro-choice and pro-life position—we have a President who vetoed a Congressional ban on the ugly and gruesome practice of snatching life away from a child just moments before he or she enters the world. That is unacceptable.

Gore responded:

What is really at stake here is whether or not women will have the right to choose. The platform on which Mr. Kemp and Senator Dole are running pledges a constitutional amendment to take away a woman's right to choose and to have the Government come in and order that woman to do what the Government says no matter what the circumstances. . . . We will never allow a woman's right to choose to be taken away.[108]

What characterized this debate was the tone of civility between the two candidates. The debate was criticized by some observers as being overly civil. "Phrases like 'with all due respect' and 'my friend Al' were flying through the air like cruise mistletoes."[109] Influential conservative columnist George Will suggested that Kemp missed an important opportunity in the debate.[110] Again, the Dole/Kemp campaign had failed to clearly distinguish itself from the Clinton/Gore agenda and did not experience the jump in the polls that they desired.

Another problem for Dole involved the Christian Coalition's voter guides. The guides endorsed Dole/Kemp and other conservative Republicans as standard bearers for the coalition's agenda. The problem arose when the national office of the coalition circulated drafts of what the voter guides would look like. A photograph of a white man was positioned above one column listing coalition concerns, including the opposition to abortion on demand, while the photograph of a black man was placed above the other column listing support for abortion on demand and other issues in opposition to the coalition's stated policy objectives. The executive director of the Leadership Conference on Civil Rights charged that the flyer revealed the Christian Coalition's attitudes toward black candidates. Ralph Reed responded that "it was a mistake made by an outside vendor and not by any member of the Christian Coalition staff."[111] The damage was done, however. The situation was reminiscent of the "Willie" Horton ads from 1988, and the coalition was forced to defend itself against accusations of racism.

Even with all this, the campaign was considered boring by most observers.[112] One woman voter from Phoenix complained, "This is not 'War and Peace,' it's more like a Harlequin romance." A Clinton supporter, annoyed by the presi-

dent's continual references to building a "bridge to the twenty-first century," de-scribed the slogan as "Chinese water torture." The campaign produced the low-est voter turnout since 1924, with less than 50 percent of eligible voters participating.[113] Clinton again failed to gain a simple majority of the electorate, but won the election with 49 percent of the popular vote and 72 percent of the electoral college. Dole won 41 percent of the popular vote. The remaining 8 per-cent voted for Reform party candidate Ross Perot, despite his being shut out of the presidential debates and barely covered by the large news organizations. Clinton's reelection was attributed to the gender gap. Fifty-eight percent of women voters chose Clinton, while 38 percent supported Dole; 43 percent of male voters chose Clinton, and 44 percent voted for Dole. Racial politics also influenced this election. If white voters had been alone at the polls, Dole would have been elected president. Eighty-three percent of the electorate was white—46 percent supported Dole, 43 percent voted for Clinton, and 9 percent chose Perot. Among the 10 percent of the electorate who were African American, 84 percent supported Clinton, 12 percent voted for Dole. Latino voters followed a similar trend. In terms of religion, the vote was split as well. Fifty-three percent of white Protestants voted for Dole, while 36 percent voted for Clinton. Clinton received 53 percent of the Catholic vote to Dole's 37 percent.[114]

The nonpartisan Christian Coalition, angered by the election results, prom-ised to be more influential in the Republican party in the future.[115] Promising to begin building the coalition's influence in 1997 in preparation for the 1998 mid-term elections and the 2000 presidential race, Pat Robertson announced his tac-tic to go after the conservatives outside "the Beltway," calling those inside the Washington, D.C., establishment "incompetent and uninterested in moral is-sues." Apparently, moral issues will not disappear from the electoral process in the near future.

Public Opinion Research

The remainder of this chapter outlines public opinion research on abortion and capital punishment, along with the social variables involved in shaping public opinion on these issues. I focus on research findings on abortion opposition and death penalty support because the best research has been conducted on those particular positions.

Demographic Factors Related to Abortion Opinions

The general public is supportive of abortion in certain circumstances: if the preg-nancy endangers the woman's health, if there is a chance of serious defect in the fetus, or if the pregnancy has resulted from rape or incest. However, approximately 10 to 20 percent of Americans consistently oppose abortion even in these circumstances.[116] When other reasons for abortion are given, the majority of respondents opposes legal abortion.

Numerous social and cultural forces contribute to variations in abortion opinion in the United States. There are demographic differences, religious differences, and varying justifications for opposition to abortion. The following variables have been studied extensively with respect to abortion opinion: income, age, education, race, gender, and religion. These are attributes around which contemporary American society is structured, and it is important to understand how this social organization may influence opinions of abortion.

Research on income and abortion opinion has varied; there is no clear overall relationship, though people with higher income have a slight tendency to be pro-choice (Cook, Jelen, and Wilcox 1992). However, Cook et al. (1992) suggest that this relationship, when present, may be attributable to education (Granberg 1978; Granberg and Granberg 1980). Jelen (1988) reports weak and inconsistent findings with respect to income in various religious groups' attitudes toward abortion. Among Roman Catholics, income is negatively related to support of abortion in traumatic (in cases of rape, maternal health threat and/or fetal defect) and elective (for convenience or financial reasons) circumstances.

As with income, the findings regarding age and cohort affect have varied, but older respondents have been found to be less likely to oppose abortion than younger respondents (Chafetz and Ebaugh 1983; Cook et al. 1992; Granberg and Granberg 1980). We might suspect that gender has a major impact on abortion opinion, but the findings on gender are also inconsistent. Cook et al. found that "there is practically no relationship between gender and attitudes toward abortion" (1992, 44). When differences are reported, research indicates that women are slightly more likely to oppose abortion than men (Arney and Trescher 1976; Chafetz and Ebaugh 1983; Granberg and Granberg 1980; Scott 1989). Jelen (1988) presents mixed results with regard to gender differences and concludes that women are more likely than men to take a pro-life position in opposing traumatic and elective abortions.

Race and ethnicity have a more consistent impact on abortion opposition than the previously considered demographic variables. In general, black Americans are more likely to oppose abortion than white Americans (Wilcox 1990). Cook et al. report research in which "40 percent of whites supported abortion under all circumstances, compared with only 30 percent of blacks" (1992, 46). This difference is confirmed by Arney and Trescher (1976) and Granberg and Granberg (1980). However, Cook et al. surmise that the apparent racial difference may be attributable to religious affiliation; African Americans are more likely to belong to fundamentalist Protestant religions, within which abortion opposition is relatively strong. Other ethnic groups have been neglected in the study of abortion opinions.

Virtually all research on abortion attitudes has examined the relationship between religious affiliation and opposition to abortion. Cook et al. report that Roman Catholics (11 percent) and fundamentalist Protestants (10 percent) are more likely to oppose all abortions than mainline Protestants (4 percent) and those with no religious affiliation (1 percent). Furthermore, frequency of religious involvement is strongly associated with opposition to abortion; the greater the attendance at religious services, the greater the opposition to abortion (Cook et al. 1992; Arney and Trescher 1976; Chafetz and Ebaugh 1983; Clayton and Tolone 1973; Claggett and Shafer 1991; Davis 1980; Granberg 1978; Granberg and Granberg 1980; Huff and Scott 1975; Jelen 1988; Johnson and Tamney 1988; McCutcheon 1987; McIntosh and Alston 1977; Tamney et al. 1992; Wilcox 1990). Furthermore, viewing the Christian Bible as the literal word of God and believing that sin must be punished are views associated with absolute opposition to abortion (Cook et al. 1992). Cook et al. conclude that "all three white denominational groupings, religious involvement, biblical inerrancy, and punitive attitudes toward sinners are all negatively related to support for abortion rights" (1992, 124).

Level of education is also related to abortion opinion (Cook et al. 1992, Tamney et al. 1992). High school dropouts are more likely to oppose abortion than people with college educations. The effect of education is very consistent and is confirmed by various research. Arney and Trescher (1976) report research in which less than 5 percent of respondents with some college education opposed abortion in all circumstances, whereas up to 26 percent of high school dropouts opposed abortion in all circumstances. Cook et al. show that as level of education increases, pro-life opinions decrease. For example, from 1987 to 1991, "only 21 percent of those who dropped out of school before completing high school supported abortion in all circumstances, but nearly two-thirds of those who had attended graduate school supported unlimited access to abortion" (Cook et al. 1992, 48).

The Cultural Matrix of Abortion Opinions

Public opinion is influenced by cultural beliefs, attitudes, and values in American society. Research on abortion attitudes demonstrates that there are three basic underlying cultural themes related to abortion opposition: believing in human life as sacred, believing in a particular form of sexual morality, and valuing traditional gender roles.

SANCTITY OF LIFE. Luker (1984) argues that opposition to abortion is strongly related to the view that a human fetus is a sacred life that should be preserved. From this point of view, procedures or practices that interfere with a fetus's development, including abortion or the use of other forms of birth control (the IUD, the Pill, RU-486, etc.) are the moral equivalent of murder and therefore should be illegal, as murder is illegal. Many opponents of abortion begin with the premise that a fetus is fully human, possessing from the moment of conception a moral stature equivalent to that of any human being.

Various aspects of this pro-life position have been examined in the research literature on abortion opinions. The research assumes that a consistent pro-life position would include opposition to euthanasia as well as opposition to abortion, indicating a concern for the sanctity of life. Several scholars have used views of euthanasia as a measure of views of "sanctity of life" (Jelen 1988; Cook et al. 1992). Jelen's findings reveal that views of euthanasia are significantly related to abortion opposition among Roman Catholics, non-fundamentalist Protestants, and fundamentalist Protestants. Cook et al. (1992) report a similar finding: opposition to euthanasia is a significant predictor of opposition to abortion.

Granberg surmised:

> If opposition to abortion represented a generalized pro-life position . . . then those opposed to legalized abortion ought to also be disproportionately opposed to capital punishment, have less confidence in the military, and to favor increased spending to improve and protect the health of people while favoring a decrease in expenditures on the military and armaments. (1978, 421)

However, Granberg found no support for a pure pro-life position among those who support restrictions on abortion. In fact, his research results contradicted his hypothesis, suggesting a weakness in the pro-life position of abortion opponents. Specifically, "the notion that opposition to abortion represents a more generalized pro-life orientation received no support" (1978, 425).

Johnson and Tamney (1988) examined several aspects of pro-life values as they relate to abortion opposition. They found that many people who support capital punishment and oppose abortion hold seemingly "inconsistent life views"—they also tend to oppose gun control, favor an increase in defense spending, and belong to fundamentalist Protestant religions. One of the more salient characteristics of those who hold "inconsistent life views" is a belief in the use of physical force to solve problems (Johnson and Tamney 1988). Tamney et al. (1992) found that belief in the overall preservation of life was not significantly related to abortion opposition.

Research findings supporting the existence of a pro-life philosophy as a foundation for opposing abortion are, at best, inconsistent. While a deep concern for sacred human life may be the most acceptable and humanitarian justification for opposing abortion, there is considerable empirical evidence casting doubt on this justification.

SEXUAL MORALITY. Many abortion opponents believe that sexual licentiousness is a root cause of social problems, including abortion. Luker (1984) addressed issues of sexual morality in her conversations with anti-abortion activists. The activists expressed their belief that too much sexual freedom leads to an increase in unplanned pregnancies and that legalized birth control (contraception and abortion) allows sexually active people to avoid the most serious consequence of their actions—pregnancy.

Cook et al. (1992) find, similarly, that people who view traditional sexual morality favorably are most likely to oppose abortion, a relationship that remains strong when controlling for many other factors. Granberg (1978) measured "personal" morality as a combination of favoring large families, disapproving of premarital sex, and opposing divorce, birth control, sex education, and pornography, and found that such views are significantly associated with anti-abortion opinions.

Jelen (1988) defined sexual conservatism as opposition to sex education in schools, premarital sex, and adultery. Overall, sexual restrictiveness significantly increases the likelihood of traumatic abortion opposition, even more than "sanctity of life" among Catholics, non-fundamentalist Protestants, and fundamentalist Protestants. Johnson and Tamney found that sexual conservatism is significantly related to abortion opposition, concluding that abortion opponents "are not so much 'right-to-lifers' as 'sexual moralizers'" (1988, 44).

Overall, traditional sexual morality is consistently indicative of abortion opposition. The view that birth control allows the sexually promiscuous to avoid the consequences of their actions is an important component of abortion opposition. The majority of the general public supports abortion in the cases of maternal health risk, fetal defect, incest and rape, where the woman is considering abortion through no "fault" of her own. However, a significant proportion of Americans oppose abortion in cases where consensual sexual intercourse has led to an unintended pregnancy. Many abortion opponents believe that termination of pregnancies that occur in these conditions lessens the "price" people pay for their immoral behavior.

TRADITIONAL GENDER ROLES. Luker argues that the current abortion debate is a "referendum on the place and meaning of motherhood," (1984, 193) in American society. The world view of anti-abortion activists, in Luker's study, includes the belief that women's natural, biological, and emotional capacities make them better-equipped than men for primary child rearing responsibilities. Furthermore, women who "control" these natural capacities through artificial birth control are seen as effectively denying their proper roles in society. As one pro-life activist asserted, "I believe that there's a natural mother's instinct. And I'm kind of chauvinist this way, but I don't believe men and women are equal" (cited in Luker 1984, 160).

Cook et al. (1992) found that people who hold traditional gender role beliefs are more likely to oppose abortion. Granberg (1978) and Granberg and Granberg (1980) confirm these findings with a similar study of traditional gender roles and abortion attitudes. When women accept traditional gender roles, motherhood is central to their lifestyles. According to anti-abortion activists, support for the centrality of motherhood reasonably leads one to oppose abortion because abortion "devalues" motherhood (Luker 1984). Therefore, if motherhood is an option, not a requirement, women have a greater ability to deny the centrality of motherhood in their lives, thereby disrupting the "natural" order of society.

Other Factors Related to Abortion Opinions

The literature on abortion opposition reveals two more factors related to this point of view: political conservatism and obedience to authority. Since 1976, the Republican party has espoused an anti-abortion platform (McKeegan 1992). Republican political candidates appeal to socially conservative "blue collar" voters, and thus the Republican party has become the home of pro-life politics in the United States, especially for fundamentalist Protestants. Public opinion research demonstrates that political party affiliation is related to abortion opinions. Cook et al. (1992) found that among conservatives, 10 percent are opposed to abortion in all circumstances and 58 percent are opposed to abortion in some circumstances, whereas 5 and 43 percent of liberals hold those views, respectively.

Research has identified authoritarian themes in the anti-abortion movement and suggests that the prevalence of abortion may be due to the diminished respect and reverence for traditional authorities (Luker 1984; Blanchard and Prewitt 1993; Blanchard 1994). Luker (1984) found that anti-abortion activists are committed to women's subservience to their husbands' authority in the home. Often citing the Bible, they believe that women are to obey the authority of their husbands, and that all must obey the ultimate authority of God. If conception is viewed as a gift from God, to terminate a pregnancy is to disobey the authority of God. Blanchard and Prewitt (1993) follow up this analysis with evidence that abortion opponents see the world in strictly dualistic terms. The world's problems are seen as a struggle between the forces of good and the forces of evil, with legal abortion representing the victory of evil. When this worldview is shattered or seriously challenged, Luker claims, vindictiveness becomes "the order of the day" (1984, 159). Anti-abortion activists view their attempts to end legal abortion as their service to God's authority. The activists convicted of bombing abortion clinics in Pensacola, Florida, on Christmas Eve, 1984, claimed that they did so in order to give a "birthday present to Jesus" (Blanchard and Prewitt 1993).

Death Penalty Opinions

The death penalty has been studied extensively in the United States (see Radelet and Vandiver 1988, which compiles much of the literature), and public opinion on this issue has been charted since 1936. From 1936 to 1953 general support for the death penalty rose from 61 percent to 70 percent; support waned to 53 percent in 1956 and 42 percent in 1966, rose to 75 percent in 1985 (Bohm 1991); and rose again to 79 percent in 1988 (Bohm 1991) and 1989 (Gallup 1989). Using the General Social Survey, Fox, Radelet, and Bonsteel (1990) report that death penalty support reached 80 percent in 1985. Ellsworth and Gross pointed out in 1994 that the "support for the death penalty [was] at an all time high" (1994, 40) and that people's attitudes toward capital punishment were "hardening." The general public, legislators, judges, and other elected officials have been demonstrating a solid endorsement of "tough on crime" agendas. Clearly, the majority of the American public supports the use of death sentencing for convicted first-degree murderers. However, when respondents are probed for specific circumstances under which they would support the death penalty, support for capital punishment is reduced overall, although a slim majority remain supporters (Durham, Elrod, and Kinkade 1996). Durham et al. conclude that the majority of respondents in their research "would like to see the death penalty used for a wider variety of murders, such as those involving voluntary manslaughter" (1996, 728).

Public opinion can be used as a barometer of the evolving standards of decency in society. Legislators refer to public opinion when debating retention or abolition of the death penalty in their states (Zeisel and Gallup 1989). Public support was a factor in Supreme Court decisions such as *Furman vs. Georgia* and *Gregg vs. Georgia*. Supreme Court Justices have used public opinion research as a barometer of the public will in many controversial decisions, especially capital punishment, where gauging the "evolving standards of decency" is of paramount concern (Epstein and Kobylka 1992, 22). When considering the *Furman* cases, Justices Brennan and Marshall "put [their] clerks to work, gathering whatever they could to show that the death penalty was passé and, as such, should be adjudged unconstitutional" (Epstein and Kobylka 1992, 75), including public opinion research. When the *Gregg* cases came before the Court several years later, Solicitor General Robert Bork argued on behalf of the government to retain capital punishment and based his argument partly on public opinion research which demonstrated that the majority of Americans favor the death penalty (Epstein and Kobylka 1992, 106–107). This strategy worked; the Justices voted to reinstate capital punishment, with some strict procedural requirements. According to Zeisel and Gallup "the death penalty might become unconstitutional if prevailing standards of decency condemned it unmistakably" (287).

Demographic Factors Related to Death Penalty Opinions

Support for the death penalty varies with income, age, gender, race, education, religion, and regional differences. The summary of findings presented here is a combination of longitudinal analyses of thirty years of Gallup polls and fifteen years of General Social Surveys, as well as of various cross-sectional opinion surveys of distinct populations.

People with higher incomes have been shown to have greater levels of support for capital punishment. A Gallup poll (1986) found the strongest support for the death penalty (79 percent) among people with a household income of $50,000 or greater, and strong support (78 percent) among those with a household income between $35,000 and $49,999. The lowest level of support for the death penalty (60 percent) was found among people with a household income of less than $10,000. Respondents whose household income was $50,000 or greater preferred the death penalty (61 percent) to life without parole (30 percent). Preference for death sentencing waned as income fell; among those whose household income was under $10,000, 41 percent favored the death penalty, while 48 percent favored life without parole (Gallup 1986).

There appears to be no clear pattern of association between age and support for the death penalty. Kohlberg and Elfenbein (1976, 1981) assert that as moral development (a partial function of age) proceeds, support for the death penalty decreases. However, Vidmar and Ellsworth (1982) found consistently higher levels of support for the death penalty among older Americans. Bohm (1991) found that approximately 60 percent of Americans of all ages supported the death penalty throughout the years of the Gallup poll. Gallup (1986) found that across all age groups there was consistently high support for the death penalty (greater than 64 percent).

There appears to be an association between sex and death penalty support. In his longitudinal analysis of Gallup polls from 1936 to 1986, Bohm concludes that for "all 21 polls, the percentage of males who favor the death penalty exceeds the percentage of females" (1991, 123). Other research confirms this trend (Vidmar and Ellsworth 1982).

From 1936 to 1986, blacks had consistently lower levels of support for capital punishment than whites. The lowest was 22 percent in 1966 and the highest was 65 percent in 1953 (Bohm 1991). Combs and Comer (1982) found that while overall support for the death penalty rose from 1966 to 1980 there remained a large racial gap in support (45 percent black support and 70 percent white support). Aguirre and Baker found that "there is a very close association between white racial prejudice and support for the death penalty" (1995, 152).

Christian religious affiliation has no obvious relationship to death penalty support (Bohm 1991). Gallup (1986) reported that 72 percent of Protestants and 70 percent of Catholics favor the death penalty, and the majority of both groups (56 percent and 54 percent, respectively) support the death penalty over life without parole. Other research has confirmed this relationship (Vidmar and Ellsworth 1982; Johnson and Tamney 1988; Young 1992).

Residents in western regions of the United States show higher levels of support for the death penalty than people in any other region. Gallup (1986) reported that 76 percent of respondents in the western states favored the death penalty and that 60 percent supported the death penalty over life without parole for murder. The lowest levels of support are seen in the southern states (Bohm 1991). Since most executions occur in the South, this low level of support may seem surprising. Bohm attributes this to

> the disproportionate percentages of blacks and the poor in the South (both groups are less likely to support the death penalty), along with an almost totally white gentry judiciary (both groups are more likely to support the death penalty). (1991, 129)

The typical supporter of the death penalty appears to be a white, upper-middle-class male who may be fundamentalist Protestant or Catholic.[117]

The Cultural Matrix of Death Penalty Opinions

People who support the death penalty often believe that it deters crime, that it is necessary to wipe out crime, that it is cost-effective, that it is what murderers deserve, and also that it is morally correct for society to get revenge. This set of justifications can be examined in light of the utilitarian and symbolic elements of death penalty support. The utilitarian explanations include beliefs in the deterrent value of the death penalty, the instrumental use of violence as a response to criminal activity, and the cost-effectiveness of death sentencing as opposed to life without parole. The symbolic explanations include retributive justifications and belief in the moral correctness of being "tough on crime" and on criminals.

UTILITARIAN EXPLANATIONS. The belief that fear of capital punishment will deter others from committing capital crimes is the most commonly offered justification for capital punishment (Ellsworth and Ross 1983; Thomas and Foster 1975). However, in one study of death penalty supporters, "two thirds (66 percent) claimed that they would still favor capital punishment even if it were proven to be no better than life imprisonment as a deterrent" (Ellsworth and Ross 1983, 147).

Gallup claims that although most people refer to deterrence as a primary reason for supporting capital punishment, "the principle of deterrence plays a relatively minor role in shaping basic attitudes" (1986, 11). In addition, Thomas and Foster (1975) claim that the belief in deterrence is based on the simplistic idea that the harsher the punishment, the less likely people will be to commit the offensive behavior. They explain the reasons for a belief in the deterrent effect of the death penalty as "a utilitarian socialization system, and the pervasive belief that severe punishment serves an effective deterrent function" (1975, 646). Therefore, harsh punishment, including capital punishment, is viewed as an effective way to solve the problem of crime.

American culture promotes the use of violence as a means to an end. Evidence of this is abundant (Archer and Gartner 1984). President George Bush enjoyed the wide support of the American public in the use of military force in the Persian Gulf War. The American public widely supports spanking and paddling young children as a means of discipline, and even feels that such punishment is necessary and good (Straus et al. 1980, Straus 1994). Not surprisingly, most Americans support capital punishment as a rational-instrumental tool for the state to use in controlling and punishing criminals (Vidmar and Miller 1980). Gelles and Straus refer to this as the "calculus of administration" (1976, 234). That is, the use of violence can be rational and calculated as a response to behavior that is perceived as socially unacceptable.

Ellsworth and Ross (1983) present findings regarding the instrumental value of capital punishment. Eighty-two percent of death penalty proponents in their research agreed that "we need capital punishment to show criminals that we really mean business about wiping out crime in this country" and 84 percent agreed that "society benefits more if the murderer is executed than if he is sentenced to life imprisonment" (1983, 151). Likewise, 94.2 percent disagreed with the statement "The death penalty serves no purpose" and 83.7 percent disagreed with the statement "Executions set a violent example which may encourage violence and killing" (1983, 153). Research shows that supporters of capital punishment see it as an instrumental solution to the problem of crime in the United States (Ellsworth and Ross 1983; Thomas and Foster 1975).

Most Americans support the death penalty because they believe that it costs less than life imprisonment without parole. Ellsworth and Ross (1983) report that over 80 percent of death penalty proponents believe that life without parole is more expensive than capital punishment. Tyler and Weber show that some people believe that "it is important to have the death penalty to save the price of life in prison" (1982, 32). While this belief may initially appeal to common sense, research shows that it is erroneous (Nakell 1982; Garey 1985). On the average, a death sentence is five times more costly than a life-without-parole sentence. This is due in part to the complicated nature of capital trials, which involve expert witnesses and generally last longer than non-capital murder trials. In addition, there is a mandatory appeals process, which is tremendously expensive for states and the federal government.

Most Americans, then, claim to support capital punishment based on their rational and instrumental beliefs in its deterrent effect, social utility, and cost-effectiveness. Ellsworth and Ross argue:

> People believe that they know the facts about deterrence and that the facts support their opinions; however, it is clear that factual evidence is extraneous to their opinions, since they also say that if the facts were different, their opinions would be the same. This is particularly interesting in regard to evidence about deterrence, since this is usually the first evidence that people (especially Retentionists) spontaneously present in support of their opinions. It may be that the belief in deterrence is seen as more "scientific" or more socially desirable than other reasons; people mention it first because its importance is obvious, not because its importance is real. (1983, 149)

SYMBOLIC EXPLANATIONS. Retribution has been identified as one of the more salient justifications for supporting capital punishment (Haas 1994). Haas defines retribution as punishment "guided by considerations of proportionality, fairness, and equality" (1994, 127). Vengeance, on the other hand, is "aimed at satisfying the victim's and society's desire for retaliation" (1994, 127). According to Gibbs, the "retributive doctrine is not haunted by [rehabilitation] problems . . . largely because it is not *utilitarian*. Since its goal is 'doing justice' rather than prevention of crimes, it makes no instrumental claims" (1978, 293). Warr and Stafford (1984) report that retribution is the most commonly stated primary goal of punishment (42 percent of respondents). Interestingly, only 5 percent of respondents in their research claimed that normative validation, defined as "maintaining moral standards in our society . . . the maintenance or intensification of norms resulting from punishment," is a primary goal of punishment (1984, 98). However, normative validation is achieved, by default, through retribution. That is, the cultural meaning of punishment is to reaffirm the moral standards of propriety and acceptable behavior. Therefore, supporters of capital punishment view it as a powerful means of maintaining social order (Warr and Stafford 1984, 104).

Through socialization and acceptance of culturally defined justifications for punishment, people come to believe in the cultural propriety of executing criminals. Vidmar and Miller (1980) assert that retributive attitudes are a consequence of the socialization process, which instills the belief that criminal activity is an assault on the social system and that punishment is just and proper.

> Public punishment or at least public knowledge of the punishment, also allows reactors to exchange expressions of approval over the fate of the offender and the "rightness" of the violated rule, thereby reaffirming and solidifying social consensus. (1980, 582)

Public knowledge and expressions of approval serve to marginalize those who do not support the use of a particular punishment and unite those who do. Essentially, "the offender is merely an object through which group solidarity and consensus are achieved" (Vidmar and Miller 1980, 582). Support for the death penalty can be viewed as an appeal to the popular sovereignty of retributive justice.

Retributive attitudes are an expression of the punitive ideology of American culture. Most people offer rational-instrumental justifications for supporting the death penalty, but research shows that close to half of those individuals would continue to support capital punishment even if it were demonstrated that capital punishment had no rational-instrumental effects (Fox, Radelet, and Bonsteel 1990). Ellsworth and Ross report that 44.9 percent of death penalty proponents in their research agreed that "society has a right to get revenge when a very serious crime like murder has been committed" (1983, 151). For those who staunchly support capital punishment, retributive justice is the basis of their support (Vidmar and Miller 1980), and the legacy of punitive justice in American culture provides ample justification for these sentiments.

Tyler and Weber (1982) argue that predispositions in political and social attitudes have a significant impact on support for the death penalty and for other punitive penal policies. The "law and order" syndrome and support for punitive policies is a reflection of the dominant cultural and political ideology, which generates wide support for capital punishment based on the "morality" of killing criminals (lex talionis). Support for capital punishment can be viewed as an indicator of support for "law and order" political agendas. This "wave of punitiveness" (Gross 1993) has spread throughout the population, which now endorses such policies as "three strikes and you're out" and "truth in sentencing," effectively eliminating parole for all offenders (Rothman 1995).

Ignatieff asserts that there has been an evolving partnership between the state and civil society and that "public rituals (executions, pillory, whipping and branding) required completion by the opprobrium of the crowd if they were to have full symbolic effect" (1983, 85). Public opinion is formed as a result of a similar partnership, with the voice of the state being echoed by average citizens.

Purdum and Paredes argue that capital punishment recalls traditions of human sacrifice in pre-civilized society.

> [M]odern capital punishment is an institutionalized *magical* response to perceived disorder in American life and in the world at large, an attempted magical solution that has an especial appeal to the beleaguered, white, God-fearing men and women of the working class. And in certain aspiring politicians they find their sacrificial priests. (1989, 153)

Common Empirical Foundations

Scholars have been curious about the seemingly inconsistent views of those who are pro-life and also support capital punishment (Luker 1984; Blanchard and Prewitt 1993; Claggett and Shafer 1991; Johnson and Tamney 1988). Luker has commented that this difference hinges on the due process of law (1984, 263). Essentially, abortion opponents are concerned about what they consider the arbitrary taking of life and see capital punishment not as arbitrary but as safeguarded by the due process system. Blanchard and Prewitt suggest that these views are shared by "culturally conservative American readers of Hebrew law and narrative" (1993, 24), which promotes the "eye for an eye" philosophy as well as obedience to God's authority in all matters of morality.

Claggett and Shafer group their research respondents into four categories, one of which is "Just Deserts," which includes those opposed to abortion and in favor of capital punishment. This group "supports the taking of life for the guilty, presumably those convicted of sufficiently heinous crime, but not the taking of life for the innocent, those who cannot be said to be sufficiently conscious to make choices—and pay penalties" (1991, 34). These respondents were identified as those who approved of "a mandatory death penalty for anyone convicted of premeditated murder" and "changing the laws to make it more difficult for a woman to get an abortion" (1991, 35). Thirty-five percent of Claggett and Shafer's respondents were categorized as "Just Desserts" [sic].

Extending the concept of Just Deserts, Cook (forthcoming) used the 1988 General Social Survey to test the theory that those who are punitive (i.e., agree with the statement "Those who violate God's rules must be punished") would be more likely to oppose abortion and favor the death penalty. The findings demonstrate that a punitive individual is twice as likely to oppose abortion and favor the death penalty as someone who is not punitive. The findings in this research question the existence of the "value of life" ethic that some people claim underlies opposition to abortion and support for capital punishment (Cook, forthcoming).

Abortion research indicates that opposition to abortion is more a matter of cultural beliefs than a matter of structural boundaries. Death penalty research indicates that those who have more vested interests to protect, those with societal power, are more likely to support capital punishment.

General Social Surveys, 1977–1994

The General Social Surveys are used here to outline abortion and death penalty opinions in the general public. Respondents were asked their opinions on abortion and capital punishment separately. In 1994, the most current year for which these data are available, responses to the question of whether "it should be possible for a pregnant woman to obtain a legal abortion" were as follows:

1. If there is a strong chance of serious defect in the baby (no: 17.7 percent)
2. If the woman's health is seriously endangered by the pregnancy (no: 9.4 percent)
3. If the woman became pregnant as the result of rape (no: 16.4 percent)
4. If the woman is married and does not want any more children (no: 51.7 percent)
5. If the family has a very low income and cannot afford any more children (no: 49.6 percent)
6. If the woman is not married and does not want to marry the man (no: 52.4 percent)
7. If the woman wants an abortion for any reason (no: 53.7 percent)

When asked if they "favored or opposed the death penalty for someone convicted of first-degree murder," 79.2 percent of respondents in 1994 said they favored the death penalty.

In order to condense these data into usable form, I constructed a variable measuring public opinion on abortion in "social distress" circumstances (low income, when the woman wants no more children, when the woman is single, and on demand). In 1994, for instance, 41.9 percent opposed abortion in all social distress categories, while 58.1 percent supported legal abortion in at least one of the social distress categories. Next, a cross-tabulation of this social distress measure of abortion opinions and the respondents' views on the death penalty was

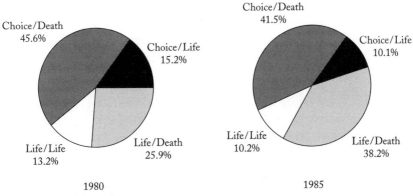

Figure 2.1 Abortion and Death Penalty Opinions, 1980, 1985

Choice/Death
45.6%

Choice/Life
15.2%

Life/Life
13.2%

Life/Death
25.9%

1980

Choice/Death
41.5%

Choice/Life
10.1%

Life/Life
10.2%

Life/Death
38.2%

1985

Source: General Social Surveys

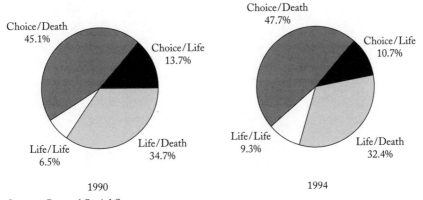

Figure 2.2 Abortion and Death Penalty Opinions, 1990, 1994

Choice/Death
45.1%

Choice/Life
13.7%

Life/Life
6.5%

Life/Death
34.7%

1990

Choice/Death
47.7%

Choice/Life
10.7%

Life/Life
9.3%

Life/Death
32.4%

1994

Source: General Social Surveys

calculated. Figures 2.1 and 2.2 illustrate these cross-tabulations as pie charts for 1980, 1985, 1990, and 1994. The statistics indicate that a plurality of respondents in every year can be categorized as pro-choice and pro–death penalty, while the next most common set of opinions is pro-life and pro–death penalty. The less common sets of opinions are pro-life and anti–death penalty and pro-choice and anti–death penalty. The category of pro-choice and pro–death penalty remained fairly stable over the seventeen years of surveys. However, there was a notable increase in the pro-life and pro–death penalty group from 1980 to 1985, with modest reductions in 1990 and 1994. The group comprised of those who are pro-life and anti–death penalty was reduced by half from 1980 to 1990, and had increased slightly by 1994. The pro-choice and anti–death penalty group fluctuated from 1980 to 1994, as shown in the pie charts.

These survey data should be viewed as broad outlines of opinions in the general public. The following chapters will help to illuminate the texture and complexities of these opinions and will show how the people come to their conclusions about abortion and capital punishment.

CHAPTER THREE

Pro-Choice and Anti–Death Penalty

Abortion and capital punishment are examined in this chapter through the eyes of those who support legal abortion choice and oppose capital punishment. Figure 3.1 shows the fluctuations within this opinion set from 1977 to 1994. In the late 1970s more than 15 percent of GSS respondents supported legal abortion while opposing capital punishment. The proportion fell to 10 percent by 1985 and remained below 13 percent through the rest of the 1980s and into the 1990s.

There are two men and six women in the pro-choice and anti–death penalty group: Sonny, Sara, Leigh, Wayne, Emma, Mildred, Madeline, and Felicia.

Summary of Interviewees

I talked with Leigh, a nineteen-year-old college student, at a university library in Mississippi. She has spent most of her life in the Deep South. Leigh describes her extended family members as "very conservative" Christians, but says her parents were not, so that "may be why I've ended up the way I am; a lot more open minded than the rest of my family." She attends services at a theologically liberal church, but says her abortion and death penalty opinions have not been strongly influenced by her religious beliefs. Leigh is very critical of Republicans and expresses her belief that the political right tries to use the poor and ethnic minorities as scapegoats for societal problems. She describes herself as a feminist.

Figure 3.1 Pro-Choice and Anti–Death Penalty, 1977–1994

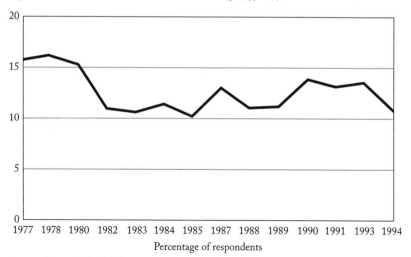

Percentage of respondents

Source: General Social Surveys, 1977–1994.
Note: No surveys were conducted in 1979, 1981, 1986, and 1992.

I spoke with Sara, also a nineteen-year-old college student, at a university library in Mississippi. Like Leigh, Sara has spent most of her life in the Deep South. She was raised with a diversity of Christian traditions, including Episcopalian, Catholic, Presbyterian, and Baptist. She attends a theologically liberal church and is very critical of traditional Christian practices that, she says, systematically marginalize women. Sara asserts that "most traditional small churches are still patriarchal organizations." Sara studied religion in college and describes herself as a "modified deist,"[1] but says religion has not strongly influenced her opinions on abortion and the death penalty. Sara says she has been "pretty much within the Republican party. But, I can be a bleeding heart when it comes to sexual issues." Despite George Bush's pro-life position, Sara voted for him in 1992 because she perceived him to be the more respectable candidate.

I talked with forty-seven-year-old Sonny at his university office in Mississippi. He is a full professor of science who has lived in Mississippi for more than ten years. He has been a citizen of the United States since 1988, having emigrated from India. Sonny is married and has a teenage daughter. Although he was raised in a Hindu family and schooled by Jesuits, Sonny is an atheist. He says, "As a scientist you have to [be]; the two things are negations in terms, they're mutually opposed." He says, "I don't believe there's anything pre-ordained. I don't believe there's a superior being sitting there like a puppet master, moving things around . . . The other thing is, as Karl Marx said, [religion is] the opiate of the masses, and God and all that is a figment of man's imagination." Sonny

CHAPTER THREE

describes himself as "ultra liberal" and a "card-carrying member of the ACLU." Sonny explains that he writes letters about social issues to the editors of local papers and has received some "nasty letters" in response. "I'm a dark-skinned foreigner, too," he adds, which he believes further complicates his political reputation.

I talked with Wayne in my university office lounge. He is a fifty-two-year-old white man who has lived in Maine all his life. Wayne is a sporadically employed mechanic who speaks with a very thick "down east" accent; our conversation is punctuated with "ayuh" and other Maine colloquialisms. Wayne was raised a Methodist, but says, "I have more Catholic views than anything." He has attended many different churches. Wayne is a liberal Democrat who believes that "the Republicans and the Libertarians are very dangerous people. We need kindness in our nation, we need to start looking at home in our nation, because people are still looking abroad, sending our stuff to Mexico. We need socialized medicine. I don't think the minimum wage should be a political football." Wayne cites passionate opposition to the death penalty as "one reason why [he] won't live in Florida [where the death penalty is used]."

I talked with thirty-four-year-old Madeline at her office in Maine. She is a married white woman, with two children. Madeline is a lawyer in a large firm who has also worked as an assistant district attorney. She was raised in the Episcopal church but attends Catholic mass with her husband and children. She describes herself as being "at a truce" with the Catholic church because "I don't accept what they think about abortion and some other issues, and they don't accept what I think about it, and that's OK. We can go on from there. There are still other issues that we have in common, other facets of the church that I think are important. We go from there." Madeline describes herself as a "socially liberal and financially conservative" Democrat. She considers the amount of money spent on the defense industry "outrageous" and would prefer to see a "shift in priorities in the money that we spend away from defense, away from [farm] subsidies, away from travel for our representatives, and all this stuff, and to support education and social services."

I met with Mildred, a fifty-year-old African American woman, at her home in Maine. Mildred is not married and has no children. She has worked in "traditionally male occupations" all her life, which has given her some insights about gender and race issues. Mildred was raised as an Episcopalian, but was encouraged by her mother to learn about other religious traditions as well. Consequently, she is familiar with Catholicism and Judaism. She views God as loving and compassionate, a view that has an important influence on her opinions on abortion and the death penalty. Mildred has been a Republican, an Independent, and a Democrat. She says, "I suppose basically I'm a Democrat, but when I become a Republican it's to work from the inside. My philosophy of change is not to pound on the door and try to bring about change from the outside, but to go inside and effect change from the inside out." Mildred sees abortion and the death penalty as related in an interesting fashion. She feels that when a woman makes the choice to have a child, we as a society ought to do our best to support that decision by making material contributions to the woman and her child, which will in the long run help to prevent crime and thus prevent the need for the death penalty. Mildred describes herself as a "founding mother" of the women's movement and sees the contemporary feminist agendas as too fractured and in too much disarray to be effective.

I talked with Emma at her home in a rural town in Maine, where she lives with her son and daughter-in-law. She is a sixty-seven-year-old widowed mother of thirteen children. Emma is a very well-read and talkative woman whose life experiences have laid the foundation for her opinions about abortion and the death penalty. She was raised Catholic, and raised her children Catholic. Emma's father was "very anti-clerical," while her mother was a devout Catholic; as a result, Emma has developed her own independent faith. She is "very comfortable in the church, but I don't agree with everything they want me to believe." She attends mass less often than she would like because of her work schedule. Emma does not identify herself politically, but says she would not vote for a pro-life politician.

I talked with Felicia at her home in a quiet neighborhood in Maine. Felicia is a talkative and energetic twenty-six-year-old married woman without children. She works part time, and her husband has a sizable income. Though she was "baptized Catholic," she no longer attends Catholic masses. She believes in God and "everything; karma, fate, destiny, but I think they all might be one and I'm just getting them confused. And I think that they're wonderful, it's wonderful to have some sort of belief system." The most important religious tenet that Felicia tries to incorporate into her life is the "golden rule" to be "a good person"—the "do unto others type of thing." Felicia sees herself as an Independent. She says she would vote for the "best man for the job." Felicia normally "looks at taxes and programs, what's [the candidate] doing for programs, if he wants to increase this and increase that [and the impact] on my pocketbook." She feels that abortion and the death penalty should not be political issues at all; to her, they are moral issues.

Abortion Opinions

The abortion opinions in this group are often based on personal experiences. One of the first things Madeline relates is her own experience with abortion about twelve years prior to the interview. She was in college at the time and in a relationship with a young man with whom she was not seriously considering spending her life. She chose to terminate a pregnancy and was glad that the procedure was safe and legal. She says

> In my mind at the time, [having a child] was not an option. My feelings about that now do involve some regret, but it's still my decision. It's no more someone else's decision to say you can't have one than someone's decision to say you must have one. I really feel that it's up to the person, based on that person's own beliefs. And there are people who feel very strongly that abortion is wrong, and without being trite I feel like saying to them, "Then don't have one."

Madeline says that for a young woman with an unwanted pregnancy, "there are no great choices," but to legally eliminate one choice is to "virtually guarantee that women will die." According to Madeline, "Women will [have abortions]; I did it. If you make abortion illegal women will die; they will go to people who are not professional and they will get infected and die."

Emma's pro-choice position is largely based on her experiences as a mother. She gave birth to nine children and took in four others. She says she knows the joys and the heartaches of raising children and that the law should not mandate that a woman become a mother against her will. Emma tells a story about her teenage great-niece, who had returned home after being a nanny for a pastor and his wife. After talking to her great-niece, Emma came to the conclusion that she had been raped by the pastor and was pregnant with his child. Emma's great-niece did not tell anyone about the pregnancy and gave birth prematurely in a bathroom. The baby died of a rupture in the umbilicus. Not knowing what else to do, Emma's great-niece put the dead baby in a duffle bag, where it was later discovered by the girl's uncle. No charges were filed against the girl, but in Emma's opinion, this is clearly a case where abortion would have been the preferred option.

Wayne's opposition to the death penalty is loosely based on his experience with racial discrimination. As a white, working-class man, he dated an African American woman and was verbally harassed while out with her in public. In a dispute with another person over money, Wayne's companion refused to pay what she owed him. A pushing match ensued, and the police intervened. Wayne says, "I kind of put two and two together. I was with a black girl and the cop didn't . . . tell me my rights or anything. They just handcuffed me and put me in the cruiser, and I went to jail." Wayne is opposed to anything he perceives to be racially discriminatory, which includes the death penalty.

For the most part, opinions are expressed in terms of the interviewees' personal beliefs and values related to life and death. An overriding concern among this group is the quality of children's lives. These interviewees generally agree that the government should not be in the business of regulating personal choices of when women should give birth and when people should die.

Abortion opinions are largely based on specific beliefs about life, including beliefs about when life begins. According to some of the interviewees in this group, life begins at conception. Even so, they do not think that this "life" should be legally protected. According to Emma:

> Because that life has not been born yet, that life may be spontaneously aborted. The laws that might be instituted, might develop to protect that unborn life, may adversely affect lives that are already in motion and functioning. . . . Who knows what's going to happen if this woman indeed cannot have an abortion. . . . No, I just don't think that laws like that should be instituted.

Madeline suggests that life might actually begin before conception because "women have eggs and men have sperm in them, and they are instruments of future life." But she believes that it would be wrong for her to impose that definition on other people. Sara thinks that because life begins at conception, abortion is "kind of an evil" but that sexual abstinence is not a realistic option for many people either. Leigh considers both the rights of a fetus and the potential for dangerous illegal abortions:

> That's another thing that I think is very important, is that how [women] were hurt from illegal abortions, some of them were sterile, and women who bled to death. I know that pro-life people hold up the pictures of the aborted fetus, and there's a photo that I've seen of a naked woman, dead, with blood all over her, who bled to death from an illegal abortion. And it's really pretty awful. It's bad, I think.

For Wayne, life begins precisely at the beginning of the second trimester, at which point he feels abortion should be illegal. For him, abortion is acceptable in the first three months because "it's early and the child wouldn't know." Mildred likens the time shortly after conception to a seed: "Do you call that seed the specific plant, like basil? Because it happens to be the seed that has the potential of being basil, but at that point it's not basil." Leigh comments:

> I don't think that life begins at conception. I think when I start to have a problem with abortion, as I understand it, third trimester is illegal unless the woman's life

is in danger. I start having a problem with abortion when, if the baby were born prematurely, when it could survive outside the womb. That's when I start to have more ethical problems. But as far as I'm concerned, [before the third trimester] it's cells.

Felicia and Sonny believe that life begins at birth. "When it's come out and alive and kicking is when it's a baby," according to Sonny. Felicia shares this view, and says that a person's birthday sums it up: "It's your entry into the world. I always think, you don't say he was conceived on Easter, he was born on January 6, 1986. You don't celebrate his conception days. You celebrate his birth days. Which means life begins at birth." Felicia believes that "something magical happens at conception" but feels that it is up to the individual whether to call that life.

Madeline says it is a matter of the "woman's jurisdiction . . . to choose what happens to her body." No one else, including a legislator or judge, can decide what is best for an individual woman; "it's none of the state's business." Privacy is an important concern of these interviewees; they believe the state should not interfere with a woman's private decisions.

Another common theme throughout the conversations is a major concern for the quality of life of the pregnant woman, as well as the child. Madeline says:

A big factor in [deciding whether to have a child] has got to be how [the woman is] going to care for the child, what kind of life the child's going to have. Now if the child's going to grow up with, if the partner that she's with, for example, is a very abusive person, as the woman looks at the future of this child and says "No, I'm not going to submit the child to this." If the mother is a crack addict. If the mother is an alcoholic. If the mother has other things going on in her life that are going to make the child's life an unsafe one. I think those are factors that go into the decision. That are going to go into the decision. And should she be prevented from having an abortion when she wants one, the child will grow up with a lot of risk factors, and she's going to resent the heck out of the kid, and it's not going to be a productive situation for anyone. Not only for her or for the child, but for their community.

Mildred echoes this concern by saying that abortion accomplishes nothing more than the termination of a pregnancy, "but in broader issues it's providing a means of ongoing life for the current life. I mean for the person that happens to have the pregnancy." Wayne, Sara, and Leigh share these quality of life opinions also. Leigh comments, "There are so many children that are born to children them-selves, who can't take care of them. And I think that's wrong. And there are children that just sit in orphanages or that are stuck in foster care because they're unwanted." Sonny, however, is also concerned about his own quality of life, as well as that of the potential child, saying that he supports legal abortion,

> primarily because I don't want to burden that woman. Because I can present it in societal costs. Because it's going to cost me. If that child, especially is born to an indigent person, or somebody who can't afford to have children, then of course it's going to increase the cost to society. Because now we're going to have to start paying welfare and aid to families with dependent children. All these things will start increasing as well. So I'd much rather, as a selfish guy not wanting to have any more taxes to be paid, I'd much rather have them go have an abortion.

The interviewees disagree, however, on whether there ought to be legal restrictions on access to abortion, such as parental consent, spousal notification, or waiting periods. Madeline, who does not support any restrictions on legal access to abortion says that "going to a judge is not a realistic exception, [it's] still putting women in danger." As a lawyer, Madeline is concerned about the Supreme Court's *Webster* decision, in which Sandra Day O'Connor (writing for the majority) did not specifically define "undue burden." According to Madeline, "A lot of things can cause an undue burden to a fourteen-year-old that to the Supreme Court may not appear to be an undue burden. And they may cause an undue burden to a woman that is in [rural Maine] that they wouldn't cause for a woman living in New York City; a twenty-four-hour waiting period is what I'm talking about there."

Sonny favors the current law, as outlined by the Court in *Roe v. Wade*, because "there is a physiological effect that is much more devastating and a psychological effect that is much more devastating as you go more and more into full-term pregnancy." Under *Roe v. Wade* access to legal abortion cannot be prohibited in the first trimester, can be restricted in the second trimester and can be prohibited in the third trimester by state law. Wayne agrees with Sonny's view that the trimester scheme is appropriate, but would prefer to see fewer women choosing to abort pregnancies, especially after the first trimester.

Felicia, on the other hand, feels that "there definitely has to be some kind of guidance," and supports some of the abortion restrictions that have been passed in the United States.

> Maybe we should have a waiting period like we have a waiting period for hand guns, which is like five days, because five days won't really affect the trimester business. Five days shouldn't be a problem. And I think maybe by the time you schedule [an abortion] and see the doctor and everything it's got to be probably

that long anyhow. I would think. You can't just walk in off the street and get one. As far as parental control or parental consent, I don't know, because I think that would hinder some girls. Maybe under a certain age, I mean if a girl is thirteen, fourteen years old, perhaps the parent should be made aware of what's going on, because who knows? It might not be her boyfriend that got her in that position. It could be something else, like incest or rape.

Felicia opposes federal funding for abortions in the United States, except on military bases.

Only in extreme cases, such as rape or maternal health threat, would these interviewees encourage someone to have an abortion. Most fundamentally agree that abortion is "something you have to decide for yourself," as Madeline states. Felicia says:

> I don't know if I'd ever encourage it. I think it's, I think I should support. I couldn't encourage. Like I say, I'm pro-choice, but that doesn't necessarily mean I could live with myself having one. But I think that a woman who's gone through, who's arrived at the decision to have an abortion has gone through enough soul searching and enough beating herself up, that's what I'm hoping, that she doesn't need any more shit then, when she finally decides to go and do it. She doesn't need anybody with a sign calling her a murderer. That's the thing. I think it's probably a very hard decision. And I know a lot of people get frightened.

Felicia would encourage an abortion if the woman were pregnant as a result of rape: "If I were raped, can you honestly tell me that I would love that child? The first time that it showed hostility or anger or violence, I would say, 'My God, it's going to be just like him, that terrible man.' I would probably raise a child that I was afraid of. Wouldn't that be terrible?"

Sonny would encourage abortion if his teenage daughter were pregnant as a result of rape: "If we are prevented by law, which could potentially happen in this country, I'd be willing to take my daughter to any place where they could go ahead and perform an abortion. My daughter believes in such a thing as well."

Sara would not necessarily encourage abortion in cases of rape, because she feels that ultimately the decision depends on the pregnant woman's own conscience and what she can live with. But Sara says she would encourage abortion under certain "social circumstances, social pressures. Our society has just grown so rapidly in the last twenty years that it's amazing that there's still places that aren't, small communities that aren't [full]. . . . And children also kind of take away economic freedom. So if that's your choice, you have to take that into account for the child."

Leigh would not necessarily encourage anyone to have an abortion, but feels abortion is justified in cases of physical trauma, including drug addiction, abuse in the family, and poverty. She is concerned about the trend of abortion legislation "because there's no way that you can ever take into account all the different circumstances."

According to Mildred,

> It's what that person feels is best for her, and if anyone says that "I want to have an abortion," it wouldn't be up to me to say, "Well think about it. Think about what you're doing." I might say that to everyone, yes. But to say you shouldn't do it, that's not up to me. I don't have any children, but even if that were my daughter, I couldn't say to her that I don't want you to do this. Because again, I may know her economic circumstances, I may be supportive of her having a child, but still that's not my decision. Everyone has to live with their decision. And I don't think that's up to me to determine which way what your choice should be. And I wouldn't want to influence it.

On other hand, some of the interviewees would discourage women from having abortions. Emma feels that she would discourage a woman from having an abortion if the woman "were secure enough" to have a child. Using herself as an example, Emma says, "I would like to think that I could deliver, if that had happened to me." Felicia says she would discourage a friend from having an abortion if she "could financially afford a child, and she was married, say just like an average woman named Kate, twenty-six years old, works part time, her husband makes good money, he works full time, her husband's thirty, and they're decent, healthy, athletic, good-looking people. . . . [A pregnancy] should be good news." Sara and Leigh both feel that if the woman is in a "good position" in life, they would discourage her from having an abortion. It is interesting to note that these "good positions" are largely based on an ideal of American living: a home, a decent income, two parents who are stable, athletic, and good looking.

Another common concern among the interviewees is the role of men in the abortion decision. Madeline would like to see a good cooperative relationship between the pregnant woman and her partner, but "there are relationships, I'm sure, where it would be unsafe for the woman to tell the father of the child that she was pregnant, for her own safety reasons. Ideally, they would be able to discuss and come to a mutually agreeable decision, but there may be circumstances where that's not the most reasonable thing for the woman to do. So I think ultimately it's the woman's decision alone. Hopefully that's a very small percentage of the cases." Felicia is bothered by men who presume to make abortion decisions for women, because "they'll never be pregnant. They'll never have to ultimately make that choice. And they'll never have to deal with the consequence of that choice. It's very easy, I think, to spout off about something that you know you'll never have to be in that position to make that decision. We all do it every day. We say, 'Well, if I were her, I'd do this.' When you know damn well you're not her."

Emma and Wayne think that men should be supportive partners to the pregnant woman. Emma says, "The father, in my opinion, has something to say there. I know that it is the woman's body and she's the one that carries the pregnancy. But except for rape and incest again, the fact that you consented to this sexual relationship is giving him permission. And if he has permission then it seems to me he has something to say in the outcome." Wayne says, "They both should agree, and the man should stand by her, and say 'Don't worry, hon, everything's going to be all right.'"

Sara brings up the issue of parental "rights." "I think the father also has parental rights. Saying that he should pay a portion for the child's upbringing, and he should also have the right to raise the child if it's unwanted. So I think if there's a father who wants [the child], then I would discourage an abortion but I realize that's [the woman's] body and that's her decision."

Abortion Politics and Activism

Madeline declares, "I would never vote for somebody who was pro-life. Never. I mean absolutely." Other interviewees echo this sentiment. Mildred says, "I'm not going to vote for Pat Buchanan. But it depends upon how [candidates] place [their pro-life views] in the campaign. Most of the people I'm inclined to look at are pro-choice, yeah, definitely. Because when I see someone who's pro-choice it's someone again who is willing, again, I think, to take a more broad look, not only at that issue but at all issues." Sonny adamantly opposes any politician who is pro-life.

> Obviously what's happened is that, living in Mississippi, it's a moot issue. But at the local elections I always make it a point to go to the. . . . For example, elections are coming up. They'll have the League of Women Voters or somebody's gonna have "a debate." It's not really a debate, but the candidates will get up there and they'll give a little short spiel about something and people submit questions. And I always submit questions about, "What's your stand on abortion? And what's your stand on capital punishment?" I get a kick out of doing something like that. I believe in voting, that you have to exercise your vote. And I believe you have no

business complaining if you don't vote. You have to be an active member of society. If you want to make changes, you have to work your butt off to make the changes.

The abortion issue guides Leigh's political choices, as well. "I won't vote for a pro-life politician. The only case that I can see that I would vote for a pro-life politician is if he or she were running against someone like David Duke[2] who is even worse. I absolutely will not vote for a candidate who will not support my rights as a woman."

To Emma, pro-life politicians and activists seem "kind of religiously fanatical. And I don't think that's the place for, the presidency is certainly not the place for a religious fanatic. Or a fanatic of any sort."

Wayne also favors pro-choice candidates. Felicia is more influenced by abortion politics at the local level than at the federal level. For instance, Felicia said, "If I have an abortion, who cares what the President says? The President doesn't know me personally."

The interviewees exhibit varying degrees of pro-choice activism. Madeline, Sonny, and Leigh contribute money to Planned Parenthood, pro-choice campaigns, and national women's organizations. Wayne has been active in Democratic politics in Maine for years, and, like Sonny, has volunteered for campaigns. Sonny says, "I believe in the adage that if you don't do it, you can't be bitching about it." Leigh is a member of the National Organization for Women, and Madeline has attended several pro-choice demonstrations. Mildred shares the activist spirit: she has been politically involved all of her adult life.

Feminist consciousness is apparent among the interviewees. Leigh, Sara, and Madeline identify themselves as feminists. About feminism, Leigh says:

> I think it's wonderful. A lot of people have warped ideas of what feminism means, that it means militant lesbians trying to convert everyone, this kind of weird organization and they hate men and they don't want any kids and women who stay home they think are bad, but that's not what feminism is about. Feminism is about choices for women.

Leigh also expresses deep concern about the misperception of feminism by the general public, a misperception she says is largely fueled by public figures such as conservative commentator Rush Limbaugh and Speaker of the House Newt Gingrich.

> A lot of people blame the decay of society on women, because women went to work and everything. And I don't think that's right. I think that women ought to

have the choice. I mean, I think it's definitely a difficult decision. If I were married and had a child it would be a real struggle for me to decide whether to work or not or just stay home. Or who would stay home. But I don't see why the man can't stay home and take care of the child. Some people need two incomes to survive. . . . I think Rush Limbaugh is a hate monger, like a lot of other people. Like Newt [Gingrich] and stuff. I totally don't agree with them. It appalls me that people actually listen to him, but I belong to NOW, and I've gotten some literature from them about Rush and some of the things he's said, and a lot of his stuff is just really incorrect. Like he says that feminists are women who want other women to have as many abortions as they can. That's wrong. They're lies. Some of the stuff is just twisted or is just typical perverted logic. But some of his stuff is just wrong. Bad facts.

Madeline says, "I'm a feminist to the extent that I believe that there's been, there is in our culture, an unjustified lack of respect for women, and that should change. And an unjustified taking of women's authenticity and power by men, frankly."

Although Emma does not describe herself as a feminist, she expresses concern about the gendered legal system.

Look at our lawmakers for years and years and years. Look at the ratio, women to men. It's small, isn't it? I think that if men carried the pregnancy, I think it's a matter of control also. I really don't think that the men who have helped pass these laws, how do I want to say this? It's a matter of control, of keeping women where they have been, which is, I don't want to say a second-class citizen, but certainly under [male] control. I don't hate men. I think [women] can help change the world. Have a few more women in there who have something to say, instead of just men.

Mildred describes herself as a "founding mother of the women's movement" and as a "concerned woman" but not as a feminist. She believes the modern women's movement in the United States is "in disarray," with each faction competing with the others in order to garner the most resources for their particular agenda, "even though it's supposed to be a non-competitive grouping." Mildred's awareness of gender discrimination is closely tied to her awareness of racial discrimination. She has been active in the civil rights movement and spent childhood summers with her grandmother in the segregated South. She describes a time when she was sitting in the "blacks only" balcony of a movie theater as a young child.

It was just amazing to sit there—I think I was nine years old—and to watch the reactions of the crowd and the differences. We sat in the balcony, and you had the white audience below you which I couldn't figure out, because as a kid you loved sitting in the balcony anyway. But in the movie I remember there's a, Althea Gibson was in the movie, and she slapped a Union officer in the movie. And this was a black woman slapping a Union officer. And everyone downstairs started cheering wildly for that, because it was a Union officer being slapped. But I was nine, so I had to think about these things. I had started out to be a doctor in my life. The conversations that I had with males, and again go back to the early '60s; I was discouraged, you know [with comments] like "you really should become a teacher or social worker or something like that."

Felicia does not consider herself a feminist: "I don't at all. But I really am turned off about anything that degrades women, and I don't consider that feminist. I consider that, well I want to say common sense." Felicia repeatedly expresses her concerns about pornography and wife abuse. Both Sonny and Wayne declare themselves to be supporters of womens' rights, but do not label themselves feminists.

Perceptions of Pro-Life Agendas

Felicia is very troubled by the concept of "pro-life" versus "pro-choice" because she sees herself occupying both categories

A lot of people have equated pro-life with anti-abortion. And I feel that if I'm pro-choice and not anti-abortion I'm not able to say I'm pro-life. But I'm both. I'm pro-choice and I'm pro-life in the sense that I'm pro-life. I'm for life, I'm for enjoying life. You should be alive, you should be healthy and happy and if I can help you out doing that, that's great. That's why I don't like it when these pro-lifers are anti-abortionists. So if I were to say to somebody I'm pro-life, they'll automatically assume that I'm anti-abortion. And I'm not. I'm pro-choice. That's why I don't think it's fair that they got to use that. You know what I'm saying? It's like it's not fair. Of course, I think everybody should be pro-life. What you do with your body is your own choice. I'm pro-choice. So if somebody were to say to me, "Oh, you're pro-choice, you're not pro-life?" Of course I'm pro-life. What am I, am I starving myself to death? Am I going out and killing? No. I'm for life. Isn't that what pro-life means? For life? That's what bugs me about [the use of the term "pro-life"] . . . It's sort of like false advertising.

Madeline, however, has the most "complaints" about pro-life agendas:

> One complaint that I have about it is that it's all run by men. [Another] complaint that I have about it is that they are imposing their views on people when I don't think they have any right to impose it on. [A third] complaint that I have on it is that they're primarily the Republican conservative political orientation people, whose underlying theory of life is that government should take their hands off. And yet in their hypocrisy they say that government should put their hands inside my womb, OK? And I'm extremely offended by that. I think that they're imposing their religious views on people, and if there's anything that this country stands for, it's religious freedom. And to say that based on my religious views that say that [abortion] is a sin, I'm not going to allow you, who may have completely different religious views, to make your own decision. They're also the same people that are saying cut off welfare and cut off aid to families with dependent children. What do they think these women are going to do? What do they think they're going to do? They want to cut social services, they want to cut out the support network completely to assist single parents or women without any kind of financial security, and yet they say that they can't make this decision which is going to profoundly affect their life. And the numbers of households headed by single mothers that have children that are living in poverty is just appalling. I mean it is appalling in this country. And I'm offended by their position for that reason as well. Not to mention trying to make people feel guilty for making this kind of choice. I mean guilty? Harassing them, threatening them, killing them. It's absurd. To be pro-life and say that this cluster of cells in someone's body is a life that must be protected at all cost, and disregarding everyone's opinion, and yet in the extreme groups feeling that it's justified to kill other people? I mean that's the most absurd position I've ever heard. It basically leaves me speechless. I think it's insane. I think it reflects a psychosis. It reduces any shred of respect that I possibly could have had for that group, or eliminates any shred of respect that I possibly could have had for that group. I like to think of myself as an open-minded person and respect the opinions of others, but I do not respect their opinion. Based in large part on the attacks on clinic workers.

Sara expresses her opinion about the pro-life agenda by pointing to a contradiction that most anti-abortion people support terminating a pregnancy that resulted from rape. "I don't see how all the people who are pro-life, pro-life, pro-life, except if it's a child conceived in what's termed as rape." She is also concerned about the unrealistic emphasis on adoption as an alternative to abortion because "you can sell [white] newborns but you have trouble adopting out

African American newborns." Leigh also believes that "[people] want healthy white children. They don't want a handicapped child. They don't want to have a child of a mixed race. And I don't agree with that but that's just the facts of life. What is in demand is a healthy white baby."

Sara is also concerned about the stigma attached to children born outside of marriage and says that it's "the same pro-life people who are [saying], this is an innocent precious being that you're going out and murdering, but once it becomes a child a lot of them don't see it as so innocent and precious. These are the same people who would stand up on Sunday and talk about abortion and go out there and look down on their children's classmates who happen to be illegitimate."

The interviewees sharply disagree with members of the conservative right who perceive abortion, divorce, and out-of-wedlock births, as signs of moral decay. Madeline says she would "politely" respond that such a point of view is "a lot of hooey." Mildred sees the argument of "moral decay" as a political ploy to gain votes by instilling fear in voters. She sees evidence of moral decay in the absence of community life.

> God, there [used to be] all types of programs. And we don't provide that again. We're more interested in property taxes being paid and what we're outlaying and what we want to keep for ourselves. That's I think one of the reasons why I decided I didn't want to become a parent, because I saw a lot of things happening as I was growing up where there was less and less willingness to provide, as a community. And I just determined that I didn't want to bring a child into that.

Mildred thinks that modern morality has stayed pretty much the same over the years: "selfish."

Emma also does not equate abortion with signs of moral decay in modern society. In her historical view of morality, Emma points out that what is seen as moral decay in one era may not be in another. "Before St. Augustine became St. Augustine, [his mother] Monica was very worried about his delinquent behavior. Breaking windows in the church was moral decay. I think that there are thousands of people. They've been having abortions forever and a day." Sara comments:

> Throughout history you're seeing up to twenty-some percent in the Middle Ages of brides were pregnant. The fact is that women have become more economically free, and society has become free enough to allow women to have status without a man, so marriage is no longer forced upon a woman. So illegitimacy soars, and other options. I can see how they consider that moral decay, but it's also a very liberating thing. People would say, a girl like myself going off to a city where we

have no family and there are no chaperones, and living in the same house with guys, fellas in coed dorms and everything, that was moral decay a couple of years ago, but now it's an accepted social practice.

Leigh also disagrees with the idea that abortion is a sign of moral decay, but states, "I think a lot of things that other people think are signs of moral decay I don't think are signs of moral decay. Such as homosexuality or the women's rights or more liberal child rearing, things like that. I don't think that is moral decay."

Another significant disagreement these interviewees have with pro-life agendas is the theme of "family values." All of the interviewees in this group express concern about the "family values" agenda because, as Leigh states, "I don't think that's realistic. I don't think that that's the only good family that there can be. Because there are a lot of bad situations in the typical heterosexual family with kids. A daughter's abused, bad situations that happen in those families that are supposed to be so ideal. But other people are raised really happily by single moms or in different circumstances." Wayne sees "family values" as an unattainable ideal because "reality sets in. Some people have to work two jobs to make it, and that's when there's two [people] in the family, or three in the family. The mother has to go to work, the father has to have two jobs too, to make it. Rents are high, food's high, medical cost is high. That's why I stress socialized medicine."

All the interviewees in this group feel that rather than stressing traditional family values, society ought to simply value families in all the diverse forms present. Family values should "include people with alternative lifestyles," according to Sara. This would include adoptive families, single-parent families, families with gay parents, and families with different cultural traditions.

Death Penalty Opinions

All of these interviewees express a desire to see the death penalty abolished. Wayne, a passionate opponent of capital punishment, says he would like to "abolish it right away." Wayne states that "two wrongs don't make a right." For Emma, the issue involves a question of who has the right to judge another's value to society: "I don't think that there is any one of us here on this earth that is in a position to judge what happens and why. I do honestly believe that for a long, long, long time now, that the penal system needs to be completely overhauled." Madeline struggles with her emotional reaction and her rational reaction to violent crime.

I'm against the death penalty. A funny thing happened though. I mentioned to my husband that I was having this interview, and that you had asked me what my position was and I had told you. And he said, "Now wait a minute. The other night when the news was on, and they were talking about some child molester, he had gotten the death penalty, and you were saying 'Right on.'" And I have to say, to be perfectly honest, I did have that feeling. And I've been thinking about that, and thinking about that contradiction and the conclusion that I came to is that my reaction like that is the same reason that the death penalty even exists today, and that is that I think fundamentally we as human animals have this desire for retribution. Desire for payback. "You hurt me, I'm gonna hurt you." And that's a really strong sort of underlying basic emotion that many people have. Now I think in most cases, I would like to think that we've risen above that, and that we can use our minds and look at things more rationally. And for a lot of reasons I think that the death penalty is simply pandering to that emotion as opposed to a reasoned, rational choice. So, I am against the death penalty, and that we as a society should not have the death penalty. That we should suppress this basic emotional response for a lot of reasons. For instance, when my daughter hits my son, my instinct is to slap her little behind. But I'm saying at the same time, "Don't hit." How can I be telling her and teaching her "don't hit" when I'm hitting her too? And how can we be telling people and teaching them "don't kill" when we're killing them too? I mean, it somehow sanctions killing as sometimes justifiable. Sometimes it's OK to kill someone if they're really, really bad, in our wisdom and consideration. I don't think it's a good way to educate our society. If what we're trying to do is reduce killing, then let's not kill.

Mildred shares this concern about the emotional basis of supporting capital punishment. "For us to be vengeful as a society, I just don't think that's a positive influence." Sonny thinks that the idea of "an eye for an eye and a tooth for a tooth, it's all baloney." He goes on to address one of the dilemmas Madeline had discussed: what they would think or feel if their child was a victim of violent crime. Sonny says, "I hope it never happens. But what I would ask for is that the person that did it be thrown in prison. I don't believe prisoners should be coddled. They should know that they're in prison because they've done something bad. We get Mike Tyson rapes, and he gets off. Look at this, I mean all this adulation, this hero's welcome. This says something terrible about this society that we live in that things like this can happen. No, I would not ask for the death penalty for my daughter's rapist. I would ask that he be thrown in prison and throw the keys away."

For Sara, "capital punishment is so barbaric" that she cannot support it, even for the person(s) responsible for the Oklahoma City bombing because "apparently it was more a rebellion kind of thing, again it's hypocritical for me to say this because we revolted from England, we had the Shays' rebellion, we had the

Tea Party rebellion, and that's what this country is founded on." Leigh expresses ambivalence about the death penalty. She is opposed to it, but can understand why people support it for serial murderers like Ted Bundy and John Wayne Gacy.

Each of the interviewees expresses a desire for the penal system to rely more heavily on life sentences without the possibility of parole, which in Emma's view is more punitive than executing someone. However, the interviewees disagree about the amenities provided to inmates. Emma suggests:

> There should be a system where they are going to be employed at things that really need to be done, and that they are going to be paid a good working wage and they can continue to support their family on the outside and take care of their children, the same responsibilities that you and I are responsible for, except they have lost their right to freedom. And you can go to school and you can become a physician and you can become a priest and you can become a professor, whatever you want inside those buildings. But you will live and work inside. And to me that would be rehabilitation. Right now it's simply punishment, and we certainly don't know how to punish very well. I don't even believe that you punish your children. You're here to discipline them, not punish them. And that to me makes such good sense.

Madeline favors the removal of cable television and most of the other amenities offered in modern prisons. Wayne and Sonny agree, but Sonny adds:

> Don't throw them in prison for frivolous things like some guy stealing a pizza and because it's the third time he stole a pizza you throw him in for life, like it happened in California. You gotta have really, really strong reasons for why a person's going to be thrown in prison. And many of the things that people are thrown in prison is some stupid little misdemeanor or something, you get thrown in prison. Or, and then on the other hand, you have a guy and a white collar crime that's been perpetrated, and a million dollars are lost, a billion dollars are lost, and he gets away scot free.

All the interviewees in this group express concern, as Wayne does, that "mistakes can be made," which further cements their opposition to the death penalty. Mildred says this is "the key" reason for her opposition of capital punishment. Madeline expresses her concern about innocent people being executed and about the flaws in the whole criminal justice system, such as racism and guilty people being freed on technicalities.

Felicia and Leigh would make exceptions, allowing the death penalty in extreme cases such as serial murders. Felicia points out that even in prison, "if these people are still alive they could kill again. They might not be outside. They might kill in prison." But then she refers to the possibility of erroneous execution: "The problem is though, how can you be sure?" Leigh considers whether serial murderers can be rehabilitated an important issue. She struggles with the idea of qualified support of capital punishment for someone like Jeffrey Dahmer, "but then I think again, if someone did something like that, are they really sane? And does killing him take away the crimes he did? No. It's kind of like vengeance or revenge. Does that really make it any better? But then if he did all those bad things, does he deserve to live? But then who decides who deserves to live and who doesn't?"

Felicia states, "I think that it doesn't take a genius to figure out that [minorities are] suffering from racism now, they're getting harsher penalties, they're getting stiffer penalties as far as the law goes," expressing the concern many interviewees have about the problems of racial bias in capital sentencing. Madeline says, it's "just appalling to me." Felicia comments, "It's a terrible thing if your brother gets a capital punishment sentence, and would that be a terrible thing if there is also racism involved and your brother is black? Chances are that's what's going to happen. It's like kick them when they're down. Maybe I'm an underdog rooter."

Mildred says that the issue of racism in the death penalty does not influence her opposition to it, but sees racial tensions being exploited in the political arena through support of capital punishment, particularly in the case of the 1988 Bush campaign ads that featured "Willie" Horton. "Well, if I were white, male, and moderate to conservative in this nation and I wanted to pursue a specific bent . . . I mean look what it did for George Bush who, in my opinion, was a weak candidate. But he wasn't running against a heavy-duty candidate at the time, either. Look what it did to sway the country. Because it became a black/white issue, and the votes were there. Makes it very easy." Mildred was in Los Angeles during the Rodney King trials and post-verdict rioting, of which she says, "For me and my own personal experience, it was just unbelievable. I mean here we had a videotape of the event that was occurring, and to come back with this, it just, as an African American myself, I just felt almost . . . Well, I'm re-reading [African American author Ralph Ellison's novel] *Invisible Man*. And it did. It makes you feel invisible in the nation, as if you didn't matter as a group. And I think that I understood the riot."

Leigh says:

One other problem I have with the death penalty is the high percentage of African Americans that are on death row as well as the people that are court appointed attorneys. And because I know, I listen to [National Public Radio] and the other big debate is we're only going to have one appeal and you're going to have to get them some good legal counsel because they pay the public defenders a pittance when O.J. Simpson's lawyers are making millions of dollars. I mean they can get O.J. off, but what about some poor person who was accused of the same crime? Can that person get off or not? I have a big problem with that. I don't know how to make it equal justice or anything, but I think that, I mean, somehow they need to do a better job of getting poor people better representation.

The issue of disparity in representation, as demonstrated by the O.J. Simpson case, caused many of the interviewees to reaffirm their opposition to capital punishment. Having been accused of murdering Nicole Brown Simpson and Ronald Goldman, Simpson hired the most prominent defense attorneys in the country to represent him in the criminal trial. He was acquitted of the charges, later to be found liable in civil court and ordered to pay $33.5 million to the victims' families.

Wayne recounts an incident that occurred when he was with his African American girlfriend of twenty years.

We ran into these gangsters that her daughter was with and they said, "Well Sandra owes us X amount of money." And this had been happening two or three or four months in a row. I said, "Oh, she don't owe you anything." So they stuck up some scissors in my eyes, and I got out the Mace. I Maced them good, right in the eyes, before he got me, and I got banged on both sides of the head. He shook his eyes like that and his brother came up and gave me a left cross and ran all the way down Main Street, all the way back, stopped in front of that place. . . . Stopped right there. And they said, "We want to get this guy here. We want to make a citizen's arrest. He's spraying Mace at everybody." The cop didn't ask me, I wasn't allowed to say anything because I was with a black girl. I kind of put two and two together. I was with a black girl and the cop didn't ask me anything or didn't tell me my rights or anything. They just handcuffed me and put me in the cruiser, and I went to jail. I showed up in court three times and they never showed up once. So, they threw it out of court.

Wayne views the justice system as flawed because of the racial bias permeating the police, judges, lawyers, and corrections officers.

These interviewees differ in their opinions of how important the death penalty is as a political issue. Madeline sees it as a less prominent issue than abortion, while Felicia sees a pro–death penalty candidate as "a tyrannical person that's like an Attila the Hun; lawmakers shouldn't be killers." Wayne is disappointed in Bill Clinton's support of the death penalty because he sees himself as being "like Bill Clinton all the way!" Wayne believes that Clinton's use of the death penalty while Governor of Arkansas protected him from some of the "Willie Horton–type ads" that plagued presidential candidate Michael Dukakis in 1988.

Sonny views the death penalty issue as a regional dilemma: "I voted for Clinton. He is pro-choice, but pro–death penalty as well. Whereas the alternative to that was anti-choice and pro–death penalty. But the national scene is the only area where we do have that sort of a choice. At the state level in Mississippi, we don't have that. Absolutely not. Because who in his right mind would go around espousing such views and get elected in Mississippi? Not gonna happen."

Sara tends to avoid death penalty supporters in her political choices because she sees support of the death penalty as symptomatic of other positions that she opposes. She believes death penalty supporters "tend to be very much against women's rights to choose. They're very anti-woman generally. Some of them are racist bigots too. I guess it tends to be the people who are most unlike me in ideology [who] tend to be for capital punishment." And Leigh says, "I could vote for someone who was for the death penalty. I mean if there were two people that had mostly the same views, and one was for it and one was against it, I would vote for the one against it."

Connecting Opinions on Abortion and the Death Penalty

Several themes emerge as important connections between these two issues. Most interviewees express a deep sense of distrust in "the system," a belief that it is not proper for the government to make abortion and capital punishment decisions, a concern for underprivileged people in society, and a feeling of "anti-control" over others. Their opinions about Paul Hill and John Salvi also are important.

There is an overriding concern among these interviewees that the legal system in place is so terribly flawed that abortion and the death penalty cannot be effectively controlled through legislation or the courts. Wayne says, "The system is totally unfair. They're gonna go crazy if they ever pass the death penalty [in Maine]. I mean, oh boy, there's our first electrocution, something like that, you know? I don't think it's fair and I don't think it's right, and I hope I never see the day that law will be passed." Leigh thinks that "when you try to start legislating [abortion and the death penalty], that it just gets a little too sticky." Madeline expresses concern that illegal abortion would be "dangerous" to some women who "will die" from procuring an illegal procedure, and that the legal system that promotes death sentencing is dangerous to ethnic minorities and the poor.

Another common theme connecting abortion and the death penalty is the sense that life and death are not casual decisions to be put in the hands of government officials. Leigh expresses a common concern about these decisions being in the hands of the state.

You never know who's going to be in power. I mean if Newt Gingrich gets elected, think what he could do with those kind of laws. He could take away my right to choose. He could start executing a whole lot of people. Of course no one would be able to be allowed to use euthanasia. He could take away my right to choose what I do, and other people's right to choose what they do. He's very popular, just like Rush [Limbaugh]! I don't know, I mean, it scares me that people like that are popular. It scares me what people will mindlessly and blindly believe. People that, because they're appealing or they strike some common theme or chord within them that they're, someone's done them wrong or especially more lower class like people that can't get ahead and blame it all on the minorities or men blame it all on the women or on the "feminazis." Blame it on somebody. Because everybody, I think if someone's in a bad situation they just want someone to blame, and I think that Rush and Newt give them someone to blame. Whereas the proper blame should be placed on patriarchy. I mean who's been in control of the world for so long and look how it's going!

Concern for the societally disadvantaged is another common theme in the conversations. Madeline expresses her dissatisfaction with the "second class status" that women occupy and with the fact that women are vulnerable to being controlled by "male-dominated" legislation. Madeline has similar views with respect to racial discrimination that leads to inequities within the legal system, particularly in criminal sentencing. Emma says it makes a "big difference where you are on this ladder, the social ladder, how tough people are going to be on you. I think if people have better living conditions, better jobs, more money, if it was easier to live some kind of normal life, you might find less crime."

Mildred outlines her concern for disadvantaged people (women and ethnic minorities) in terms of socio-economic and political priorities.

We either have to make a choice that we're going to support a child born in this country, every child, and support them well, or we have to always make sure that the individual who knows has the key to that choice and either prior to getting there, as I sort of alluded to before, we have to provide proper sexual education for them.

Sonny expresses disapproval of any government action that interferes with a person's civil rights, including anti-abortion and pro–death penalty laws.

Emma says she cannot support laws restricting a woman's right to choose abortion nor advocate capital punishment because she is "so anti-control." In her opinion, punishment "simply breaks the spirit, and then what do you have?" And since punishment fundamentally "has to do with control," Emma believes that laws that eliminate choice for women open them up to being controlled completely by punishment from the state. "Maybe I'm even more anti-control than I thought I was, especially with the abortion bit, and as far as the death penalty goes, I don't see that that has ever served any good." Emma says that she is "so anti-police it just isn't even funny." She elaborates:

> From what I have seen, they don't seem terribly well educated. And there was no status attached to being a policeman. I don't know if there is now, even. And the pay was not very good. And I've always felt that the person who became a policeman was the one who needed the security of that uniform, and a gun if he carries a gun, or, they needed something other than what they themselves could provide for. My opinion is, they're out to punish. The cops are out to punish. That's it. And I don't think that should be their role.

Mildred expresses concern for personal autonomy, while Sonny voices his suspicion of government interference with life and death decisions. Leigh simply feels that people ought "not judge people so harshly because they're not like them, I think is just really fundamental to everything."

Opinions about Paul Hill and John Salvi

Despite their support of legal choice, these interviewees agree that Paul Hill should not be executed for the anti-abortion murders he committed in Florida in 1994. While they understand Hill's logic, most of them view his actions (and the actions of other extreme anti-abortion activists) as "fanaticism." Sonny, however, views the issue in terms of complacency and perhaps fear among the pro-choice activists.

> Unfortunately, what's happening is that the people of my ilk are not standing up. You find that the pro-lifers are much more vocal and much more prone to violence. And that's the irony of the whole thing. On the one hand you claim that you are pro-life, but you don't mind running around, as they claim, "by whatever means," like Operation Rescue, and all these folks claim "by whatever means." Unfortunately what's happening is that the people who are pro-choice have not, other than the National Organization of Women and NARAL and all these groups and Planned Parenthood, which have been trying to vocalize their opinions. But the typical run-of-the-mill person who believes in choice does not stand up on the rooftop, screaming and yelling about it. This morning I mentioned a woman who's on the board for the Sierra Club, and she's really, really environmentally conscious, and she's definitely pro-choice, definitely against the death penalty

and things like that, and she will espouse those beliefs when I'm talking to her. But I've asked her, "Why don't you write letters to the editor, or go and get on the radio, or talk about it?" She says that she may be hurting herself, banks may not give her a loan. . . . She's afraid that there may be some repercussions.

Sonny recommends stricter gun control laws to prevent violent pro-life activists from getting guns, and stricter enforcement of anti-stalking laws as they relate to clinic workers. Referring to the Freedom of Access to Clinic Entrances law, Sonny said, "What Clinton did was very good, but in spite of it, Boston had that Salvi guy." Sonny feels that putting Paul Hill to death "would be a really, really stupid thing; by killing another person you're not going to get that first life back."

Sara first became aware of anti-abortion violence when she met a man who is a clinic escort. "He was a huge guy who walked the female fence [entrance to the clinic] here in Mississippi. [Protestors] threw acid in the eyes of people going in, they had to wear protective gear, it was just so inhumane." While she says she cannot feel too sorry for Paul Hill, she does not think using the death penalty would be the right thing.

Madeline discusses what she would have done had she been a prosecutor on the Paul Hill case. "Under the law a twelve-week-old fetus is not a life. Under the law it's not a protectable life. Now if you fall down the stairs and miscarry, you can't sue the stair person for the wrongful death." She continues:

> I never prosecuted a capital case, so I don't know, but I would have responded by, I would have liked to have responded by putting on expert witnesses to establish that at twelve weeks we're talking about something that's as big as the tip of a pen. Maybe the end of a pen. We're talking about a very loosely organized group of cells. We're not talking about a person. That there are something like two thirds, or at least half, of pregnancies miscarry at twelve weeks. It's not something that rises to the level of homicide. It just doesn't in my opinion.

Madeline feels, however, that sentencing Hill to death was "absurd." "It's just such a circle, so ridiculous."

Solutions

These interviewees offer various solutions to the problems discussed in our conversations. All would keep abortion legal and would abolish the death penalty, replacing it with a system of life in prison without the possibility of parole. Two suggested solutions emerge as most prominent: improved education with a solid communitarian ethic, and the fostering of tolerance for diversity in society.

The education aspect of Mildred's solutions to abortion and capital punishment problems is a unifying theme:

> I'd provide education for people so they could make an intelligent decision before they got pregnant, and give them means of preventing that pregnancy, so they're not driven to that decision necessarily. And if they are driven to that decision, not only provide them with the means of having a completed abortion, but if they chose not to have an abortion to provide them with support in the society for their being able to take their pregnancy to term and have that child and then make a decision what to do with that child beyond that, whether to keep it and raise it themselves or to have a society that's willing to raise it for them. And again, follow that child through that society to be able to give an opportunity for success for that child, that individual, so they don't end up in a system that's going to eventually place them in a position where they're going to commit crime and end up on death row.

She continues to discuss solutions by recounting an incident from her own childhood. A stranger approached her in a car, asking for directions. She did not feel comfortable talking to him, especially after he offered her money to show him the place he was attempting to find. Mildred's mother and a female neighbor came outside to intervene. The fact that the neighbor appeared to help her demonstrated to Mildred that a sense of community is important for the safety of children and everyone else. "It takes a village," she says.

> And I think that is a black idea. And very often, and that was one of the unfortunate things with the migration north, that within the structure of the black family began to change, because you didn't have your aunts and uncles, your grandmothers, and all of these individuals were helping to raise that child, that you had previously. Not only the black community. I think that was very true of the agrarian communities too. I think we have to replace that with a society that has that mind-set where we are taking care and helping as a society to raise that child. Because that's the only way that that child really, truly has a chance and an opportunity. When I view it, that's how I have to view it.

Sonny feels that education should focus on measures to prevent unplanned pregnancies, as well as preventive measures for crime. "As the old cliche goes, prevention is so much better than the cure. That's always the case. That's another one of the ironies, is we have people talking about not allowing women to have abortions, but they're also unwilling to allow for aggressive sex education and things like that, and making available condoms and birth control pills, and things like that." For Sonny, education extends beyond "book education" and must include "life skills" such as "values and the work ethic"; prevention must include corporate responsibility, with flextime and family medical leave so that employees will not have to neglect the demands of family life.

Promotion of tolerance for diversity is another commonly mentioned solution. Madeline advocates

> respect for your fellow human beings. And that goes to the whole death penalty thing too, and I think that goes to abortion on the personal level. And that to teach people respect would hopefully teach them to respect themselves, and to not feel that they need to control other people to build themselves up. It would help them treat people more fairly and more generously, and more caringly and lovingly, if you respected them, and hopefully not kill them so much. And as a mother, as a pregnant woman, my personal view is that an act of respect would be not to have an abortion. That's my personal view. But it's not to say that someone else's view is wrong, because I'm not the authority.

Leigh would "change people's minds and make them accepting of diversity and people that are different. And not judge people so harshly because they're not like them. I think that is just really fundamental to everything. I mean, a lot of religious wars, a lot of oppression and things are because people are different and others don't understand them." This extension of tolerance would include women's rights, gay rights, and civil rights for all people, as well as abolishing nuclear weapons and all pollutants that destroy the environment. Leigh realizes that this is "idealistic, but it seems like if everybody would just accept all our differences that we could basically get along, and understand each other. I think if we all understood each other, and if we were all free and equal and stuff, then why would there have to be any more wars? And people wouldn't be oppressed."

CHAPTER FOUR

Pro-Choice and Pro–Death Penalty

In this chapter, I examine abortion and the death penalty through the opinions of people who support both. Figure 4.1 shows the fluctuations in this opinion set, based on GSS respondents from 1977 to 1994. Pro-choice and pro–death penalty is the most common of all the opinion sets, although it has not reached a simple majority. Between 1977 and 1994 the proportion of U.S. residents who supported legal abortion choice and also supported capital punishment ranged from 40 percent to 50 percent. The level of support remained fairly stable over this seventeen-year period.

There are five women and a man in this group: Autumn, Maria, Olivia, Johnnie, Courtney, and Rick.

Summary of Interviewees

I met with Autumn at her home in Maine. Autumn is a sixty-two-year-old retired federal worker, divorced after thirty-eight years of marriage. She believes in God but is opposed to organized religion, and believes that the Bible "was written by men," not by God. Autumn attributes her divorce in large part to religious differences with her husband. He "became a real Baptist" and she was always a feminist. This led to many disagreements, though the divorce was amicable. Autumn is very concerned about freedom of choice, taxes, gay rights, and

Figure 4.1 Pro-Choice and Pro–Death Penalty, 1977–1994

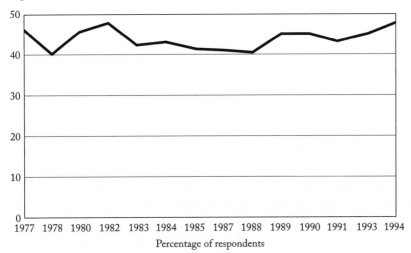

50													
40													
30													
20													
10													
0													

1977 1978 1980 1982 1983 1984 1985 1987 1988 1989 1990 1991 1993 1994

Percentage of respondents

Source: General Social Survey, 1977–1994.
Note: No surveys were conducted in 1979, 1981, 1986, and 1992.

welfare. She does not label herself as either liberal or conservative. She watches national politics closely and is well-informed about the Republican presidential candidates in the 1996 primaries.

Maria is a twenty-six-year-old mother who lives in a wealthy suburb in Maine. I met her at her home, where she spends her days caring for her one-year-old daughter. She is expecting a second child. Her husband is a small business owner who makes a good living; the couple decided that Maria would stop working and raise their children. Maria is a Catholic who attends mass regularly and thinks it is important to raise children within the faith. "I use the church more as a guide than as a strict set of laws. I know my belief goes against that Catholic view, but there's a lot of things that the Catholic Church does that I don't believe in wholeheartedly. And so, I think religion should be used as a guide, not as a law and that's how I choose to use religion." Maria is a registered Republican, though she does not identify herself as conservative. Even though she is pro-choice, Maria does not vote strictly on the issue of choice. Other issues are more important to her and she expresses support for the legalization of marijuana for medicinal purposes, reduced federal government, and lower taxes.

Olivia is a thirty-eight-year-old woman with three children—an eighteen-year-old son from her first marriage and two small children with her present husband. I talked with her at a university library in Maine. Although she was raised in the Church of Christ, Olivia does not believe in organized religion; however, she believes that there "are higher beings, but I don't believe that one person is the messenger of everything." Olivia also states, "I am not a Christian, and I find that Christianity is a really antagonistic and controlling [faith]." Olivia is "not very political," but abortion is an important issue to her and plays a part in her voting decisions. She has been an abortion counselor for eight years. The death penalty is not an important political issue for Olivia.

Courtney, age twenty-four, has won many beauty pageants. Her image is seen on calendars and pinups in her region of the country. I interviewed her at her home in the evening. Courtney has left college and is working at a bank. She grew up in an abusive home and her father was unfaithful to her mother. She recalls the day she caught her father in an affair as the day "when I became opinionated." Courtney was raised a Baptist, but does not attend church. She considers herself "saved," but "it's nothing that I have to swear or confess or anything, I don't have to pray every day. I don't believe that if I don't pray bad things are going to happen." Courtney is "the only Democrat in my family" and she voted for Perot in the 1992 presidential election. Abortion is an important issue for her and she says she would seriously consider a candidate's position on abortion before casting her vote. Courtney talks for the first time about her own abortion, which she had had nearly eighteen months before our conversation. Her former fiancé was furious with her for terminating the pregnancy. He had been raised in a prominent, actively pro-life family. Courtney's decision to abort was made in spite of bitter disagreements with her fiancé and his family.

I met with Johnnie, a forty-five-year-old medical technician, at her office in Mississippi. She is divorced. Johnnie has suffered severe child abuse and wife abuse, which influences some of her opinions. Though she does not actively participate in an organized religion, she counts herself as "God's child" and believes her life is "God's choice" because of a remarkable childhood experience. At age ten, Johnnie was rowing a boat alone in Florida when a sudden and strong storm appeared, through which she stayed dry. Johnnie describes the experience:

As the storm came flying at me there was this little flicker of light up above and I thought, How strange to see the sun once more before I die. And I looked up and it wasn't the sun. It was God. . . . This happened faster than the proverbial wink of an eye. I just sort of looked up like this to see the sun, and the clouds just kind of spun apart like a vortex, and a shaft of light just cut down through and was in the boat. I didn't even have time for my jaw to drop. It hit the boat just as the storm ran across. It was light. It flowed, it did not shine. And it was God. It was the most love I have ever felt in my life. I have never been loved. It was just like a thousand mothers just put their arms around me. . . . [I know] I am God's by his choice. My life is his choice. Because I actually was supposed to die many years ago, and I'm alive by an act of God.

Johnnie is politically active; she votes regularly and has written letters to legislators informing them of her opinions and voting intentions. Johnnie is an Independent who voted for Bush in 1992, despite her disagreement with him on abortion; his opposition to gun control won her vote. Welfare is an important issue to Johnnie. She feels that the government is promoting "houses of prostitution" in supporting single women with children.

Rick, a forty-six-year-old disabled Vietnam veteran, served in the Special Forces. I went to his modest home in Mississippi for our conversation. He owns a small business, which, in addition to his military income, provides enough income for him to live on. Rick takes strong medication to battle the pain of his war injuries. He is divorced and has two children. Rick refers to himself as a "freelance Christian," which to him means that "I don't put a label on it, I believe in a supreme God, and I believe Jesus Christ died for my sins, and I don't put Methodist, Catholic, Jew, Baptist, Presbyterian, Lutheran labels on it." Organized religion has become more of a social club, in Rick's opinion, and he thinks that there is some hypocrisy in modern religions. Rick tends to vote for Republicans and expresses deep hatred for liberal Democrats, especially Senator Edward Kennedy.

> I'd vote for anybody but him. I'd vote for a convicted criminal before I'd vote for him. He's [a criminal], just not convicted. I predominantly go Republican because of their conservative views, although I disagree on their abortion stance. It's not just Kennedy, it's all the liberal Democrats. They're all the, quote unquote, "liberals." There's liberal Republicans. There's liberal whatever elses. The giveaways, the free spending, the be damned. Just outright liberal, just all these just total giveaway programs. I understand there's a need for assistance and help when it's needed, yes, but they've just turned the dadgummed thing upside down, and I'm quite frankly tired of paying for it. I'm doing good to provide for myself and my family. Why should I have to provide for these foreign countries and these people here that are just sitting on their butt not even making, hell, I'm disabled and trying to work.

Abortion Opinions

All of the interviewees support a woman's legal right to choose abortion for several reasons. The most common theme that emerges is that motherhood is a huge responsibility and should be taken seriously by those who choose to become mothers. Furthermore, if women are not prepared to care for their children, these interviewees think that they would be better off not having children, who would end up on the welfare rolls. Another common theme is the belief that every child should start out in life being wanted by his or her parents, or else face a life of neglect and/or abuse. Olivia, Rick, and Courtney have had an abortion experience in their own lives, which confirmed their abortion opinions. Olivia describes her experience with abortion as helping her to figure out when life begins: "I've had an abortion and I've had children, and I know that when I made the choice to conceive the pregnancy of my children, as far as I was concerned, they were kids at that time. Because that was my way of looking at it. Suddenly I was growing a baby. When I was pregnant and chose not to continue with the pregnancy, I chose to believe that it wasn't a baby at that point. Obviously it's not viable that early."

For Rick, the abortion experience occurred when he was married.

> I had a son from a previous marriage and she had two from a previous marriage. And we had one together. I was struggling in the banking business. She was struggling to get her master's degree. We were struggling with house payments. She became pregnant. The IUD didn't work, and I didn't use any protection. So we ended up, she was pregnant. She was a card-carrying, hard-core Catholic. So we talked about it and I persuaded her to have an abortion. Economics, already too many children that we were struggling to raise. She was going to have to quit school, I might have had to take a second job. Her career and her educational pursuits would have been challenged. It wouldn't be fair to the other children. She didn't want to, but we just looked at all the sides and so she finally decided [to abort].

Rick, years later, still feels some regret for the decision and is "afraid of what [God is] going to say." He feels the decision might be a "black mark in my book." But he also believes that God is a "loving and forgiving God" who is supposed to forgive him his sins, "if this is even a sin, and I'm not sure it is."

Courtney and her fiancé "lived together almost two years. My father was very violent, and in turn it makes me that way. I cannot be with someone that brings that out in me, that knows what buttons to push and pushes them anyway, knowing what they're going to bring out in me. It was so ugly I knew I couldn't be with a man like that and ever raise children." She discovered she was pregnant after she and her fiancé had broken off their engagement.

> I said [to my mother] I don't want to have it. Knowing whose it is, I don't want to have it. She said, "Are you sure?" And I said, "Pretty much." And I called him up and told him and he got mad, and anyway, I hung up the phone and he called me back. It was a Sunday and I told him, I already have it scheduled, my mom's coming down. We're paying for it. I don't want any money from you, I've never wanted anything from you. I'll handle this myself. It's my decision and I've made

this decision and I'm going to handle it myself. I don't want anything from you. I just don't. He said, "You're going to have a hard time dealing with this. This is going to come back to haunt you." He said so many things that were so mean. He was saying, "I can't believe you murdered my baby. My family hates you. I hate you. How could you kill my baby?" A lot of things. See, I haven't talked about this since it happened. That's the first time I've said it. I don't feel guilty. I feel like I made the best choice for everyone involved.

On the morning of anti-abortion murders, Courtney was on her way to work and had to drive by the clinics where she had been a patient. She saw the police covering bodies with sheets and saw people being taken out of the clinics and put into ambulances. She was "really, really scared."

Autumn commented, "There is a pin that the NOW—National Organization for Women—puts out that says, 'If you can't trust me with a choice, how could you trust me to raise a child?'" She says this reflects her pro-choice opinions. Autumn feels that motherhood is an "enormous responsibility" and that it's "the most important job you can take on, and if you don't think you want any children, I don't think you should have any." Autumn has worked as an interviewer for the Census Bureau, and in her work she saw a lot of children being neglected and abused by parents who did not want them. "And I saw enough of it that I thought, there are a lot of children around who weren't wanted. Or aren't wanted now. Maybe they were wanted originally. I still think it's such a big responsibility that the woman should make that choice. The husband should have some say in it, of course, if there's a husband. But basically, I think she carries the biggest load emotionally." Autumn does not think that people "have a right to have as many children as they want" because of population problems and because some people may want seven children, but can only afford to have two or three.

Rick echoes this perspective and expresses concern primarily for economic support of children.

I'm not saying buy it the most expensive clothes and buy it the most expensive toys and join the country club and buy a yacht and boats and take trips and eat steak and caviar. But at least provide some basic shelter, food, and clothing, and educational opportunities. She wants to have a child, she ought to have one. But take care of it. If she can't take care of it, she shouldn't have a child. I should have to take care of that child? I'm doing all I can to take care of my children. Why should I take care of somebody else's? If she says, "OK, the government's not going to subsidize me for having this child, I can't take care of it, and I got pregnant, I messed up, the boy didn't take any protection, I didn't take any protection, what are my other options?" Then I will consider the abortion option. She should have the right to choose that option.

Maria thinks that motherhood is a "much more challenging job than any other" and that "people do not take enough responsibility for their children." Olivia explains:

I just don't think that any of us has been very much accountable, or would consider themselves accountable. If you went to your parents today and said, "This is how you treated me when I was a child," probably the response you'd get would be, "Well, that's the best I could do." And I do believe our parents did the best that they could do, but I think that parenting now is a much bigger deal. . . . It's not just because you need another set of hands on the farm. Or because three people are going to die of TB this winter, or something like that. That's not realistic any more. So we have to arm our kids with other skills, and that's a big responsibility. Skills such as independence and self-esteem and nurturing and responsibility for your own decision making. But understand consequences of decisions, too.

Johnnie thinks that "[pregnant women] should have to manage the situation themselves or with their family."

In other words, if you're pregnant, that's your responsibility. It's not that you run and say, "I want tax money to support a child, or I want tax money for this or that whatever." I think in some respects for women who are financially strapped, they should be able to get assistance if she wants an abortion. It should be within her grasp to not have to have a child if she doesn't want to have it. But if she chooses to have the child, then she's responsible for it.

Courtney made her decision to abort her pregnancy based on this idea of maternal responsibility. She was reluctant to "take anything from anybody" in support of herself and the child. "I'd rather sell my stereo to have something to eat than have somebody buy me dinner. I thought about all the things that I wouldn't be able to have. I know that sounds really selfish, but that means I wouldn't be able to give it everything that I wanted to, if I didn't have things for myself I couldn't afford two of us or three of us. I did not want to be with [my fiancé]. I was trying to get away from him. That's why I moved away in the first place. This meant I'd have to go home and get farther into it than I was in the first place. It upset me, needless to say."

Closely related to this belief that motherhood is a major responsibility is the idea that in order for children to be raised properly, they ought to be planned for and wanted. Most interviewees express this point of view, though for different reasons. Johnnie and Courtney recall their feelings as unwanted and abused children. Johnnie recounts, at length, the suicidal thoughts she has entertained since childhood.

There was a railroad track went across, we lived on a big river. The railroad track went across the river. And Mom told us, "Never go out on that railroad bridge, because if a train comes, you can't get off fast enough and they'll kill you." Hey. I spent almost, I don't know how long I spent trying to figure out how to get to that railroad track. I was going to climb out on that bridge and wait for a train. But it was a case of I couldn't figure out how to get there. I could see the bridge. It was maybe half a mile down the river. But you could see the bridge because the river was so wide. And I just couldn't figure out how to get to the bridge. That was probably the one thing that kept me from dying, was the fact that I couldn't figure out how to get to the bridge. But my mom said, "Children have been caught out on there and been killed." And to me that was like, wow, one way to get out of here. It was a case of, my dad worked on the police department, and you knew if you ran away and they caught you they'd just bring you back. He'd beat the hell out of you for that too. There was no way to win. So if people don't want children, why force them to bring them into the world and go through what I went through? If a person doesn't want a child they're going to abuse it. Or if it's a child of rape or something like that, or they're forced to have a child, I think that's where a lot of abuse comes from, because the child was never wanted in the first place. I think that's part of what happened with us. My father never really wanted kids. My mom wanted children in the family.

Courtney relates her experience.

I know how it feels to grow up when you're not wanted, because my dad always wished I was a little boy, and I wasn't. I'm not going to have a child that I regret because I had to give up my life. . . . I would never want to push someone into this world when they're not wanted and they're resented. If I ever, if the thought even crossed my mind that I can't have something because of that other person. That would be my fault for ruining someone else's life or making someone else insecure as long as they live.

The interviewees would, in some circumstances, encourage a woman to have an abortion. Olivia says, "If my daughter were sixteen years old and I thought having a baby would ruin her life, I might really try to encourage her to lean towards choosing an abortion, but again, I think I'd have to respect that and she has the right to make her own choices." Olivia "would never try to discourage anybody" from having an abortion. Courtney explains why she encouraged a seventeen-year-old she knows to have an abortion:

[She and her boyfriend are] not dating any more, but she can't move back home because she doesn't get along with her mom. Anyway, found out she's pregnant, and said she was going to keep it. She hasn't graduated high school, she has never worked, [she and her boyfriend are] not together anymore. Her mom isn't making money, she doesn't have an education. She has nothing. No car, no experience, no money, no future. She has nothing. She is still a child. She has nothing. She's never been independent, and she was thinking about having it. I said, I cannot believe she's even thinking about having the child. She has nothing to give that child. Nothing. It would have nothing, she would be a nothing. You can't get a career living off somebody else. I mean, that's awful. I would never do that. I would never want to do that to myself or anybody else. I'm not having a baby and then having my mom raise those two children [herself and her baby]. There's just no way.

Johnnie recalls her experience of childhood abuse in discussing whether she would encourage a woman to have an abortion. Johnnie and her sister were so badly abused by their father that their pelvises were broken, leading to a very difficult time in childbirth for her sister. Johnnie says her sister "died three times on the delivery table having her first kid."

Her pelvic bones were fractured and rehealed over and over again. I have scoliosis. From "spanking," that's what he called it. But you have to understand, this was a man who came back from World War II and had been blowed up, and his hand right here was badly damaged, and he could use his hand but it was numb in the fact that he had no feeling, hot, cold, anything, no pain, and that's what he used to beat us with. He laughed because it didn't hurt him a bit. Of course, he didn't know how hard he was hitting us and he didn't really care. But I have a deformed back and pelvis, and I opted not to have kids. I just knew, after my sister told me, from the doctor talking to her. He had told her to tell, he asked if she had any sisters. She said yes. He said, "You be sure and tell them not to have any kids unless they've been X-rayed and have a very good doctor because they're possibly going to be just like you." The other two children she had, she had by cesarean section. I opted not to have any children.

Quality of life of women and children is important to these interviewees. Autumn says, "I want women to have a choice to grow and get educated and live a full life and have children when you're ready." Olivia thinks that every child deserves to be "born into a loving home, I figure every child deserves all kinds of things—love and safety and security and food and cleanliness and all these things, and a lot of children don't get that." Johnnie feels the same. "Your childhood shapes your life in an awful lot of respects. I formed some early opinions because I had to, you know, I had no choice but to survive," she said. About anti-abortion laws, Johnnie asks, "Are we human beings or are we just cattle in a chute? And if we're just cattle in a chute, what are those things we're producing? It's like I told my Mom one day, when I was a child why didn't you kill me? Because I didn't like being alive." She goes on to recount a horrifying story of abuse and its aftermath, which bolsters her conviction that all children should have a good quality of life.

I potted at the wrong time, typical child thing, you get nervous, you get scared, you pot at the wrong time and the wrong place. They say most children get abused for that very reason; poor timing, you know. And so I got the hell whipped out of me. I was six. It was one of the sad points of my life. You feel so useless, you're in such pain. I realized later in life, and still I sometimes have trouble dealing with the fact that my mom didn't protect us, she wouldn't get between us. Of course she was, you know, "the man is the lord of the castle" crap. But that time she did intervene. After he finished whipping me he told me to go to bed, go to my room. I knew I wasn't going to get supper or breakfast or anything. And mom intervened and said, "I don't want her going right to bed." And my mind just sort of went blank and said, "Mom's going to help me." For that brief moment I had this thing that Mom was there for me. She said, "I don't want her going straight to bed." And I'm kind of like, somebody wants me. And then she said, "I don't want that blood all over my sheets. I have to wash those sheets and hang them out, and I don't want the neighbors seeing those spots all over my sheets. I work too hard to have white sheets. She's got to have a bath before she goes to bed and gets that blood all over my sheets." And I realize that part of it was she wanted to doctor me up before I went to bed. But it just sort of blew everything out of the mind. She got me by the hand and took me upstairs and stood me in the bathtub and tried to wash the blood, to stop the bleeding, you know, all like that. Like I say, I was six, what does a six-year-old know anyhow? And I remember that night, you know, of course I was in bed the rest of that afternoon, whatever, and that was the first time that I ever, I was raised like I say in the Methodist Church, they raise you up "Jesus loves the little children" and all this stuff, and it was the first time that I really had had all I could handle. And that night when it got real quiet, I knew that God loved little children, and that he could help people, if you really prayed. And so I prayed that God would let me die. Because I knew people died in their sleep. And so I prayed to God that he would take me and just let me die in my sleep. The most horrible experience was waking up in the morning and knowing that even God didn't want you. And you're only six years old, and you think you must really be the shit of the earth. There was no reason left to have any hope, or for anything, because even God didn't want you. And that took a long time to get over.

These interviewees also express concern about teen pregnancy. They believe that teens are not capable of providing for the material needs of growing children. Autumn saw many teen parents in her occupation as a Census surveyor. "It's very upsetting, she's going to raise this baby when she's still a child? You can't do that." Olivia says that every type of contraceptive method fails at some point and "I did see a lot of teens and unmarried women in the [abortion] clinic, and for those people I think it is a much bigger problem than for women who are in a marriage, or a real concrete relationship." Johnnie, who had also worked at a family planning clinic, recalls a time when a single mother came into the clinic with her four teenage daughters. The mother had noticed that there were too many sanitary napkins left at the end of the month, so "she brought [her daughters] to us and we confirmed a three-month pregnancy in her daughter who was just turning thirteen. I don't know how it came out, but for a thirteen-year-old girl to carry a baby to full term, there's going to be some destruction there."

Perceptions of Pro-Life Activism

All of these interviewees express concern about anti-abortion protesting. Most believe that anti-abortion activists have no right to force their views, beliefs, and opinions on others. Olivia calls their stance "stupid, pious, moral, and self-serving." She sees the activists as "fanatics" who "used to surround the [clinic where I worked], and they'd stand up near the client and they'd show little plastic fetuses to our clients, and show them their signs." Furthermore, Olivia says:

People who live by doctrine that they feel is rigid, like the Bible . . . I think the Bible is easily interpreted by people in any way they want it to be. And I don't think people have the right to use their interpretation as an argument for political choices or personal choices of other people. If they want to make that choice for themselves, if they say, 'I've read the Bible and it says, God says you can't have an abortion,' fine, but I don't even think they should put that on their kids.

Courtney wonders, "How dare anyone judge me?" In her decision to abort, she was concerned about her own well-being and her ability to provide a decent life for herself. Maria recalls growing up with her pro-life parents, whose message to her was "If you want to play you've got to pay." Autumn refers to this as a "punishment attitude."

> I have a sister who is so opposed to abortion but the reason she is so opposed to abortion is because she thinks somebody should be punished if they get pregnant and they're not married. "They get pregnant they should have to have the baby." . . . That's a punishment attitude. It isn't thinking about this child, this baby. It's hard to explain, but she acts like only married people have a right to sex. And only married people who want children have a right to sex. Because the rhythm method worked for her. She has two children. But she believes that her way is the right way, and nobody else should do it any other way, and if you're not married you should not be having sex. And if you do you should be punished.

Autumn and Olivia believe that pro-life advocates are opposed to contraception and opposed to sexual activity in general. Autumn says, "You see, these people don't even believe in birth control. A lot of them don't. They believe that's a sin. What do you want us to do, OK? No sex. Forget about sex."

Olivia has a very personal reaction to John Salvi's attack on two abortion clinics in Brookline, Massachusetts.

> When that happened, when the people were shot in Massachusetts last year, it was December 30th, which is my birthday, and I don't know how many times I've looked up from the desk [at the clinic where I worked] and someone would have walked in and said, 'Is this Dr. [Smith]'s office?' and I would have said 'Yes.' Just like that's what happened to the young woman at Planned Parenthood. Someone said, 'Is this Planned Parenthood?' and she said 'Yes' and he shot her. So it just really brought it close to home. So I would love to be a clinic escort or something, but I can't afford to do that. I have a life.

Paul Hill is a common subject throughout these conversations as well. All the interviewees feel he should be executed for his crimes. Maria "put him in the same category as [John Salvi]. Totally wrong." All agree that Paul Hill and others have a right to their personal beliefs, but do not have the right to forcefully and violently impose those beliefs on others. Courtney was working in a city at the time of one of the fatal acts of anti-abortion violence. She used to go to one of the clinics for her birth control pills.

> I used to work right across the street. I drove by and saw everything that happened and I heard it when it happened and I drove by there. I drove by the one [street] that had the last [attack] and, I mean I had to go in there and get my exam. That's

where I got my birth control pills from, because they were cheaper there. There were TV cameras there everywhere. When I went there for my pills I parked around the corner and walked in the front door because I didn't want to drive in there, because there was all these people blocking, and they like, you know, talk to you right as you go in there, like knock on your window or something when you go in, like why do you come here? Don't you know the devil's working here? And all that kind of stuff. It was weird. So I just kind of put my sunglasses on and put my head down and I said, and I would say, I'm right with you, I'm just getting a checkup, I'm just taking care of my body. I'm not here on a Tuesday, or a Monday, or whatever it was. They go OK, will you read this literature? And I would. I would take it and read it every time.

Johnnie compares Paul Hill to Adolf Hitler.

It wasn't his right to take someone else's life. If that person that he figures is killing other people was to die, he wasn't exactly following any Christian belief, because the Christian belief does not say "Go out and murder thy brother because he's doing wrong." That's exactly what Hitler said. A little bit different line. It only takes a little lie, and if you convince enough people that it's right, pretty soon you have a bigger lie. But it's still a lie. God's gonna decide who's right. On this earth we're given our thoughts and our emotions, and we all carry our history and our baggage around with us. We are what we are. But the long run is, if you can read the Bible and understand it, which is one of the hard things for some people to do, and you don't follow a lot of rhetoric, and you read it for what it says, and you kind of look at it in both ways, it says, "Thou shalt not kill." OK, he went in to kill someone that he decided was killing someone else. And he claims this was preserving life.

Olivia says, bluntly, that Paul Hill "should be gunned down in a parking lot." She says she would prefer that society view things strictly in a "black and white code of ethics" because it "would make things a lot easier if we did and everyone believed the same way."

Rick says that Hill should be executed quickly and as painfully as possible, and adds, "I'd probably torture him first."

We established the United States of America based on those religious foundations. You may not go out and kill your neighbor, for whatever reason. So he did and he should die. He shouldn't be put in jail and a free ride. I don't want to pay for him sitting in there playing Ping-Pong and lifting weights and watching TV and eat-ing better than I do. I have to go buy stuff on sale and warm up leftovers. I don't want to pay for him sitting over there for thirty years.

Abortion Politics

While most of the interviewees consider abortion an important political issue, few consider it the most important of all political issues. However, a candidate's position on abortion influences their voting at the polls. Autumn would not let abortion influence her presidential choices because she feels that presidents can do little to undermine the freedom of choice. But she says that "in the state legislature I probably wouldn't let [a candidate's position on abortion] be the deciding issue, but it certainly would help me lean."

Johnnie and Rick, who tend to vote for Republicans, feel that other political issues, such as gun control, take priority over abortion. Both are opposed to gun control legislation and prefer to see people in office who reflect that belief. Johnnie learned "a long time ago to pick your fights, and you can't fight them all." Abortion is very important to Johnnie "because it's a woman's right to choose, and after having mine thoroughly stomped over, the most important thing is for a woman to have a choice." For Rick, a candidate's abortion stance is not "the critical driving force behind my decision, it is one of the considerations, [but] I've voted Republican and they have been consistently pro-life." Maria declares that she has some difficulty voting for pro-choice candidates, because she is a registered Republican, and many Republicans are opposed to choice. "So, when I go to the polls I try to make an informed decision, and I take usually the politician's philosophy and if I agree with the majority of the points that will be the person I would vote for." She is a supporter of Senator Olympia Snowe from Maine, a well-known abortion rights supporter.

Olivia, on the other hand, bases her voting decisions almost exclusively on abortion rights issues. She is "not very political" but has been an active supporter of abortion rights on the state level. She "definitely finds out who's pro-choice" before voting.

> My feeling is, if they can start telling us what to do with our bodies, they can start telling us what books to read and all kinds of things. I believe that people should have the right to make choices, so I always vote pro-choice. I spoke before the legislature once, many years ago. There was a parental consent bill, kind of like '86 or '87. We all got together, went into our office, and wrote our little speeches, and we were all really nervous, and wore these really conservative clothes because all the right-to-life people were going to be there. The first right-to-life person that

got up was this chubby little grandma type lady, who I'm sure is a wonderful woman, but she got up and she said, "My sixteen-year-old granddaughter got pregnant, and she wanted to have an abortion. The family didn't let her. We all decided that she should have that baby, and that baby is so cute. . . ." And I just wanted to smack her. I wanted to say, "So what? Of course the baby's cute. All babies are cute." It's like a puppy. Puppies are cute. It doesn't mean we should all have a house full of dogs. I just wanted to smack her.

There are many other political issues that are important to these interviewees. While abortion is an important political issue to these interviewees, it is not as important as some others. For instance, welfare dependency weighs heavily on the minds of this group and three (Rick, Johnnie and Courtney) feel that legislation limiting access to firearms is more important than abortion. With respect to welfare dependency, these interviewees believe that when women have children they should do so in the context of financial security in order to avoid government aid. With respect to gun control, these interviewees believe that access to firearms is critical for self-preservation in a world gone awry with random violence.

The most commonly mentioned political issue is welfare, which all of the interviewees agree should be radically changed. All express some resentment toward those who live on government assistance. Johnnie's view has been influenced by the actions of a member of her family.

But I think in some ways it shows the more openness of our society at the facts that [unplanned pregnancies] happen. But I think one of the biggest problems we have with accepting the fact that, we accept the fact that accidents happen, is overlooking the fact that somewhere you've got to establish rules and try and maintain them. And I don't think that providing money and housing and stuff for pregnant teenagers is the way to do it. I know Mississippi considers from the time a woman is pregnant that she is an adult. They would provide housing and food and all this other stuff. I think there has to be some sort of burden placed on these people. I have a niece who ran around with a junkie, got pregnant, married him, moved out of state. Of course, their relationship was not one that was going to last. It broke down, they got divorced. She since has had two bastard children. So now she has three children. She lives entirely on welfare, and she makes more money than I do working six days a week. She flies here and there where she wants to go visit. The state that she lives in pays her rent and pays her utilities. She has to pay for her own phone, oh shuckydarn. And she has to pay for part of her food. She banks, every month, more money than I can imagine being able to bank. She lives in Minnesota. They have a great welfare system for unmarried single women.

She's in her twenties now, and the youngest is two and a half and then there's one about a year and a half older than that, and the older one would be another year or year and a half older than that. To me, she is a disgrace. As far as I'm concerned, I mean, it's not like she doesn't know what causes children, at this point. Because she has literally had these kids to increase her welfare. She's a welfare queen. And as far as I'm concerned, some of these women who are just doing, they are just having babies so they never have to work. . . . I think they need a work farm for these people with barracks. I don't think there should be a free ride for doing something that I consider is immoral. Having children out of wedlock, in my opinion, is wrong. We shouldn't subsidize these things, because in my religion it clearly says, "Do not support the whores of Baal." And that's what we're doing when you're giving money to unwed mothers with bastard children. This is part of what is preached against in my Bible, Old Testament and New Testament. Do not support the whores of Baal. As far as I'm concerned, when you're supporting prostitutes, and that's what my niece is, basically, you're supporting the opposite of what my religious views are. And to tax me to pay for these whores and their bastard children really ticks me off.

As far as Rick is concerned "I think they all ought to take them all [welfare mothers] outside and shoot them, I know that's hard core, but by God I'm tired of paying people to have babies when they can't afford to have them." Maria is not quite as "hard core" in her views about welfare recipients, but thinks they ought to work for the money they receive from the government. Having volunteered at a local community service agency she knows that there are "some people that come in there that truly need assistance; just have really thin jackets on and they're skinny and they look like they haven't eaten a decent meal in a while. Other people come in and they're pulling up in late 1994 cars, looking to get Thanksgiving dinner or some kind of gas vouchers or something like that. It just doesn't seem right. The welfare system definitely needs to be looked at." She makes a distinction between those people who are out of work because of economic cycles and those who are "just saying OK, I'll watch another Maury Povich or Sally Jessy Raphael and eat bonbons, I think they ought to do something in return."

Olivia's concern about welfare is based on her experiences with clients in the family planning clinic where she worked.

They're living on AFDC [Aid to Families with Dependent Children] assistance, they're having another baby because their AFDC payment goes up. I heard over and over again, "Well, if I have another one . . ." They're already so entrenched in the welfare system, they see no way out. They're so out of control already. And not that control is such a big issue, but they feel they have no goals. They don't have a goal, belief system that they can do it, that they deserve better, that their children deserve better. They're already so deeply mired in that system that the only light at the end of the tunnel is, "Well, if I have another baby . . . I had one baby and I'm getting all this help. Why not have another one?" But then those babies are not getting what they need. They're not getting a quality of life. I'm not saying their moms don't love them. They do. And some of them were in relationships with the same partner. The guys didn't all run off and abandon them, although that does happen much of the time.

Autumn considers the larger picture. She is opposed to people using welfare as their way of life, but is "not opposed to all welfare," recognizing that some people "genuinely need help because they're disabled or whatever." Autumn is more distressed about what she calls "corporate welfare."

But corporate welfare, they will give you money, your corporation, to promote your product overseas. Where's the justice there? Did you hear the news this morning, or last night, or yesterday about the congress people that are taking trips all over the world, costing us hundreds of thousands of dollars, and for no real purpose, even though they say it's part of their job. I mean, it doesn't make sense, some of them. When you get a chance, read about it. And it's your money and my money that they're using to do this.

Courtney, Rick, and Johnnie mention gun control as a political issue important to them. Courtney and Johnnie view guns as an equalizer between the genders. Johnnie says:

I'm not for violence and that sort of thing, but I am pro-guns. As a woman I know for a fact without a gun I am defenseless. I have been in that position. I didn't like it. I've been shot at. I've had my own husband try and kill me. If I hadn't had a gun, he probably would have. No woman is strong enough to fight off a man. It's the only thing we have that can prevent us from being killed and raped and our children murdered, because women, we don't have the strength. And I especially, with my scoliosis, you can hit me on either shoulder and I'll go down like a brick, because of my back. And so I've learned. Of course I learned how to use a firearm when I was fairly young. My mother taught me. Her father had given her a .22 and taught her how to shoot a rifle and a shotgun and she taught me.

Courtney explains that her pistol, in addition to her self-defense classes, provides her with a sense of security.

I go out by myself, I like jogging by myself. It's almost like I dare somebody to touch me. Because they're gonna have to kill me before they touch me again. Or I'm gonna kill them. I carry a pistol and it's registered. I'm taking classes. My daddy is a marksman. He taught me well. I'm not scared of a gun. I think all women need to be familiar with guns. I think we all need to, I think we should be allowed to carry one in our purse at all times. I know it's a concealed weapon, but I think we should all get registered. Just to be prepared for anything that might come your way. Because everybody thinks, not me, not me, not me.

Rick is concerned with the Constitutional rights of citizens of the United States. The issues important to Rick are "freedom of choice issues, whether it be education, whether it be religion, whether it be abortion, whether it be the right to own weapons in your own home. I'm not saying I want everybody to go out and get them a gun and go on a shooting spree. Just because you have a gun doesn't mean you have to kill somebody."

Death Penalty Opinions

These interviewees believe that the death penalty is appropriate for murderers. Related to this opinion is concern for the failure of the criminal justice system to protect society, a willingness to tolerate some level of error with capital sentencing, and a belief that the death penalty saves taxpayers money. Rick has served as a juror in a capital case in Mississippi, where the defendant was convicted and sentenced to death. "It was my civic obligation, and I felt like whatever the evidence was I was going to listen to it and make as fairly an intelligent decision, based on the laws of our courts. Had there been sufficient evidence to merit otherwise, then I could vote not guilty or voted for a lighter sentence." The case was that of a young black man accused of killing a white store clerk during an armed robbery. The evidence presented was a security videotape, the weapon used, with fingerprints, and an uncoerced signed confession. The defense failed to present mitigating circumstances. "They got his grandmother up there and his Sunday school teacher and high school, family members saying, 'Oh please don't take my son's life. He's guilty. Lock him in jail.' That was their only argument, their only defense, whether it was going to be death or life in prison." Only one juror, a black woman, was uneasy about the death penalty. She had "moral convictions" against the death penalty, but "we went back over the fact that the man [victim] was pleading for mercy for his life, that he had a wife and small children," and the jury eventually agreed on a death sentence. Rick says that no matter how good the lawyer was, or if "God himself" were up there arguing for this defendant, "it would not have mattered, I would still have broken it down to the simple basics of the evidence that was presented." The fact that the defendant was African American and the victim was white "had nothing to do with it, if he was white, green, purple, blue, it wouldn't have mattered. They had it on videotape, they had the weapon, had his fingerprints, he took them to the weapon, he confessed, and the [victim had begged] for his life."

> I really, really don't think that [race] ever entered into it one way or the other. [The victim] was a man who had a wife and a family and was running a business. It was a punk off the street that had a history of crime, but not much. He'd never killed anybody before, but he did have a little tainted history. It might not have been very severe, but he was a criminal, a punk off the street, walked in and robbed a man point blank and shot him in cold blood. So he could have been white, he could have been the richest man in the counties, had the best schooling, driven the best cars, whatever, and shot a black student or whatever trying to make a living and support his family. It would not have mattered one bit. Here's an honest, decent human being and here's a punk, and this one took this one's life. This guy needs to be eliminated. He is no longer a valuable contributing member to society. He needs to go. Not in jail where I have to pay for it. If God wants to forgive him, that's fine. Society shouldn't have to forgive him. We made the laws based on what we believe God's laws to be, and we need to enforce those. We ought to let God deal with all of it.

Variations on these themes are expressed by the other interviewees in this group. Support for the death penalty for "horrendous" or "heinous" crimes begs the question, "What is a horrendous crime?" For Autumn, and all the others, the answer is "Charlie Manson, who killed many. Jeffrey Dahmer who killed many and cut them up. In my opinion [they are] not safe ever, ever again to be around people. I would go with the death penalty for [them]." Beyond the serial murderers, however, Autumn also thinks that the death penalty is justified for those who profit from the sale of illegal drugs. "Now we're talking about the death penalty. What you do to that young person when you get them hooked on cocaine to me is almost as bad as killing them. And when you're selling it you're doing it to a lot of them. And that's murder. When you get somebody hooked on stuff like that you've wrecked their life. A few of them will come out of it, but I don't think many can." Maria believes that if the evidence presented at trial proves the defendant guilty beyond a reasonable doubt, and if the defendant "cannot be rehabilitated," then execution is justified. "I'm almost in a line with 'an eye for an eye.' If you murder somebody then your life should be of equal value in exchange. But if you beat up a guy in a pub one Friday night, you shouldn't get the death penalty." On the other hand, Maria says:

I always try to put myself in the place of a mother of a person on death row or in a certain circumstance. If it was my child, you always hesitate and say they don't deserve that. But if you step beyond your own fear and look at what the person has done, whether it's your child or somebody else's child, because everybody's a child of somebody, if you go beyond yourself and look at what they've done, then I think that it might be less of a burden to know that that person's not suffering every single day in jail and the physicians in there aren't the greatest, that the death would be better for them than having to linger in life forever in jail. I think that if a person's able to step beyond themselves and look at what was actually done, then they might also agree that the death penalty would be right.

Olivia thinks that "crimes against kids, like child abuse, rape, and really violent crimes," are sufficiently heinous to warrant capital punishment.

People who torture and make people go through hours of pain and agony till they finally kill them. I mean, what must Nicole and Ronnie Goldman have gone through in that few minutes of being surprised and attacked like that? Unless it's happened, I don't think you know that kind of horror, even the person who does it, even the perpetrator. So I think that person should get it back, personally. But then, who's going to do that? Who's going to sneak up on O.J. and stab him in the night?

Johnnie feels that drunk driving is a horrendous enough crime to warrant execution. "If they're drunk driving and they kill someone, I think it should apply, because we make choices. If you choose to drink and drive you have murdered someone, because you knew it was a big possibility, when you got in that car, you're going to hit somebody. And you didn't really give a damn." She would also apply the death penalty to "crimes of passion and rage."

I have had rage. I understand rage. And if I should take someone's life, I don't feel that I should have the right to enjoy life, and go on with my life, when I deliberately took someone else's. A blind passion or a blind rage is just anger. It's "I want my way." That's not good for society. That's not good for anybody. Especially the person they killed. And when you say, "But it was blind passion," I say, "Bullshit." You did it because you wanted to.

Rick echoes Maria's "eye for an eye" sentiments. For Rick the horrendous crimes that warrant the death penalty are "hideous, almost sick, mad, insane. . . . You take the serial killers, you take the Jeffrey Dahmers, you take the people that just at random kill, I think those people need to be eliminated. You go into a store, and you hold the store owner up, he's on his knees begging for his life, 'Take my money, take anything you want, just don't kill me. I'm not going to hurt you. Here, my hands are behind my head, I can't get to you or hurt you. Take it and go.' POW! They should die." Furthermore, Rick thinks that "second offenders, rape, child abuse, armed robbery, any violent crimes against people, property, their person, their welfare," are worthy of capital punishment.

> I really think first offenders—child abuse, molestation, rape—they should just shoot them. Get them out of society. They're no good to society. They just ought to be eliminated. But that's carrying it a little too far. I'd say second offense definitely. First offense, put them in jail. If they get out on parole for good behavior, blah blah blah, if they're supposedly, quote unquote, "rehabilitated." If they do it again, shoot them. We don't need people like that in our society. I want my family and my child and their children to walk down the street safely without fear of anyone.

When asked what crimes are sufficiently heinous to warrant the death penalty, Courtney begins, "Well, I'm kind of one for castration too. You want to throw that in there, or something to that effect? Another thing that's kind of shaped the way I am, as far as not being naive, is my first time . . . I was raped. My first time. And I was still a child." Courtney was raped at fifteen, while babysitting. "I looked like I was ten, I weighed only eighty pounds or so and still looked like a little kid. . . . I just bled and bled and bled, I had just crawled to the bathroom crying, and [my best friend] came in." Courtney did not go to the hospital or press charges. She faced the knowledge that the rapist bragged about how he "got another virgin." She recalls, "[The rapist] was so much bigger than I was, he was so much stronger than I was, and I know that one day, one day he's gonna get what's coming to him. And now that I'm older and I have a loud voice of my own, I wish I could be the one to give it to him."

Courtney goes on to talk about the rape and murder of Polly Klaas. She believes that Davis, the defendant in that case, "needs to be put to death now. You know, hook it up. Fill that chair and just get it over with. I'm tired of paying for him. He's had enough play time. He's done enough damage for one lifetime. Let's not give him a chance to do some more. Look at how many people's lives he ruined. He killed a little angel."

Interviewees also express a deep frustration with the criminal justice system, which they perceive to be inept at providing security to society. Courtney expresses this in her view of the murder of Polly Klaas.

Look at Polly. I mean he got worse and worse. That would never have happened if the system would have worked. I would have done something to that man to make him not feel that desire to control like that if he didn't have the ability to hurt a woman like that then they would not have happened. It would either humble him to where he didn't do that or maybe he would just go crazy and do something worse, I don't know. But I think that chain could have been stopped, you know, if they would have looked up. If the police officers were given the authority to look up a criminal record when they stop someone, which they're not. If I got stopped, if I was acting funny or was suspicious or, I mean, they can check for outstanding warrants right now. But, you know, they can't look up your police record. Your history. Which is accessible in seconds. And they would have known who that man was that they had for thirty-five minutes. They questioned him for thirty-five minutes before they let him go. They found him in the woods, right just like fifty feet from where he killed her.

Autumn saw numerous flaws in the system when she was doing research for the Census Bureau, examining the conviction and sentencing of felons. "And one day I actually had to leave and go home, I got so upset because of rape convictions, where they were given six year [sentences], all suspended [after] six months. And it happened repeatedly, not with the same person, but in different cases." She believes the system treats rape cases "casually" but also feels that rape does not warrant the death penalty. However, Autumn says, "If I gave them ten years, they'd be in there for ten years." Another aspect of the system that bothers Autumn is the delays in carrying out the sentencing.

I think it needs to be soon. If you tell a child twelve years old that he's not to whatever, you don't want him to have other people in when you're not there. I don't want you to have your friends in unless I'm here. You come home, and here he is, he's having a party. I think the penalty or the punishment for that, whatever, should be soon. I don't think you should say, 'Eight months from now you're going to be grounded for a week.'

Rick places the failure of the system to rehabilitate offenders in the lap of the offenders themselves.

You can put them in a room full of all kinds of counselors and therapists and give them all kinds of training to go out and earn a decent living, to get them off the street and away from crime. But they've got to make the conscious choice to absorb that and do something with it. I can go sit all day out here in the classroom and listen to all sorts of lectures, but if I don't absorb any information and do something positive with it, then it's been wasted. I can go sit in the church all day long and listen to a stream of preachers come through here, but if I don't choose to listen to what they're telling me and do something with that information, and I just ignore it and go on . . . If they had the chance and they blew it, or they don't make the choice to utilize this to some positive good, and they're going to go out and re-create the same mayhem and havoc that got them in there to begin with, get rid of them. They're damaging society, and they're hurting me, and I'm tired of it. I'm paying for all this. And then my life, and I've got two or three hundred dollars cash and I worked hard for it. I don't want somebody lurking in them bushes out there figuring to knock me in the head, after he's just done it two or three times previously, and been in jail and out doing it again. I don't want to have to look over my shoulder.

These interviewees are willing to tolerate some level of error with the death penalty. "I'd like to not tolerate any, I'd like to think that there wouldn't be any [mistakes]," Olivia says. When informed of the research findings on miscarriages of justice in capital cases (Bedau and Radelet 1987; Radelet, Bedau, and Putnam, 1992), Olivia says, "Well, that's like one every three years or something. I guess when you look at it on a percentage basis, it's not that high." Courtney says of the possibility of executing innocent people, "Then it happens, and somebody's going to sue the government and get a lot of money. Or sue the city. It's going to happen. I mean, nothing is flawless."

Autumn feels that there are more guilty people going free than innocent people being executed. Rick feels the same way, and elaborates:

If there's going to be some innocent people, OK, look at the war with Japan. There were innocent women and children and civilians that died when we dropped those bombs on Hiroshima and Nagasaki. There were innocent people that died. I'm sorry. It ended the war. More innocent people didn't die. OK, so then you say because the means justify the ends. A lot of these things are decisions that I can't make. [God has] got to make that. You're gonna have those that fall through the cracks. I'm sorry. I think that 98 percent of the time if a person is convicted and sentenced, it's gonna be right. You're gonna have 1 or 2 percent of the time, I'm sorry. I think in the end, the majority has been served. We're trying to protect the rights of a very, very small group of people over here, and that's fine if you can do that without sacrificing the rights of a whole bunch of people. So if you let ninety-eight hardened criminals go free to commit those crimes again, then ninety-eight more people are going to be violated, as opposed to the two people that were innocent that died that didn't kill anybody to begin with, and they were sentenced to die wrongly. They wouldn't have killed anybody anyway. But then these ninety-eight that didn't get sentenced to death and that did go free and that did kill again, then you got ninety-eight people that lost their lives as opposed to two over here that lost their lives.

Most of the interviewees share the belief that the death penalty is more cost-effective than life-without-parole sentences. Autumn is the only person in this group aware that the death penalty is more expensive than life without parole: "They tell me that it costs more to give a death penalty than any other penalty, but you see, I think that's a mistake. I think the death penalty should be . . . If it's given to you, I don't think it should take twenty years. No wonder it's so expensive." Maria recognizes that due to the public financing of corrections, "it's the taxpayers that are going to have to support the prisoners and pay for their health care and food and housing and rehabilitation." Olivia sees it as a "real drain on taxpayers" to support criminals and believes it is more cost-effective to execute them. She says that "that money could be diverted" into a program for hungry children instead.

Rick and Courtney express a deep resentment toward convicts who receive benefits that they do not have access to. Courtney explains:

> $500,000 [for life without parole]. This man ate better than I do, he has an opportunity to have a better education than I do. I can't afford to be in school right now. He has better health care than I do. He has probably better athletic facilities than I have access to. He has opportunities in prison, for taking someone's life, that I don't have. Nobody gives me those things. Nobody pays for my education. Nobody. Nothing. And these men in jail that have been on death row for like twenty years and have killed like thirty-seven people and have admitted it, chopped them in little pieces and done whatever with them, children, you know, wives, moms, babies, and to know that they're sitting there having opportunities that I don't. I'm not saying we should like kick them and make them eat dirt and beat them up or anything. Let's just get it over with, and quit taking my money to pay for this shit for these people. It just . . . It's not fair. I don't want to pay a penny in taxes to this government because of what they're doing. I hate it. It's not fair. It's so not fair. I can't stand it.

These interviewees are not very concerned about the death penalty as a political issue. Rick and Courtney are the only two who go out of their way to find out a candidate's stance on capital punishment before casting their votes. Rick refers to the death penalty as a "definite criteria" for deciding his vote. Johnnie considers it important, but not as important as the abortion issue.

Connecting Opinions on Abortion and the Death Penalty

Interviewees in this group feel that abortion and the death penalty are "not at all connected," as Autumn put it. Maria thinks the issues are "two separate things" and should not be connected at all. "It cannot be compared. Because I've thought too, at some times, if you support life and you support not having abortions, and then you support the death penalty, it seems like it's a conflict of interests, because one time you're saying death and the next time you're saying life. But I don't agree. I think that they're two separate issues and can't be combined." Olivia also believes that the two issues cannot be compared.

Johnnie sees these issues as connected in terms of "accountability" for behavior. "You have to be accountable, whether you're having a child, not having a child, killing someone, not killing someone, being drunk and driving. The biggest failure of our society is to hold people accountable for their choices. He raped seven women and they finally catch him, these were all choices he made. They say, 'Oh, he was sick. He didn't understand.' Bullshit. Most people will do just exactly what they can get away with. It's part of the human mentality."

Solutions

Since abortion and capital punishment are viewed as separate issues among these interviewees, it is not surprising that their proposed solutions to the problems are distinct. Autumn asks, "Solution to the death penalty? It should be, if it's given, it should be given only in extreme cases, but it should be soon. With abortion I still think if you can't trust me to make a choice you can't trust me to raise a child. If I'm not mature enough to make this decision I'm certainly not mature enough to raise a child."

Maria presents her solutions:

Let's take each issue separately. The death penalty issue, I think there needs to be a restructuring of the criminal justice system. I think that they have to set down a specific set of guidelines so punishments would be swift. For example, if you get caught with one pound of cocaine, this is your sentence. Or if you get caught molesting a child, this is your sentence. If you get caught murdering somebody, this is your sentence. Because right now, the criminal justice system does give not equal punishment for equal crime. So somebody who molests a child may get five years in prison, and somebody else who molests a child may get twenty years in prison. So that's not equal. So I think you really have to really look at the criminal justice system and try to restructure so there's some kind of equality to it. And I think that you have to specifically define where capital punishment will be used, and I think that it should go for all of the states. Not one state has a specific set of rules and another state has another set. Because you can go to one state and commit the same crime and go to another state, and the punishment would be different. You need to have a general set of guidelines. If we're going to live as a united nation, all states, then I think that the federal system should all be the same for each of the states. The abortion issue? That issue I would take more to an educational level. I think that schools should educate, or start educating at a very early age, about birth control methods. First grade and kindergarten. I think that the issue of gender and sex and health should all start at an early age. . . . So I'd start there. I would try to educate at the very earliest ages possible about health issues and sexuality and then in terms of government involvement, again I don't think that each state should have a specific set of laws, because someone can get pregnant in New Hampshire and go down to Massachusetts and have an abortion and not think anything of it. And I don't know how much government involvement should be allowed in that particular area, because like I said, it's a personal decision. It's a health thing. It's just . . . It's a health issue, it's an individual issue, it does have an impact on other people. It's a woman's decision to choose how and direct how her life should go, and so I think that it should be taken away from the government and that it should be more of a medical procedure.

Olivia would eliminate weapons, especially nuclear weapons, and clean up the pollution and destruction of the environment. She would also eliminate organized religion and replace it with a free spirituality movement. Rick believes that getting back to the "grassroots American principles," upon which the United States were founded, is needed above all else.

Break it back down to the basic principles. Here they are; if you violate these basic rules, here are the penalties for them. And yeah, there might be some innocents that fell through the cracks, but still, the overall good would have been served, and it would eliminate . . . And I might even be . . . If I remove my soul from my body and I'm sitting out here in judgment of everybody else, I might even be one of the ones I'd eliminate. Those are some of my views and my opinions. I can be real irrational at times, and emotional, and strong, adamant about things. But I'm not going to go out here and rob a bank, I'm not going to go out here and kill somebody. Let's say that I look back on my decision to terminate my wife's pregnancy, and that I look back on my decision that I made to send that boy to the death penalty, and I'm sitting over here in judgment then, and I'm the ultimate one out here then and he's got all the answers, see. Right now sitting here I don't have all the answers. But if I were omnipotent and I did have all these answers, let the chips fall where they may, sweetheart. Roll the dice . . .

When looking below the surface of these opinions, however, it is apparent that these interviewees share a punitive mentality toward irresponsibility. Irresponsibility, for this group, involves having children when one cannot afford to raise them independently, committing crimes in general, and committing capital crimes in particular. Underlying this punitive mentality are sentiments toward individualism and accountability. Each individual is directly accountable for his or her own decisions and therefore should be punished for failing to take responsibility for those individual actions. Punishment serves two purposes for these interviewees: it holds people accountable as individuals and rectifies a wrong that has been committed. None of these interviewees see abortion as a "wrong" worthy of rectifying, but they do see irresponsible parenting in such terms. All of these interviewees see capital crimes as the most serious "wrongs" in society and demand rectifying those crimes through capital punishment.

CHAPTER FIVE

Pro-Life and Anti–Death Penalty

This chapter examines the anti-abortion and anti–death penalty opinions of six interviewees: Jeanie, Connor, Glenn, Louise, Marcia, and Bob. Figure 5.1 illustrates the fluctuations in this set of opinions from 1977 to 1994. The proportion of people in this category has never been more than 14.5 percent or less than 6 percent. The fluctuations have been wide, but with an overall downward trend.

Summary of Interviewees

I met with Jeanie at her home in Mississippi. Jeanie is an active member of the Church of Christ, and her children were at the vacation bible school sponsored by her church on the morning of our conversation. She is thirty-seven years old, divorced, and has two small sons, whom she is raising alone. Jeanie works full time as a special education teacher in a public school, where she teaches mostly in the "gifted and talented" program. During her troubled marriage and later her divorce, her congregation was critical of her. "To many Church of Christ people being divorced I'm going to hell. I mean, I got divorced and my husband did not commit adultery." Subsequently, Jeanie is critical of fundamentalists. She feels that they are overly concerned with rigid dogma and that they do not pay attention to the spiritual message of love in the Scriptures. However, she maintains her own religious faith. Jeanie normally votes for Republicans because of their

Figure 5.1   Pro-Life and Anti–Death Penalty, 1977–1994

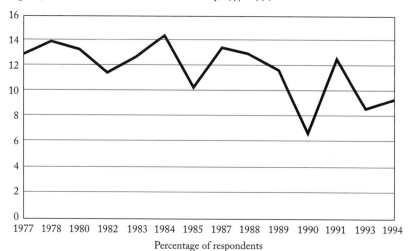

Percentage of respondents

Source: General Social Survey, 1977–1994.
Note: No surveys were conducted in 1979, 1981, 1986, and 1992.

pro-life platform, despite her own "liberal heart and soul," which leads her to support social service programs for the underprivileged and better funding for public education. She thinks that financial support should be extended to women who are pregnant in order to discourage them from having abortions.

I met with Connor at his office in Maine. He is a forty-year-old accountant who is married and has two small children. Connor has deep religious convictions and expresses a desire to be "right with God" and to live a "Christ-like life" with his family and his community. His family attends a Congregational church, the denomination in which Connor was raised. He describes a time when he "strayed" from his faith, during college and later. He was nearly paralyzed at age twenty after a "hellacious" car accident. It was a "miracle" to him that his spinal cord was not severed. He told me of a dream his mother had had just before the accident, in which a deceased aunt warned her that her son would be decapitated. That, and years later a painful breakup with a girlfriend, cemented his faith in spirituality and spurred him to begin praying, "and I haven't stopped." Connor is a Republican. For him the important political issues are "reduction of the size of government, reforming Medicaid and Medicare, reforming Social Security, reducing taxes, reducing government spending, things like that." Social issues are less important to him than fiscal issues; as an accountant, he feels that tax policies over the years have gouged personal income, thereby reducing the quality of life for the average person.

CHAPTER FIVE

I talked with Glenn at his modest home in a neighborhood in rural Maine. He is a forty-four-year-old, married father of five children ranging in age from eleven years to seven months. He is a "writer by nature" and spends a good deal of time caring for his children while his wife works away from home and he works at home. Glenn and I talked to the children while we discussed abortion and the death penalty. At a few places in our conversation, Glenn asked the children for their opinions, which reflected his own. Glenn is a devout Roman Catholic who attends church regularly with his family. But, he says, "I do not speak for any religion. I do not speak for the Catholic Church or any religion, but the spirituality is what concerns me. I think it's easy to be cornered into a perspective and say OK, you're a Catholic, so this is your view, or you're undecided." Glenn is adamant that he not be categorized as a blind follower of Catholic beliefs. He has thought religious issues through, prayed about them, and come to his own spiritual understanding. He feels that his views should be seen as complementary to the Catholic Church, not as a reiteration of the Pope's positions. Glenn normally votes for independent candidates, after carefully examining their positions on various issues. The reasoning behind those positions is more important to him than the positions themselves. Despite their pro-life platform, the Republicans have been a "big disappointment" to Glenn. He feels that they have not adequately addressed the issue of abortion, within the context of the woman's life and the circumstances which make abortion the preferred solution for the pregnant woman.

I met with Louise at a university library. She and her husband had recently moved to a remote island off the coast of Maine. Louise has two grown sons and is in her late forties. Before moving to Maine, she worked as a community services nurse in a large northeastern city and had largely low-income patients. This influenced her opinions a great deal. Louise is a "social justice" Catholic—a Catholic who works to assist the poor and underprivileged and believes that the Church has a moral obligation to alleviate economic, racial and gender oppression—but has been "lapsed" for a number of years. She says there are many reasons for her absence from the church, such as the role of women. She is "uncomfortable with the Church's view of women. I think [women are] starting to rise above the level of pea brains. And as I get older I kind of just laugh when I run into the old thoughts about it. We are thinking, intelligent human beings, yet we're not treated that way. So, anyway, because of that my husband and I gradually found, ourselves, that we just could not relate to the Church, and yet at the same time I always felt deeply about the good that the Catholic Church does in a lot of ways." However, Louise retains many of the "good things" she learned from the Catholic Church, such as their emphasis on social justice con-

cerns and providing for the poor. Since moving to Maine she has become involved with Catholic Charities, a more "liberal" wing of the Church. Louise has
always been a Democrat, "though it's getting hard to tell" these days. She sees
the two major parties as ideologically merging into each other, but refers to Newt
Gingrich and Jesse Helms as her "longtime [political] foes."

I met with Marcia at her home in a wealthy coastal Maine neighborhood.
For many years she had worked as a highly paid engineer at a large company,
while her husband stayed home raising their young son. When her son was four,
she left her job in order to spend more time as a mother. At the time of our
conversation, Marcia was working part time as a real-estate agent and her husband was building his own business as a carpenter. She and her family are "culturally Catholics" and they participate in the Catholic Church because it is the
religious community in which they are the most comfortable. She feels that it is
important to participate in the many rituals of the Church that mark milestones
in life, such as First Communion and weddings. Marcia changes her party affiliation in order to "anti-vote" as much as possible: She is certain of what she does
not want to see happen politically, so she votes against candidates or referenda,
rather than for them. For instance, "I registered as a Republican once just to anti-
vote against Linda Bean, I thought she was a screwball." (Linda Louise Bean is
the granddaughter of L. L. Bean, who founded the famous retail store. She is a
very wealthy and very conservative Republican who ran for office in Maine in
1988 but was defeated in the primary. In 1996, Bean was instrumental in the Pat
Buchanan political campaign in Maine.) Marcia tends to favor Democrats, but
does not feel a deep loyalty to either major party. "I would have to say socially
I'm more of a liberal. Like I strongly believe in equal rights for homosexuals. I
would vote for or against a candidate based on that. I think I do feel strongly
about that. That's another thing in life that just mystifies me. People who just
have these feelings about homosexuality. I just don't know why it's become such
this issue to them." She also favors better welfare benefits for those who want to
stay home to raise their children. "This taxpayer would write them a check to
stay home with their kids!"

I met Bob at a bustling cafe and bookstore in a small town in Maine. He is a
sixty-four-year-old, retired advertising executive. He has been married and divorced twice and has three children. When I spoke with him on the phone, prior
to our meeting, he described himself as a "non–angry white male." One side of
his family were practicing Lutherans while the other side were "brewers" and not
religiously active. Bob describes his religious heritage as "wonderfully simpatico";
he enjoys drinking beer with his pastor and watching football games. He currently attends a Congregationalist church, wherein there is much disagreement

about "who and what Jesus is." About his own beliefs he simply says, "I'm a work in progress." Bob has always defined himself as a conservative, but these days he says he is more likely to be labeled a "moderate"—not because he has changed but because "the goalposts have changed." He says that people like "[Pat] Buchanan and [Bob] Dornan [former Orange County, California, congressional representative] scare the hell out of me." Bob is extraordinarily logical in his opinions and very well-informed about sociopolitical issues and their histories. He says his friends describe his brain as an "attic" where all kinds of interesting things are stored; he describes his mind as a "velcro ball to which information just sticks."

Abortion Opinions

The anti-abortion opinions expressed by these interviewees is largely predicated on the belief that life begins at conception and that it is wrong to terminate that life. Many would tolerate some abortions, in extreme and rare cases, such as when abortion is medically necessary in order to save the pregnant woman's life. The three men in this group are very concerned about the role of men in the abortion decision. A few have been active in the anti-abortion movement and some have donated money to pro-life organizations. Many have made political choices based on candidates' positions on abortion.

Life begins at conception, according to all six people in this group. Glenn "always felt that what was taking place inside the womb was very sacred, and therefore had to be respected." Glenn continues:

I think it would be contrary to scientific reasoning to conclude that it's anything else other than human. To say that it's a life and not call it human life is deceptive. It can't be any other type of life but human. So therefore I would say it must begin at conception. I think the preponderance of scientific evidence is on that side of it. To assume that the soul entered the woman, or entered the child, you're getting into a spiritual level that only God can answer. In the structure of Christianity it begins at conception, because when the angel Gabriel actually appeared to Mary, he didn't give her a child. He gave her a seed. So if you want to bring it into the context of Christianity, then you have to look at Mary. Did he give her a baby or did he give her a seed? He gave her a baby, but he gave her a seed. He gave her both within the context of the seed. The child of God. When Elizabeth met with Mary, the unborn child [John the Baptist] leapt in Elizabeth's womb. The very first one to greet Jesus was an unborn child. So we only look at the world of the born child, but there's a whole world going on inside of the womb.

Bob evaluates the question in light of his belief that babies have personalities while still in the womb. Some babies are "so passive" that it's "kind of frightening" while others are "hyperkinetic" and provide "rabbit punches to the kidneys here and karate kicks to the liver there, very active, and a lot of times these characteristics are seen in the child later, in adult personality." Bob also comments that at fertilization "a whole bunch of things have been determined; gender is determined at that instant, so we're not talking about an asexual fetus, we're talking about a little boy or a little girl." Connor sees conception as a scientific phenomenon, but also as a spiritual reality. "When the sperm and the egg get together and you have the little zygote, from that moment I believe that little entity is given a soul. That's the distinguishing characteristic between us and apes or fish, and when we terminate that life we rob that soul of whatever existence it was born to have." Marcia and Jeanie base their belief on their own pregnancy experiences. Marcia says,

> I know exactly when I conceived. So based on that experience I would say that it is the time of conception. I really, I can't say anything else. There's no other explanation in my mind. Six hours after I conceived I had morning sickness and I had it for nine months. So that really hit home to me that there's something going on that's bigger than me that I have no control over. And I think that really hit it home, even though it was the morning sickness pieces, that I think it really showed me that this is something that's bigger than the woman who has become pregnant. So life begins at morning sickness!

Based on their beliefs about the beginning of life, these interviewees believe that it is wrong to terminate a pregnancy. "It is infanticide," Bob argues, "and I just think that it's wrong to do that to that person." For Glenn, "Abortion is killing." Connor concludes, "I have a deep religious conviction and feel personally close to a Creator and would find it difficult to think that a Creator would want me to sanction the destruction of life that was created by the miracle of the joining of a man and a woman." Connor also believes that terminating a pregnancy is wrong because "we clearly rob that particular soul of the existence that had been planned for it." Connor says that those who are "fully developed persons" will not choose to abort because they are people "who lead a Christ-like life with generosity, tenderness, loving your neighbor, inclusiveness."

Louise feels that abortion is "a dead end" for the baby and for the woman. "If you're going to become sexually active you should be sexually responsible" by using effective contraceptive measures. Louise recalls the cases of young women who were her patients.

Going into homes where the woman would say that she's had four abortions, so "I'll just get rid of this one." And she has a couple kids running around, plus she obviously doesn't have much in the way of parenting skills. She's used to being on cocaine. I'm thinking of one particular case who's using it for a birth control method. But I don't know, there's an awful lot of work that needs to be done to change that person.

Marcia thinks that babies "are the victims in all this, this is not victimless; the unborn are the victims in this." She likes to think that she's "speaking for that one [little] unborn, not speaking for all under all circumstances, but maybe giving my part for that one." She hopes that one hundred years from now society will look back "and be appalled that abortion was legal and that there weren't other options for women and their partners."

When *Roe v. Wade* was decided, Glenn was twenty-one years old. He recalls, "I felt like a part of society had died. I feel like the future of the society is in the children and when they passed laws providing for abortion, I believe they [had] killed a portion of our future."

Any time you deliberately destroy someone else, or the rights of someone else, you're engaging in violence on a spiritual level or on a psychological level. To destroy the life of an unborn child through those means is to interrupt what was in the sanctity of that womb, and to disrupt it violently, to destroy, to kill it. There is a killing that is taking place. And you can't, I don't think anyone would deny that. And that's the heart of the matter. Mother Teresa says this, and I believe this to be true, in any act of an abortion there are two deaths to take place. You have the unborn child and you have the conscience of the mother. And any time you allow that violence to take place you are then giving breath to violence, so that it can actually, in reality violence becomes a spirit which can eventually seep outside of the woman, if you will. By allowing abortion to be an acceptable practice, you are allowing violence to take place within the heart of that woman. That's where it becomes degrading in one sense. Because now you're using violence as an acceptable form of behavior. And therefore society becomes far more violent. There's nothing more violent than the act of abortion. If you hold the view that we hold in the context of the Christianity, where every life is sacred, then the abortion itself is an abortion of God. You're seeing, as Mother Teresa would say, Christ aborted. Those who abort, abort Christ. So you have a gift that's being radically thrown back in God's face, in one sense.

A theme that emerges in some of these conversations is a comparison of abortion to either the Holocaust or the enslavement of blacks in America. As a Mississippian, Jeanie is embarrassed by the legacy of slavery in the South and the news that her home state only recently (April 1995) ratified the Thirteenth Amendment outlawing slavery. Jeanie says she is also embarrassed by a country that allows for the killing of innocent babies. In reference to the number of abortions performed each year in the United States and around the world, Connor says, "It is just . . . I can't think about it, because it is just like the Holocaust times a thousand. It is just so insane. So you can't think about that." Connor also sees abortion as analogous to slavery.

> I think that in a hundred years we're going to look back and we're going to be astonished that we could have actually had abortion as a legal thing in our society. We're going to look back and go, "My God, in the twentieth century they were barbarians." Because we will have evolved. Our thinking will have evolved, and it will be the way we think of slavery today, people will think of abortion in a hundred years.

Glenn offers the most detailed comparison of abortion with slavery and the Holocaust.

> I see [abortion] as a sinful structure. It's similar to slavery and it's similar to an action going on. Without being extremist in views, I think that when the German people realized that there was something evil taking place in the concentration camps, mainly the taking of innocent life, and they turned the other way, they turned their back on it, or they didn't know how to [stop] it, what eventually happened was, there became a justification in their psyche to permit it to happen to other people but not to them. What I see going on in society today is there's something evil taking place in an abortion clinic. Everyone is aware of the evil that's taking place. And the problems that are being created are that nobody seems to want to deal with that evil. They just want to kind of pass over it, or ignore it. They don't want to deal with the reality that something has been lost. Namely an unborn child, the life of that child was lost from the society. The spirit of the society is dying. I think what happened in Hitler's time, when you look at the concentration camps, what you begin to realize is yeah, these people who were blamed, namely the Jewish people, were the scapegoat. Now, the unborn children are the scapegoat. You have almost the same reasoning processes that permitted, from a philosophical perspective, the existence of the concentration camps, as you do for the conditions to abort. Because when you get right down to the nitty gritty, you talk about abortion inside the clinic in front of a doctor, you're talking about the death of a child. In a similar way, when you talk about the concentration camps, and you talk about that individual in that camp, you're talking about the

death of that individual. So when you put it into the very real context of what's going on, there are many similarities, striking similarities in the philosophical perspectives in terms of how you come to that conclusion that it's OK to do it. What I think happens is it becomes somewhat sinister in nature, because you have a tendency to anesthetize the terminology, if you will, and therefore you permit it. Again, without getting to the radical extreme end of it, because if you push any philosophy to its extreme it almost becomes incomprehensible, but I would say without going to too much of an extreme on that side, I think that the seeds of the reasoning process which permitted slavery, the seeds of the reasoning processes which permit any person to make a choice for another and to dominate that other person in so far as to taking that person's life. They're all similar in their philosophical structure.

Glenn goes on to discuss Adolf Hitler's policy of ensuring racial superiority as "pro-life" in the sense that it "preserves the future of the race." This is an extreme view notwithstanding Glenn's previous comments about the sinful structure of the Holocaust thinking.

> Even Hitler had respect for unborn children. So much so that he let his German girls, who were bearing their children, the "future of the race" and he would call the future superior race or the supreme race, have all kinds of benefits. He promoted that. It's hard to call Hitler "pro-life" but in essence he was very much pro-life when it came to bearing future children. He had at least the insight to know that the future of your country is based on the children. We seem to have lost sight of that, I think.

All of these interviewees would allow for abortion under certain exceptional and rare circumstances. Jeanie says, "About the only instance where I would recommend somebody to have an abortion would be if it were endangering the life of the mother, that's kind of to save life there, too." Neither rape, incest, nor severe fetal defect are justifiable reasons for an abortion in Jeanie's opinion, because "that's just playing God, to me." Connor elaborates on his view of abortion in cases of fetal defect or rape.

> I think a Down's syndrome baby has just too much life that can be, that the person can live, and I just couldn't justify that. If the fetus had no arms, then I could not support aborting the fetus. Just arms. I mean arms are great, but you don't kill people because they don't have arms. The one thing that I have trouble with is rape. My gut reaction to that is that I would not abort. But I think that it would, again, I always try to make it personal, my wife. And if she's been raped, which has been horrible, and it's taken a tremendous toll on her and it will for the longest time, what would the impact be on her of bringing this child to term? I'd have to

consider that. I would definitely not want the law to be such that I could not be part of that decision in the situation of rape. So I would definitely want the law to be that there is an exception in some way for rape.

Louise is also ambivalent about abortion in the case of rape. She "would find it really tough if somebody said they wanted to have an abortion, I would not have as much of a problem referring somebody to counseling for that."

In cases of rape and incest, Bob would "fully support the idea that a woman should not be forced to carry a child to term; that would be inhumane." But in cases of severe fetal defect, he would recommend letting "nature take its course" because there are "probably things that could be learned from studying such a child." In the case of fetal defect, such as anencephalia, Marcia "would have given birth and I think I would have had no medical intervention and just had the child die, and I know how difficult that would be, but I think that's what I would have done, and donated the organs for other children to live." Marcia is, however, very much in favor of the "morning after pill" for a woman who has been raped because "that way, you don't really know if you have conceived or not."

Glenn feels that when there is a severe fetal defect or a health threat to the pregnant woman, "every effort should be made to save the life of them both." If that can't be done, Glenn thinks "the medical community owes it to them to at least explain the options, including organ donation and including other available means to make the best out of that situation should it arise."

These interviewees offer alternatives to abortion, such as adoption, abstinence, getting married, single parenting, and contraception. Bob is "very pro-birth control; don't start [a baby], but after it gets started this is going to be a person." Bob explains that he grew up in a generation that "delayed gratification."

> I grew up in a world where you didn't get married till you finished college and were able to support somebody. This was, that's being a man, not seeing how many women you could hurt. So most of us, most guys that I knew, had no sexual experience whatever until they were married. And that might have been in their mid-twenties, mid-thirties. We were just as libidinous as the guys today, but we basically had a little more control of our lives in general, not just in that thing.

Jeanie, Marcia, Louise, and Connor agree with Bob's perspective on contraception. But Glenn believes a "contraceptive mentality" creates more abortions in the United States every year.

> I'm fundamentally opposed to contraception, but I think again, without being painted into an extreme position, one has to weigh the considerations of the situ-

ation very carefully. I think that the issue of contraception is even more complicated sometimes than abortion because it carries with it the mind-set that it's OK to do something provided you're protecting yourself. I think the deception that is taking place in you is that there are many diseases, for example, that are being transmitted through a condom, and the condom is being used as a sort of a cure-all for certain [problems] and it's not. There are many cases when contraception fails. What it's doing is, it's setting up a false sense of security for many people. That concerns me. There are many women who get pregnant while they're on the pill, or while they're using condoms, and those are the very women that oftentimes use abortion as a backup to a contraceptive method. So in general, probably the main reason why abortion is so popular is because it's a backup to a contraceptive method. The failure of contraception is far greater than people realize. That leads to more abortions. I think in the long run, and here again I think studies have shown that when you bring in the idea of contraception you promote abortion.

Adoption is the preferred solution for these interviewees. Connor feels that "[adoption] is actually a wonderful thing, which is very appealing to me," mostly because it is "not destroying a life" and would leave him in "harmony with my maker." In Bob's opinion, people are "not complete" unless they have raised children, so adoption is a good alternative to abortion. About his own parenting experience he says, "I wouldn't have been the same guy I am without my kids, I don't think people are complete. I never date gals who've never had children; they're not complete." Glenn sees adoption as a loving alternative to abortion, but in order to really promote adoption, society must "stop looking at its individual parts." He thinks there's "no unity of the community" and believes that pregnant women who don't want to raise their children should be in touch with families who want to adopt, regardless of race or ethnic grouping.

Marcia says:

I'd like it to go back to the good old days when [the home for unwed mothers] handed out umpty-ump babies a week to families who really wanted them. I wish that there was a better system, whether it's through the churches or through municipalities or states or whatever it would take to have an in-place system so that somebody having to make that decision or somebody with an untimely pregnancy had a specific checklist of what you go through to carry a baby to term and you're going to have this, this, and this for prenatal care and this is where you'll deliver and this is the counseling you'll receive around it and this is the, whether there's a money factor involved, and your baby will be placed in the state of New Hampshire, so that the woman knows these are the things that are going to happen in the next nine months and then whatever support you need afterwards. I don't think that's in place today. Where can families go if they're thinking about the adoption alternative?

The men in this group offer their opinions about men's involvement in the abortion decision. Bob says that "today if a woman wants an abortion" she gets an abortion and the father has no say; that's wrong. It should be consensual on both parts if they can find the guy." Glenn views the man as "equally liable for the situation. I think if he can stop a woman from having an abortion, he should have some right, in one sense, because it is his child. But under the guidelines of the legal system that we have today, there is absolutely nothing a man can do, unfortunately, to prevent a woman from having an abortion." Connor would like to see, if the existing law remains intact, a law that would allow a man "veto power" over the abortion decision.

> The effect of that law would be to encourage life. Again [take] me and my wife. I don't want the abortion, my wife wants the abortion. For example. And I veto the abortion. Well I veto the abortion, so no abortion happens, and now I must live with the consequences. Which would be an unhappy wife. So I would have to be willing either to do everything in my power to convince my wife that this is the right thing to do, or I would have to be willing to lose my wife. If I'm going to have veto power now, I could totally, I could veto the abortion, my wife definitely wanted the abortion, she just got back into the work force, she doesn't want to, she's done the kids, we've got kids. "Please. I mean, what? Am I like a baby factory?" And I would be adamant about it, you know, "I've got to face my maker, I've got to be able to do these kinds of things, and I'll take the responsibility." "Oh, you will. You'll take the responsibility. So what are you saying? You're going to quit your job?" So I think that although this veto power would exist, it may not happen very often, because it, in a practical sense, you do have to continue to live with your spouse. Right? If it did not result in compromise, then it would result in some type of unpleasantness in the marriage, whether it would ultimately end in divorce or whatever, who knows? But I, that's not to say that getting a divorce over the abortion issue is a bad thing. If one feels strongly about life and your mate doesn't share your feelings about it, that's a pretty deep difference.

Abortion Politics and Activism

Jeanie is the only interviewee in this group who says she would base her voting decisions on abortion "over just about anything." Connor says that abortion is "a factor, but I'm not a single-issue voter, I'm a compromising guy." Louise is more concerned about people with children losing welfare benefits than about voting for pro-life candidates, although she says it is "something I think about." She explains, "If somebody is pro-abortion I would not, not vote for them because of that, but I would be inclined to write to them and ask questions, in terms of [where they stand on] human services and everything else." Marcia does not base her voting decisions on abortion at all.

Glenn is concerned about the logic behind candidates' stances on abortion, not about the way candidates describe themselves.

> I see pro-life candidates who bother me, more so sometimes than pro-choice candidates. I think if you look at the view, and stop calling them pro-choice and pro-life, and get down to what they're saying, you may support candidates who don't necessarily agree with your perspective. Like, I notice now that [1996 presidential hopeful] Steve Forbes, for example, is being considered pro-choice, but if you listen to his view he's not really pro-choice. He's against abortion and he wants to see it eventually outlawed, but he wants to work within the context of the law, changing public opinion, and working to reduce the number of abortions. That sounds pretty much like what I want to do. I'm very concerned, though, about pro-life candidates who don't do anything when they could have done something. I see that as a missed opportunity, but I also see that as a way of controlling the pro-choice or pro-life agenda. What bothers me about pro-life candidates is, they might be able to dance. They might court the supporters of pro-life. But how sincere are they in doing anything once they get elected?

Political activism is a theme that emerges in the conversations with these interviewees, though only two are politically active. Bob explains, "I'm a part of a silent majority or the quiet generation, or whatever you want to [call it]. We didn't do that sort of thing. It's offensive to me. You won't find bumper stickers on my car, either." Connor, Marcia, and Jeanie are also in the non-activist category. Louise has been concerned about the image of pro-life activism and decided to get involved in order to do something positive.

> I just recently had an interview at Birthline, which is a Catholic charity. They do pregnancy counseling. I had been thinking of getting in, well, I had been thinking for the last couple of years, after I had decided that personally I was opposed to abortion, I felt that and saw the negligence and the violence. It's not something I could do. I don't agree with it. But I wanted to try to do something positive. So it took me a couple of years to decide to take a step. So I'm going to get involved with that.

Glenn has been involved with an organization that "provides counseling for women who've had abortions" and provides material support for pregnant women in need. Glenn believes one has to go "beyond the very simple position of pro-choice or pro-life to what's going on inside the psyche of the woman. So, rather than becoming judgmental about the issue, there is a fragmentation in the psyche of the woman that has to be healed, so you deal with that through love."

The interviewees unanimously oppose violent activism, but also feel that pro-life activists are misrepresented in the media. Connor expresses his admiration of activists who risk their well-being for the pro-life cause.

> I think that anybody, no matter what the cause, who feels strongly enough about an issue, to risk persecution, is a person that should be respected. It's so easy to slide into the background. But to risk being persecuted, especially in an anti-abortion clinic protest, because those people are persecuted ruthlessly by the media. They are the scum of the earth. And for them to feel as strongly as they do and to be able to stand up to society and say, "Hey, look, I don't care if you put me in jail. I don't care if I am ostracized at my workplace. I don't care if I am not going to get the promotion at work. I care about that soul that's in that fetus. That's what I care about." And a person that has that degree of commitment, it's a wonderful thing. I don't have it.

Glenn, on the other hand, sharply criticizes the pro-life movement.

> I see a lot of people on the pro-life side of it that are not taking care of the child and are not looking at the woman in the context of the child. In other words, pro-life. How so? Did you support the unborn child? Are you going to step up to the plate for this woman and help her? Are you going to provide medical attention? Are you going to provide counsel? Are you going to provide a means for her to live with? That's really what I mean.

The interviewees are, in Jeanie's words, "embarrassed" by violent pro-life activists such as Paul Hill and John Salvi and hopeful that the public would have a more well-rounded image of the activists, who are mostly nonviolent. Jeanie states, "It is wrong, to me it's the same thing. I believe in preservation of life; what he did was just as wrong as anybody else, anyone performing [abortions]." Connor believes that "they both [Hill and Salvi] did wrong and they both need to be punished. They have to live out the rest of their days in confinement because they've demonstrated that they are not capable of living by the rules of society." Regarding the "justifiable homicide" defense that Paul Hill was not allowed to use in court, Glenn says:

I've listened to his reasoning on television, and I'll tell you. I see a contradiction when he shot the gun. Because my question to him would be, "Should not the Christian be on the dying end of the gun and not the killing end?" I think he was wrong to kill. He reduces himself to an executioner. We are not to judge in this world. Nowhere in Scripture is it saying that we should bring down judgment upon somebody. The argument that they use, by killing an abortionist and saying that they save lives of future unborn children, I'd see that as a flawed argument, because I don't think that's necessarily true. Here you're dealing with a whole culture of death, which the Pope says, which he's right on. Paul Hill is just perpetuating the culture of death by killing, it's contradictory all the way.

Bob says he was glad he didn't "have to sit on [Hill's] jury. Although I just honestly feel that we should close the abortion clinics, but what you do to do that is you challenge it in court, you work to change laws." To Marcia the murders of clinic workers "just seemed illogical." She feels that Salvi and Hill would have been obsessed with a different issue, if not abortion.

If it wasn't this issue it would have been some other issue that [Hill] would have gone off half-cocked on. I don't think it really had anything to do with abortion in particular. He would have found something else. That he didn't like homosexuals, or he didn't like blacks, or he didn't like . . . There would have been some social bandwagon he would have jumped on that would, in a way encourage him or get him all fired up about something.

Glenn and Marcia are critical of abortion rights advocates. Marcia says that "a lot of people in that following are not really pro-choice; I think they're really pro-abortion. I think they don't really feel the way that I feel about when life begins, or that there are any moral consequences. They encourage abortion when it isn't necessarily the right thing to do." For Marcia those consequences include psychological trauma and second thoughts about the abortion after the fact. She feels that pro-choice advocates abandon women who have abortions by failing to provide counseling to help women deal with the moral consequences of abortion.

Glenn takes issue with the conceptualization of the abortion issue as one of "choice."

I always felt that the issue of choice itself was a slick marketing scam. That there is no choice once conception takes place. Because if you truly believe in the word "choice" as the society uses it, then you have to ask the question "Did you choose to be born?" and if you answer "No" to that question, then why should you choose for an unborn child? And if you answer "Yes" to that question, that you did choose to be born, then why deny the unborn their choice? So I always felt the position of choice was hypocritical in its very language.

Glenn offers a more extreme view: "If you want to deal with the individuals that are making a living by working in abortion clinics, I see them as no different than maybe soldiers that Hitler had . . . walking into the concentration camps and guarding so that no one escapes."

Death Penalty Opinions

All members of this group are generally opposed to the death penalty. For some, like Connor, this opposition is based on convictions about being "pro-life." For others, like Louise and Marcia, concern about the fairness of the legal system leads them to question the application of capital punishment. All of these interviewees think that it is very important that murderers be punished but would prefer to see a system of life sentencing without the possibility of parole replace the death penalty.

"I don't like killing anybody," Connor says, a view that is echoed by the others in this group. Louise identifies her opposition to the death penalty as stemming from her experience as a child of the 1960s. "Maybe it's because the time that I became a conscious being, like in high school, was in the '60s, and at that time in our religion classes in school and stuff, the value of life" was often discussed. She goes on to say that the principle of an "eye for an eye" troubles her greatly, but she understands "the feeling that people have wanting revenge to settle things, but it's just not a solution for me." Louise also expresses concern for the people who administer executions and considers the impact that "being killers" has on them. She became aware of this issue after listening to an interview with Sister Helen Prejean (author of the book *Dead Man Walking*, about a man on death row, which was adapted into a movie of the same name). Louise explains, "She talked about, in the interview, the guards at the prison and anybody involved with the execution and how difficult it is for many of them. And I think that's something that really has to be looked at. Because it's easy to say that the solution to a violent crime and the closure for it is an execution. But is it really closure?" Ultimately, says Louise, society "does not have the right to take another person's life, just as the criminal did not have the right to kill; I don't think we right any wrong by executing them. It does not bring the victim back, either." Furthermore, Louise thinks that a medical professional who participates in an execution violates the oaths and ethics that doctors and nurses are supposed to follow.

Glenn thinks that when the state executes someone "it takes the place of the executioner." Society "loses someone of value" when executions are carried out. "I think when you draw the conclusion that people don't have value, you're missing something. We have a society that is fragmenting. And the way it's fragmenting is it's wrong to kill somebody, and there probably was a crime that they had committed, worthy of the death penalty. Without getting into the issues of that, what you're doing when you step in and kill them is you're taking them out of the society. For what purpose? There is no good to be gained from it, ultimately you lose." For Glenn, being "tough on crime" requires forgiveness and compassion: "The toughest solution is the one toward forgiveness, the easy solution is the one toward execution."

> To be tough on crime is to ultimately come to the level of forgiveness and reintegrate that person into society. You can get into arguments of what caused that person to do it in the first place. I think when you get to that position, and you start working with that person, perhaps in rehabilitative needs, you can actually turn the society around by turning its killers around. To the society, then maybe they could be the means by which peace comes to the society. I think that "Thou shalt not kill" is a commandment, it's not a suggestion.

Marcia recalls when she first started thinking about the death penalty—at a fraternity party celebrating the execution of convicted murderer Gary Gilmore in 1977. "The decorations were coffins and black punch and people cheering on the execution, and I think it was the first time I really thought about it. I think because it was like wow, these are reasonable, although nutty young people, who think that this is a game. I think it requires more thought than that." This experience made her "stop and think" about capital punishment because it "seemed so over the edge." On the other hand, Marcia says that if someone murdered her child she would want to execute them herself "or make sure they were killed." She is glad to live in Maine, which does not have the death penalty, because "I don't want to be the one that would make a decision like that. And I think it's a punishment just not on the criminal; it's a punishment I think in their family all the time. Imagine how a mother feels to have her child die by firing squad, I think it ripples. How does their defense lawyer feel? How do their children feel? Their wives? It's in a big way, not just punishing the criminal but punishing everybody."

Bob says he has always opposed the death penalty because it is "irreversible." He launches into a lengthy explanation of his opinion.

> I see there are three kinds of people. People who want to get caught, people who don't care if they get caught, and people who are convinced they won't be caught.

I don't believe we can deter any of these. The guy who wants to get caught is a psycho. He says catch me before I kill again, and either does it in a way that assures he will get gunned down in the commission of the crime or leaves a whole bunch of clues around. The guy who is looking for vengeance or is jealous of his wife or girlfriend or something like that, he doesn't care. He's going to inflict his anger and he doesn't really care. You're not going to stop him, although you might, there is another approach that might help with him. And the third character who thinks that, about four or five percent whatever, of the people who actually commit a murder get caught, and I'm a lot smarter than those, pardon me, damn dumb cops. I can make it look like an accident. I can do this. So, deterrence doesn't work, and my understanding is that there are more murders in those states which have capital punishment than in those that don't. Now, regarding incapacitation, well, there is an alternative in that case which is incarceration. Separate that person from society or in some way or other render that person incapable of doing this again. Another thing is moral outrage, revenge. Here, now you're bringing in the whole religious concept from somewhere in the "good book" it says, vengeance is mine, sayeth the Lord, and if you usurp that particular divine prerogative, then you're in danger of playing God, and I don't think that's appropriate . . . I don't think revenge is an honorable reason for doing something like that and it therefore has no place in the schema of punishment. That is where I believe that the damage that is done to society is almost as great as that which is done to the guy that gets fricasseed. You make toast out of a guy, what have you done? I was pulling the trigger. You were pulling the trigger. We, America pulled the trigger. America flips the switch on the electric chair. America presses the plunger on the injection device. We all share in it. Including the people who protest these executions, because obviously they weren't successful, so give them an F for failure. But we, I think we become less. We look down at certain societies, the Islamic societies in which you steal they cut your hand off. You commit adultery, they sexually mutilate you. Whatever is the offending member, and we look at this and say, what a bunch of, what a primitive people, and claim we're better than they. At least. So I just feel that morally it debases the society that does the execution. Now a very practical thing, coming all the way down from religious objections down to practical matters, it's too darn expensive to execute somebody. Costs millions of dollars to pop a capsule on a guy.

These interviewees are concerned about the potential for executing innocent people. Jeanie says the fact that some innocent people have been executed "makes me embarrassed to be an American." Marcia is also very concerned about this problem. Bob feels that there is no means of "compensating [innocent people wrongly convicted], you can't really buy back years, you can throw enough money at the guy to be reasonably comfortable for the time he's got left and say 'mea culpa' but mistakes will happen. It is a fact that mistakes will happen." The risk of executing innocent people has not influenced Glenn's death penalty opinion "one iota," though it is a major concern to him. His opposition to the death penalty does not hinge on the possibility of mistakes, but on his belief that it is wrong to kill others.

The interviewees express support for life sentences without the possibility of parole instead of capital punishment. Jeanie comments, "I think being locked up for the rest of your life is harsh"—even more harsh than the death penalty. Louise would like to see those who are currently under a sentence of death in the United States resentenced to life without parole. Bob would like to see them "put so far back in the slammer you gotta pump daylight to them." This is the best alternative to the death penalty, in his opinion. Marcia says:

> I think life without parole would have to be as bad as death. Yeah. I just can't imagine being thrown in prison, knowing that you are never going to leave. To me I just can't imagine. I don't know why you'd want to live, probably. What's the point? So, if there were a way to have a true life without parole, that would be my preference.

Death Penalty Politics

None of these interviewees consider their opposition to the death penalty a sufficiently important political issue to influence their vote. Louise is the only person in this group who sees the death penalty as a more important issue than abortion. "If a candidate is in favor of the death penalty I would not immediately rule it out for that reason, but I think I would give it more weight than if they were in favor of abortion. If somebody's opposed to the death penalty their other philosophies would probably line up more closely with what I believe. I call it the value of life. But, I don't think a political candidate would use that term. I don't even know if they'd see it that way, but if they did, I think it would be political suicide."

Jeanie, on the other hand, says she "feels stronger" about abortion. "I feel very strongly against both of them, but if I were to prioritize which one I thought was an issue which needed more support or whatever, it would be the abortion issue." When asked how she would reconcile her pro-life consistency with a political candidate who is not, she declares that question "a tough one, I'm going to have to answer to that someday." Connor shares Jeanie's view of the importance of the abortion issue. The death penalty position "has less impact" on his voting choices. To Marcia a candidate's stand on the death penalty issue does not influence her voting. In Bob's opinion, politicians have little to do with capital punishment anyway, so it is a peripheral issue. All things being equal, Bob would favor an anti–death penalty candidate over a pro–death penalty candidate in a gubernatorial race because of the role governors have in death sentences.

Connecting Opinions on Abortion and the Death Penalty

The common theme that connects anti-abortion and anti–death penalty opinions is the belief in the preservation of human life from the moment of conception until natural death. To Connor, the phrase "you play God" sums up the connection because "whatever that purpose is for that one-legged fetus, or whatever it is, we presume we know, and we presume we know what's best. And that just may not be the case at all." In order to live a "Christ-like life," Connor says, people must "turn the other cheek" and must view all human life as equal in the eyes of God. Connor says that "we are all equally loved by God," whether embryo or convicted murderer. Louise believes in a "value of life" ethic and feels that people should take care of each other.

> And I just don't think we've done the job. I know we haven't. So I think that when kids are raised in an environment where for whatever reason their parents or whoever the caretaker is, treats them in a brutal way, and the brutality can be physical but it can also be emotional and psychological, and they don't value themselves. If they don't love themselves, how can they like somebody else? And if they see in the neighborhood around them or in their family that how you treat someone is in a very violent way, and if they can see that there's some gain to that, I think that's where a lot of criminals come from. And so I, that's what I mean by it's all connected. But I wonder sometimes if we as a whole society really value life, because when you look back over history of the abuse and we're funding, for any of the social services it's always a huge fight.

Glenn connects the issues of abortion and capital punishment in terms of his own ability to face God. "I would like to face God thinking that I'd at least tried to help someone else, as opposed to trying to hurt them. Society has to come out on the side of helping and not hurting. I just don't see the logic of killing. It just is illogical, to my way of thinking. The fundamental question I would ask as in the whole position is, how is society better off as a result of that action?" The biggest problem facing society, according to Glenn, is that we are not "respecting life" at all stages and ages. "It is a sanctity of life issue. If we could just summarize it all the way Jesus did, I suppose, 'Whatever you do to the least of my brothers, that you do unto me.' If we could just take that as a model and go with it, I think what you would find is a wonderful, wonderful opportunity to create a world that's worth living in." In Glenn's opinion, the capitalist consumer economy is driven "by the profit-motive" rather than by an ethic of life. "When you see a company like AT & T lay off forty-five thousand workers, and they made a profit last year, you have to ask if they're looking at their employees as unimportant." Furthermore, Glenn thinks that "something inside us is dying" when society allows for legal abortion and executions. "It kills the spirit of community in society, it robs society of the future, and takes somebody of value out of society."

Bob believes that both abortion and the death penalty involve the irrevocable extermination of life. Bob says that they both have "a negative effect on the person doing it, [and] society. I think we become less by so doing. I just feel that this is morally it debases the society that does the [killing]."

Solutions

The interviewees' solutions to the problems they have with abortion and the death penalty hinge on social change, including better welfare assistance to the poor, rather than legal change, so often advocated by people on either side of these issues. Most of the interviewees in this group consider abortion the more important problem and have less to say about capital punishment. Jeanie offers her opinions on what changes are needed.

> The answer to a lot of these things, the bottom thing is money. The bottom line to the whole criminal system and all that comes, just to me it all boils down to there's not enough money. I could get off on all kinds of little views here, just like with special education, which is what I deal with, we are required by law to provide an appropriate education. That's "an" appropriate but not necessarily "the most" appropriate. And there's a difference, and I know that. I've got parents that are coming and wanting all these kinds of services for their child and my hands are tied because we don't have the services. So, the first thing I'd do is somehow just come up with billions and trillions, large amounts of money to just go and overhaul these things, and also to provide many other options than abortion. Socially acceptable [options], I mean I would want to change people toward, because I'm thinking about if I were to show up pregnant right now [as a divorced mother of two] I would be totally embarrassed. It would be horrible, the social stigma, and everybody knows, everybody that's ever had a child, that poor child.

Connor advocates gradual legal change, which he predicts would lead to social change. First, he would give men "veto power" over the abortion decision, based on his belief that if men were able to veto the procedure, fewer abortions would occur. Such a veto would require some type of communication between the man and woman about their future together and the future of their child. "If the gradual change resulted in fewer abortions, where the goal is to get rid of abortion, then there's no need to change the law further." But, if the law giving men "veto power" resulted in more abortions, Connor would "strip the man of his veto power and go back to what it was before" and focus on other types of legal change to minimize abortion.

Part of the structural change that Bob advocates for both the death penalty and abortion is the establishment of more uniform laws that would eliminate state-level disparities. "I do believe that it is up to the legal profession to come up with national guidelines." Specifically referring to the death penalty, Bob says, "Behavior modification is part of what punishment's got to be about. You don't do that by executing. A friend of mine used to say, 'You've gotta execute them, how else are they gonna learn?'"

Jeanie, Marcia, and Louise favor expanding welfare assistance to include more underprivileged people and provide more benefits for children. Jeanie feels that welfare benefits should include job training. She feels people should have a "responsibility to show up for work" if they are going to receive aid. "Getting rid of life is not an option, we need to provide better services, and I would want to change public opinion."

In Louise's opinion, the "profit motive undermines the value of life." She sees the economy as overly concerned with profits and not nearly concerned enough with enhancing the quality of life.

> Throw some more money at human services. I think we ought to set up a system that takes a look at what's going on and give some credence to the studies that are already done out there by social service people. [Find out] what works, what doesn't work, and pick a couple of areas in human services and really make a commitment to it. Also, health care; I think it's a crime that this country doesn't have universal health care. We see more and more people at this clinic and it will just continue to be so because of layoffs. People will come, people are working and have no health benefits. That is first, and in that I'd look at preventative stuff as far as I'm concerned, otherwise you're wasting your time. Education is the second thing. I think we're in danger of becoming a nation of illiterates. I think I read somewhere that close to a third of adults cannot read. If a third of our adults are functionally illiterate, what does that portend for [the future]? And now that we're moving into, we're there, the technological computer age, that gap is going to widen tremendously.

Marcia discusses shared community responsibility. "I think it's different from just personal responsibility; I think it's involvement, really thinking it through. I mean I think I decided a long time ago, that I'm one of those people who will pick up the phone and call the police, even if I sound like an idiot. Or even if it inconveniences me." Furthermore, Marcia would prefer that mothers of young children stay home and care for the children personally rather than be forced into a workfare program, where welfare recipients are required to do public works in exchange for financial assistance, and have to place the children in day care.

> I'd be the first taxpayer to say I'd rather write them a check to stay home with their kid than write them a check to go to work and put the child in day care. I would rather do that, whether it's to the age of five or whether it's to some other, three, whatever the age is, but I definitely think for those first three to five years I would definitely be the first taxpayer to write the check to say please stay at home. If it means that in order for that check to continue you have to go to parenting classes, you have to go to cooking nutrition class, you've got to go to something. Something so that the job you're doing at home with your child you're doing well.

Glenn states, "My fundamental position is that I would prefer to see [abortion] be unwanted. I don't think it should be legally sanctioned, but what concerns me is the fact that 1.5 million women choose it. Why? Why do 1.5 million women abort? That's the more scary thing than the law. See, I think if you change the heart of the woman then the law will follow. But to change the law without changing the heart is to create more lawbreakers." The "law is irrelevant" to Glenn's perspective. He feels that what is necessary is to change the cultural emphasis that promotes death, in the form of abortion and capital punishment. "We need to change the heart of society, totally, to where forgiveness is preferred and promoted," Glenn says of capital punishment.

Clearly these interviewees are not punitive about other people's lifestyle choices, but would prefer to see society become a more humane place in which to raise children. For this group of interviewees, that means having adequate material support and spiritual guidance so that life is always the preferred option. Choosing death, including abortion and capital punishment, involves thwarting God's call to be loving, forgiving and compassionate. Encapsulated in these views is a communitarian ethic whereby these interviewees are willing to share their own time and resources in helping those who have little. In addition, they believe that as a society all citizens share a communitarian responsibility toward others; welfare benefits are an example of such responsibility. When people violate norms and laws, the first option should not be toward punishment but rather toward forgiveness and rehabilitation of the hearts and souls of violators.

CHAPTER SIX

Pro-Life and Pro–Death Penalty

This chapter examines the perspectives of those who oppose abortion and favor the death penalty. There are ten people in this group of interviewees: Carolyn, Dave, Enoch, Harold, Harry, Johann, Leo, Rebel, Suzanne, and Warren. Figure 6.1 illustrates the changes over time in pro-life and pro–death penalty public opinion. At no point in time is the proportion of the general public who fit into this category greater than 40 percent. The graph indicates a slight increase over the seventeen-year period being analyzed. In general, approximately 35 percent of English-speaking adults in the United States are pro-life and pro–death penalty.

Summary of Interviewees

Carolyn is a woman in her late forties. I talked with her in Mississippi, where she works as the director of a Crisis Pregnancy Center. Carolyn is careful to point out that her opinions do not necessarily reflect those of the center that she directs. She is married with three children. She has directed the center for ten years and is "absolutely certain" that her anti-abortion opinion is God's will. Since marrying her husband, she has been a devout Southern Baptist, but she has friends who belong to different Christian denominations. Prior to her marriage she was a Presbyterian. She believes the country's laws should reflect bibli-

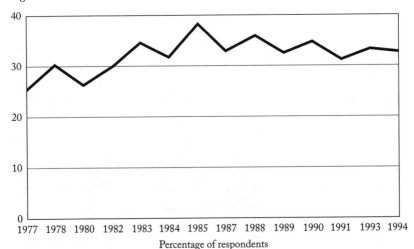

Figure 6.1 Pro-Life and Pro–Death Penalty, 1977–1994

Percentage of respondents

Source: General Social Survey, 1977–1994.
Note: No surveys were conducted in 1979, 1981, 1986, and 1992.

cal principles and morals. Carolyn considers abortion the most important political issue, but she is not a "single-issue" voter. However, she does not elaborate
on other political issues that are important to her.

Dave is a twenty-four-year-old, newly married man with no children. We
met at a university student union in Mississippi. Dave was working as a contract
electrician on campus at the time of the interviews. He was raised Catholic and
retains much of the faith. He attended Catholic schools and their teaching in-
forms his opinions. However, he does not attend religious services because of his
perception of inappropriate motives for church involvement. He believes many
people attend church to improve their standing in the community and/or business world, rather than for worship. Politically, Dave is very cynical. He does not
vote and has not registered to vote. He is skeptical of politicians' motives for
running for office and believes they say anything to get elected rather than standing firm in their own convictions.

Enoch is a twenty-three-year-old, newly married man with no children. We
met at a public lounge at a university in Mississippi. Though he is not a native
of the South, Enoch attended college there, and at the time of our meeting was
visiting his wife's family. He resides in Chicago. He is unemployed and making
plans to attend seminary. He chose Enoch as his pseudonym because it is the
name of a character in the Old Testament who walked with God for three hundred years. Throughout our conversation, Enoch refers to scriptural passages to
support his opinions. He and his wife attend a Southern Baptist church and

practice their faith daily. Reared in a non-Christian home, Enoch began to think about religion in high school and then was "reborn" in college through his friends who were involved with the Baptist student organization. He says, "I guess you could say that I'm a 4.5-point out of 5-point Calvinist." Enoch does not claim any political label or any affiliation with a political party. He makes political choices based on what he sees as scriptural mandates for public officials. Enoch also bases his political choices on the religious affiliation of the candidates. He says he would not vote for a Muslim candidate and he would vote for a Jewish candidate only if he or she was an orthodox Jew, not a reform or moderate Jew. He is displeased with President Clinton and would not vote for Democrats in general because of their support for welfare. "First Thessalonians, chapter 4, says that man who does not work shouldn't eat. There are able-bodied people out there . . . a man who does not work should not eat."

Rebel's pseudonym reflects his southern pride. I talked with him at his home in a small town in Mississippi. He is an avid antiques collector, and his house is decorated with antique Civil War items; however, he bristles at the name "Civil War" because he feels it really was the "War of Northern Aggression." Rebel participates in war reenactments, always as a confederate soldier. He is a forty-six-year-old married man with a teenage daughter. He has been a firefighter in his hometown for more than twenty years. He was raised in the Southern Baptist tradition, and when he married began attending the Assembly of God church, where his wife worshipped. He disagreed with some of the preaching and subsequently his attendance at church dropped off. He retains many of his childhood religious beliefs, however. Politically, he says, "I'm just neutral" and "not a bleeding heart liberal." He would not vote for Democrats because they tend to favor gun control. Rebel is a sportsman who takes great pleasure in his weapons. He taught his daughter to shoot at age five and has been shooting with her ever since. Rebel feels that some level of assistance to the poor is required because "there are people who really need it."

I met with Harold at his modest apartment in a senior citizen's complex in Maine. He is a white man in his late fifties who has been disabled for years. He lives on a fixed social security income. Harold has been married twice and has one son, possibly another child, and four grandchildren. His "possible" other child is a "big question mark" in his life. When he was eighteen years old and in the Marine Corps, he fell in love with a woman and she became pregnant. They married, but within four months they parted and he never saw her again. Several years later, he received divorce papers that said that "no children resulted from this union," leading him to wonder what happened to the child she was carrying. Harold is not a terribly religious man, and stopped attending church services in 1970 when, he says, the sermons were filled with politics. Harold does not identify himself as either liberal, conservative, Republican, or Democrat, but he is very concerned about his Social Security income. He was raised in very impoverished circumstances in rural Maine and is not eager to repeat those hungry days. Therefore, he pays careful attention to the laws about Social Security. He resents what he perceives to be better conditions for the "poor blacks than for the poor whites" and attributes this to "reverse racism." Harold would like to see the poor whites march on Washington, D.C., to demand better treatment for themselves and to end reverse racism.

Harry is a fifty-six-year-old man, married twice, with two children from each marriage. He is a retired Naval seaman and has been employed at a homeless shelter in Maine for three years. He also works part time as an emergency medical technician. I met with Harry at a university library in Maine. He is a Chinese-Italian American who relies on what he sees as his "oriental instincts" to explain his opinions, especially on the death penalty. Raised Roman Catholic, Harry is "not really into church that much." He is also not very political—he has never voted and is not registered to vote. He says that he plans on registering to vote in the near future.

I met with Johann at a university library in Maine. He is a twenty-three-year-old single man who had a son with an ex-girlfriend when he was seventeen years old. He works as a forklift operator in a large warehouse in Maine. Johann is not a religious man, but he is very spiritual. Raised in the Catholic faith by his parents, who divorced when he was eleven, Johann is no longer a practicing Catholic. He does, however, hold certain spiritual beliefs. "I believe in an afterlife. I believe that every human being down here has some type of mission to achieve a certain spirituality that they're trying to achieve . . . almost like a task like, to get through certain things." He has read extensively about Buddhism and eastern mystical traditions. Johann describes himself as politically independent. He is concerned about U.S. military involvement in foreign conflicts such as Bosnia and about the fall of the former Soviet Union. Johann is also concerned about what he sees as over-regulation of small businesses in the United States, especially the fishing industry on the coast of Maine, which is run largely by small business owners.

I met with Suzanne at her home in an affluent town on the Maine coast. She had recently moved there from Canada, where she had spent all of her life. Suzanne is in her late forties and has seven children; her husband has five children. They have one grandchild. Suzanne studied law in Canada but now works in the home as a "natural healer"; her work involves kinesiology, and as a healer she evaluates the effects of stress on the well-being of the body and mind. She has raised her children with home-schooling rather than sending them to public schools. Suzanne does not regularly attend religious services and says that organized religion "is not my path." Her beliefs are more spiritual than they are religious: "I guess I believe in God, or something. I try to pray to whatever's out there, and I try to meditate and I try to do good on the planet, and that's about it." Suzanne does not classify herself as either liberal or conservative, but expresses concerns about reducing taxes to encourage employment and enhancing democracy throughout the world. She is concerned about gay rights and says that while homosexuals should not be discriminated against, landlords should have the right to refuse prospective tenants who are gay if they have religious objections to that lifestyle.

Leo is a fifty-two-year-old retired surgeon whom I met at a university library in Maine. He has lived and worked in Maine most of his life and has "retired with nothing." Our conversation was interrupted several times, when Leo requested that the tape recorder be turned off so he would not be recorded sounding "stupid." Leo is a devout Catholic who attends services regularly. His religious beliefs play an important role in his opinions on abortion and capital punishment. In explaining his opinions, Leo frequently quotes the Bible and argues that anyone who disagrees with him would necessarily be wrong and stupid. "Now you see, if you call yourself a Christian, you're not free to disbelieve that [life begins at conception]. You see, it's absurd. You see, how can you say you're a Christian and at the same time you're free to disbelieve what you claim that you should believe? How stupid." In Leo's opinion there is no room for disagreement with what he philosophically "proves" to be true. He is a reader of philosophy and several times mentions the political ideas of St. Thomas Aquinas as most accurately reflecting "the truth." While Leo respects the office held by political leaders, he largely sees them as "stupid," which is also his view of the judiciary. "The way I see this is, either the courts are ignorant, so ignorant that they have no right to be on the court, or they're malignant. One or the other. And they've slain themselves with their own arrogance, their own intellectual pride." He does not affiliate himself with any political party and is highly critical of the reasoning behind many political agendas. Leo declares that he needs to "prove" to me that he is right and that studying opinions is the wrong approach because

I don't have to obey an opinion. You know what a pain it is? You know what the classic definition of an opinion is? You ought to have it. An opinion is "the holding to one side of a proposition whilst in fear that the other side may yet be right." You can't improve on that definition. That's what an opinion is. And oh, here. That's your opinion. See, you can say to me, well that's just your opinion. I came here, because you gave us the benefit of the doubt. Maybe you didn't think any of us could make any proofs or arguments. You're willing to listen to our opinions.

And they remain opinions until they move out of the realm of opinions into the realm of certainty and from certainty to truth. And I have done that.

Warren is a sixty-two-year-old retired defense and airline industry executive. I met with him at his home in Maine. Warren explains how his opinions have changed over the years. He does not participate in religious life, but annually organizes a carnation sale at local churches, which raises money for the anti-abortion group Maine Right to Life. Warren explains, "I'm what you call a lapsed Catholic. When I go into a church, the plaster cracks. But the fact of the matter is, I don't have a religion. I truly do not have a religion." Warren adds,

> I have dabbled in astronomy most of my life. You can't watch the majestic flow of the universe around you and consider it to be accidental. So I believe a supreme and original being created it. Did you ever hear of Aquinas's theory, St. Thomas Aquinas's causality? The acorn is only there because there was a tree before. You know what I'm talking about. It's impossible to get your brain beyond Aquinas's causality. There is a supreme being. You may call that God "Yahweh." . . . You may call it whatever you wish. But there is a supreme being holding you accountable.

Warren is a conservative. He points out that while he does not base his vote on party affiliation, he is more likely to vote for Republicans than for Democrats. Social and moral issues are at the top of Warren's political priorities. In addition to his anti-abortion and pro–death penalty opinions, he opposes gay rights legislation. "I think sodomy is wrong. Period. As a matter of fact, I get upset when people promote gay lifestyles when it has such horrible, negative complications. Here's a piece of society which has horrendous, death-dealing consequences."

Tying these interviewees' opinions together is a desire to secure obedience to a behavioral code through punishment and a desire to hold people accountable for their actions.

Abortion Opinions

Several important themes emerge in this group's anti-abortion opinions. First is the unanimous belief, justified through scriptural quotes, that life begins at conception and is therefore worthy of protection. There are few circumstances under which the interviewees in this group would tolerate abortion. Second, the interviewees would promote alternatives to abortion, especially sexual abstinence and adoption. Third, they believe strongly that abortion allows women and men to avoid the consequences of their sexual behavior and that abortion should be a punishable offense. Finally, there is a common concern that society is quickly losing its moral anchor. Each of these beliefs will be examined in detail through the words of the interviewees. Then, I will examine their opinions about abortion politics and activism.

When Life Begins

The belief that life begins at conception is central to these interviewees' abortion opposition. For some the belief that God creates life rests on religious faith, and for others this is simply a biological statement of fact. For still others, it is a combination of religious conviction and scientific fact. Carolyn says of the human embryo, "I believe that's human life. I don't believe that biologically that can be disputed. And, in my mind, that since it is human life, then we have no right to take that life." Carolyn finds it offensive that anyone could refer to the human embryo as "a blob of nothing because it's a person known to God who somehow fits into God's plan and God's purpose." Carolyn explains,

> We're schizophrenic to me in our society, in the way we feel about this, because it's a baby if it's wanted, and if it's unwanted it's a product of conception to be terminated. There are very few things in this life that I will tell you that I am absolutely convinced and have no doubt in my mind whatsoever, there are very few things. I am firmly convinced that this is a human being, and we must not do anything to interfere with the right to life of that human being. Therefore, if we believe abortion is murder, and I do, then we believe the person performing the abortion procedure is committing murder.

Dave thinks that "murder is such a loose term for [abortion], I would almost think it's a genocide in a sense." When asked to clarify that, he says, "It's the adult population of the United States wiping out its infants." Dave says this does not occur in the animal kingdom and that there are no known cases where an animal has deliberately aborted its own offspring. He considers abortion one of the seven deadly sins. "The question is, who do you put the blame on? The doctor that does it or the mother that allows it? The mother because it's her conscious decision."

Dave considers the courts and the legal system beyond their authority in deciding that the human embryo is not a person. "Who are we to judge when that fetus becomes human? That's what they're doing by saying 'Yesterday it was a fetus, now it's a human being, you can't have an abortion today.' Why wasn't it a human the day before and the day before that and upon conception? As far as

I'm concerned the minute the egg, the single cell splits and becomes two it's no longer just a fetus to me. There is a human being there in its growth stage."

Rebel believes that since life begins at conception, and women still choose to abort, then obviously "they have no respect for their own bodies, they figure that's a quick fix, but their child has its own right to live." Harold says, "That's life in there and there's no way you can say it ain't life. That's why I call it premeditated murder." Based on his own experience as a young man, Harold concludes that abortion is a "crime of passion."

> I'll try to explain to you what happened to me when I was in the service in 1958. I was an MP. Well anyway, I met a Wave [woman serving in the navy] and I met her on a blind date, and this is why I call it a "crime of passion" now. I wound up in Elizabeth City, North Carolina, saying "I do," within a matter of a month, month and a half. She did want to use protections or whatever at that time, and I said, "No. I want a child." Because being in the service you don't know whether you're going to be dead the next day. And I wanted someone to carry on. So maybe I might have been selfish. So I don't know. So if that wasn't a crime of passion, what do you call it? I mean, I was in a passionate mood and I wound up in Elizabeth City, North Carolina. So I'm saying that's why I call it a crime of passion. It's a passionate mood you're in, and you're not paying attention to what you're doing. It's easy to forget responsibility. And she left the service when she was six months pregnant. So I don't know. Well, she waited four years to divorce me, so I don't know. She said there was a, I asked her, I wrote her a letter when I got the divorce papers. I don't know why she waited till 1962 to divorce me. She said the baby was born, it was stillborn at birth. It was Rh factor. Because in the divorce papers it said there was no children born of this marriage. So I don't know. There's that feeling of always saying to yourself. I don't know, but I'd like to know if there's somebody out there. If somebody knocks on the door and resembles my son, maybe I'd want to know it. But I've always had that feeling inside me that there's something out there but I can't see it or touch it. So I imagine a woman must feel frustrated if she aborts it and set back and think what had it been. That's why I call it a "crime of passion."

According to Harold, since it requires passion to bring about a pregnancy and it is traumatic if the pregnancy is unwanted, it is a crime of passion to terminate that pregnancy. In Harold's view, women who have abortions are not acting rationally but rather are consumed with the emotions of the moment. Likewise, men who engage in risky sexual activity that might produce pregnancy are acting on passion rather than reason, which further justifies Harold's view that abortion is a "crime of passion." Harold can understand "one mistake," but if there is a situation of "repeat abortions, their tubes should be tied, immediately."

Warren, who has always thought that "abortion was terribly wrong and engaged in by scurrilous people to accomplish scurrilous goals," believes that life begins at conception and that abortion is "killing; it can't be anything else. You take something that's living and you kill it, there it is, there is no other definition. How could it be otherwise?" Warren was deeply influenced by an anti-abortion film, *The Silent Scream,* produced by Dr. Bernard Nathanson. "I saw a fetus being killed and pulling away from an inserting needle, repeatedly, the rage . . . That was an emotional moment in my life. I guess my rage was at the doctor who was on the other end of that needle, to start with. But, in the end, it was a rage against society that that could take place with the blessings of the law."

Suzanne, who "tries to do no harm" in the world, thinks abortion is ultimately a human rights issue. She believes that since life begins at the moment of conception and the embryo is a human being, it is entitled to the same human rights that we all value. "Why does it suddenly acquire rights just because it's in a different place, outside the womb instead of inside the womb? It's similar to the whole human rights movement; people have different rights depending on which national borders they're in. In one country, for instance, it's OK to abort a child because it's going to be female. In another country it's not. We either believe in human rights or we don't. I hate to sound like a fanatic, but your fist stops where my nose begins." Suzanne does not believe that abortion is necessarily equivalent to murder, because "it [defining something as murder] depends on the motive of the person."

Leo explains in detail his belief that life begins at conception and his criticism of the courts for the *Roe v. Wade* decision.

> The reason I'm not in favor of abortion is because the human conceptus from the moment of conception is a person. And it's inconceivable to me that the courts could have come to a decision, predicated on I know not what, that it is not a person. The fertilized ovum, within the uterus, is alive, it's human, it's got forty-six chromosomes, its sex can be determined immediately, and it's explosive in its vitality. It can hardly contain itself. It immediately divides into another cell. It's just absolutely an explosive micro cosmos. But what the courts would assume, or say, is that this has no identity. And the fact is, nothing exists without an identity. That's absolutely impossible. So by the legal definition of a person they've contradicted themselves already. That's the first thing. The second is that they've done something that is absolutely fraught with danger and it has never occurred in the history of the cosmos. They've defined something in the negative. Definitions

are never in the negative. They've done something that is incomprehensible to a rational mind, to define something in the negative. Now the problem with the courts—one of the problems, there's many problems with the courts—is their imagination has deceived them. They have said to themselves, "It is impossible for this to be a person, because it is too small." Whereas in humility they should have said, "I don't know how this is a person, but it must be. And the reason is obvious." There is no case in the history of the world, and it is self-evident, indefinitely self-evident, that like generates like. So to define something in the negative is illogical. It's a deception.

Leo goes on to explain that, in his opinion, to define a fetus as not human because of its size or because it is within the uterus is another deception. "How anybody can say that this is not alive. . . . In order for any human being to [do so] the degree of stupidity one has to say that this is not alive? It's incomprehensible to me how stupid you'd be. You can't put it into words. . . . If I see you up and about and I say you're not alive when you're moving? How much more stupid can you get? It really is so stupid it boggles the mind."

Leo believes that since abortion is deliberately ending a human life, it is murder. "That's what the definition of murder is; to kill an innocent human being." He sees abortion as undermining God's plan for the universe.

So if you want to frustrate my plan for creation, you have to do it by reducing yourselves to a bunch of murderers. And I've got plenty of time and patience. If you feel tremendous sorrow and pity for these children being ground up, I mean, can you imagine me having a giant meat grinder here and putting you on it and grinding you up inch by inch? Well that's what we do to these beings in the womb. They feel this. I mean they've got brains and they've got their nervous system, they have skin, and here, they move, they move like people. Oh look at that, they move like a snake moves when you touch it. You see? So the nice thing about this is, if there is a nice thing about it is that the souls, if you want to watch somebody dies when they're young, no one will believe this when you put this in the book, so you don't even have to bother. Just think of how many of these souls will never have had the opportunity to go to hell. You see, every single one of these souls will reside among the blessed. They will not have had, they will not have had the opportunity to offend God. That's one hell of a blessing. See even from this people think there is horror. But God is, St. Augustus [referring to St. Augustine] says the reason we know God is omnipotent is only God can bring good from evil. And the arguments about why God didn't annihilate Adam and Eve and start all over, one of the arguments is this—that would have been to say that God couldn't have brought good from evil. How horrible.

Embryonic and fetal life, according to Leo, ought to be protected more passionately than life at any other stage because it is innocent and has committed no sin or offense. As Dave agrees, "The child did nothing but was conceived, we were all born as a result of original sin, but you can't condemn a child for that, otherwise none of us would be here."

Carolyn does not see her anti-abortion position as imposing a moral standard on others.

> I don't personally see [opposing] abortion as imposing my beliefs on someone else. You could look as those mothers and doctors imposing their moral beliefs on that unborn child; if you want to look at it that way. As far as I'm concerned that is the function of law to protect human beings. You know, I think laws ought to be set up to protect for our good and I think the abortion law would do that, not just from a spiritual standpoint, but a physical standpoint, the protection of women and their bodies, and the protection of that unborn child's life.

This paternalistic view of the law is reflected in the opinions of other interviewees. Leo believes that the law should eliminate the legal right to abortion because it is bad for women. Leo asks, if it's nothing more than a "blob or a wart to be removed," then why the need for psychological counseling afterwards? "Do you do that when a woman has a wart removed from her hand? See, their very activities imply something horrible is going on, why would they have a nervous breakdown about having a wart removed from their uterus? How dare the federal government spend billions of dollars counseling people that had a wart removed from their uterus?! It's horrendous."

Rebel thinks that women who abort pregnancies have "no respect for their bodies" and should be legally required to continue the pregnancies rather than using abortion as a "quick fix." In Harold's opinion, abortion is a traumatic experience for women, which means that "ninety percent of them would feel that guilt, in my opinion, then you have that ten percent that wouldn't care nothing about their kids." In addition, Harold believes that "there's no excuse for a woman to get pregnant" when she doesn't want to and that the law should prohibit abortion because the "child can't speak for itself." Suzanne sees abortion as a problem for women in other aspects of their lives. "If a person starts treating another life as an object, she or he can decide what to do about it. They will not have happy relationships in their own life, so their life is not all that it could be."

In Dave's opinion, the Supreme Court was wrong to decide in favor of a woman's right to control her own body. "I understand that, but, what about the child's body? Who decides what it gets to do with its body? The Supreme Court? The mother?" This is fundamentally flawed, in Dave's opinion, because the child has not been afforded the right to self-determination. Rebel says that "legalize[d] abortion [puts] lives at a very low cost, and life is worth everything in the world. That child is not asking to be put into this situation, and yet its life is going to be snuffed out because the government goes 'Yeah, it's legal to do this now.' I just don't think it should be made easy for the lady to go down there and [get an abortion]."

Most of these interviewees rely on the Bible to justify their anti-abortion opinions. Some of the more common quotes come from the Old Testament books of Exodus, Jeremiah, and Psalms. Carolyn and Enoch quote Jeremiah 1: 5: "Before I formed you in the womb I knew you and before you were born I consecrated you, I appointed you a prophet to the nations" (New Revised Standard Version). This scripture convinces them that all life is known to God and therefore worthy of legal protection. Carolyn, Enoch, and Leo refer to Psalm 51: 5, which reads, "Behold, I was shapen in iniquity, and in sin did my mother conceive me" (King James Version). This leads Carolyn to the conclusion that "from the moment of conception the soul is there, from conception that person is there, it is not a blob." Furthermore, Carolyn is convinced that the soul enters the body at conception: "Psalm 51 clears that up for me." And Leo argues that "what's interesting is that [the Psalm's author] says that 'I was conceived.' I told you earlier that conception is the moment a thing begins to be what it is. Here he proves to himself there's an 'I' and how could he prove to himself there's an 'I' if he was not a person?"

Carolyn, Enoch, and Leo also cite Psalm 139: 13: "For it was you who formed my inward parts; you knit me together in my mother's womb" (New Revised Standard Version). "From there it became kind of obvious to me that life begins at conception," Enoch comments. Dave, Carolyn, and Leo agree with this interpretation.

Leo quotes a famous passage from Exodus.

> If men who are fighting hit a pregnant woman and she gives birth prematurely but there is no serious injury, the offender must be fined whatever the woman's husband demands and the court allows. But if there is serious injury, you are to take life for life, eye for eye, tooth for tooth, hand for hand, foot for foot, burn for burn, wound for wound, bruise for bruise. (Exodus 21: 22–25, New International Version)

Therefore, Leo concludes, "anything that strikes a woman is bad enough, but there's something horrible about striking a pregnant woman. And yet, you can eviscerate that blob from the uterus and it used to be that it would be something horrible." Rebel warns, "They'll pay for it one of these days. At the judgment that's coming, I see it as things sure won't be good. That'll be a bad mark on their spot."

Few of these interviewees would tolerate abortion even in the cases of fetal defect, rape, incest, or grave health threat to the pregnant woman. When asked under what circumstances she would tolerate abortion, Suzanne says none, because such exceptions are "just weasel clauses." Based on the experience of a friend who was gang raped, became pregnant, and had the child, who turned out to be "a beautiful spirit," Suzanne no longer makes an exception for rape. Enoch agrees, saying that "it must be ordered by the sovereignty of God, that God has ordered everything the way He wants it to be ordered, then there's not really anything man can do to change that. Man can try as he may to 'thwart the plans of God' and he can't do that."

Dave relies on the experiences of a childhood friend to explain why he does not support abortion even when the pregnant woman's life is in danger. "One of my best friends, his mother was only five foot one inch and ninety pounds when she gave birth to him, and it almost killed her, but she wanted him enough that she put her life up to risk to have him. If there's a mother out there that would rather live than to give her child a life, that's rather selfish, because she shouldn't have conceived the child in the first place."

Warren makes one exception. If "medical science determines that, should she continue the pregnancy it will result in her death, you're faced with a horrible dilemma. You are, in my opinion, morally correct to take whatever action is necessary to remove what I'm going to call an 'illness' which is going to take the life of the mother." However, Warren uses the famous scientist Steven J. Hawking as an example for not aborting when there is a serious fetal defect. Recognizing the valuable contributions to society that have been made by such individuals, Warren believes that fetal defects are not adequate justifications for abortion. He calls Hawking "one of the great minds of this world, I hate to think what would have been the case had he been born in this country; he'd have been put out of his misery before he ever came down the channel."

Carolyn explains why she would tolerate abortion under only one rare condition.

I don't believe in abortion in cases of rape and incest, which a lot of people will allow, because the child is not at fault for the circumstances under which it was conceived. To me, if you're going to be . . . my husband loves the term "intellectually honest," and if you're going to say this is a child, then rape or incest doesn't change the fact that this is a child. And abortion would not be right because abortion is the willful taking of innocent unborn life, innocent unborn human life. The circumstance that I would allow, the exception in my mind would be an ectopic pregnancy. I believe that is an acceptable solution. The difference is, in a tubal pregnancy the intent is not kill the baby, the intent is to save the mother's life. They have not found a way that they can safely remove the fertilized ovum, they don't know how to do that. By the time that is found, it is a life threatening situation and if it is not attended to the tube will rupture, killing the fetus for sure and maybe the mother as well. In that circumstance, I would allow, in my mind, it would be conscionable to do a procedure to remove it, knowing when you did that the fetus was not going to survive. But, the fetus is not going to survive anyway. And the intent is not to go in and kill the fetus, you're trying to save the life of the mother.

In explaining why she would oppose abortion in the case of severe fetal defects, such as anencephalia, she says that women who carry a pregnancy to term knowing that the baby will not survive "can then see the child and go through the grieving process. If they terminate the pregnancy beforehand, it kind of cuts that off for them. Also, God can always work a miracle."

Rebel and Harold would tolerate abortion in cases of rape and incest, because "she didn't have a choice in it," as Rebel says. Harold elaborates: "The rape is forced and if she gets pregnant I don't think she should have to carry it. I believe the woman has a right to an abortion. And incest is forced too, I think if a daughter got pregnant because of a father or stepfather, whatever, I don't think she should be forced to carry it."

Leo, who would tolerate abortion only to save a mother's life, says that in the cases of rape and incest, "unfortunately, you can't [abort]. That is a human person. That person, you can't kill or slay that being because of the unfortunate assault on you as a woman. It's a tragedy. But you can't. Oh, it's awful, isn't it? It's just awful. And of course it's so difficult for the human mind, or for the girl or the woman who's been raped to . . . And with all the thinking today, how can she possibly think clearly in the milieu that's occurred in the last twenty-five, thirty years in this country?" Because many people approve of abortion in the cases of rape and incest, Leo feels that women are unable to think clearly when faced with such a decision. "Thinking clearly," to Leo, means reasoning that the conceptus is a person from the moment of conception and must not be aborted.

Alternatives to Abortion

An important theme that runs through these conversations is the existence of alternatives to abortion. The most popular alternatives among these interviewees are abstinence and adoption. Carolyn says, "The ideal is not an alternative, but it's prevention." She favors abstinence until marriage. Warren offers his view of abstinence.

> Obviously, until marriage, abstinence is not a bad choice. Now I'll admit, it's a struggle for the human soul to practice abstinence until marriage. It is hard. And I'd be the first one to tell you that or the first one to admit it. That don't mean the fight isn't worth it. It is a test of moral fiber. There's no question about it. But it's not a test we shouldn't take or advise against. I know it's archaic, but I think that the mechanism by which a woman becomes pregnant today is well known. It's no mystery. And I think that in the ideal world, an adult couple can exercise restraint and practice abstinence when necessary to either completely avoid pregnancy or minimize the chances of it. Adults have that responsibility, in my vision. They have that responsibility to society. I think that there are ways to not have kids. And I'm such an old fuddy-duddy I don't like to discuss them with women I hardly know. There is also a way or ways in which couples can express love and satisfy their sexual needs without sexual intercourse. Do I have to say anything more?

Dave would also promote abstinence as the preferred alternative. "Premarital sex, to me, it's overrated, but everybody's going to experiment. In today's society it's more trouble than it's worth; you have a maximum of twenty or thirty seconds of actual hormonal excitement and pleasure that you risk losing friends, tearing up relationships, ruining reputations, contracting diseases, and pregnancies. The risk factors are too much."

Adoption is the next most popular alternative among this group of interviewees. Dave comments, "Even in [the local] paper, which is kind of a joke, you've got families advertising to adopt. And they'll pay for all the medical expenses of the birth, everything." Johann would like to see adoption used more often, too. "If abortion were stopped then more people would be able to adopt children. More people that are qualified to do so. I think abortion's a too easy way out." Suzanne and Carolyn believe adoption is a very personal and difficult choice for a woman to make, but would applaud any woman who opted to give her baby up for adoption rather than abort the pregnancy. Carolyn says:

> Adoption is a very personal decision, and it has to be made on a personal level. We feel very positively about adoption, if given a lot of thought and a lot of counseling. It's not a choice that's made I'm sure without some personal pain. Living with that choice, at least you know that you've given that child life. The clients I've seen down here, and there've been thousands since we began, of the girls that

I've seen and talked to that have had abortions, I've seen very few that don't have regrets, and some of those regrets are severe.

Suzanne sees adoption as "a very difficult [alternative]. It's very difficult to get to the adoption stage. . . . I'd like to see mandatory counseling that encouraged adoptions. It's a very emotional time, I have been through seven pregnancies, I know how emotional it can be."

Accountability

Most of these interviewees believe that access to legal abortion allows women and men to avoid the responsibility of their sexual activities, that people should be held accountable for their behavior, and that harsh punishments for abortion are reasonable. People have to "face the music, take responsibility for their actions" when they are facing an unintended pregnancy, according to Dave. Johann, whose former girlfriend aborted her second pregnancy three months after their first child was born, recounts his own experience. "[Abortion is] an easy way out, or it seems to be. The scar it leaves when it's done, that won't be easy. So, I don't think there is an easy way out to avoid your responsibilities. Sure you won't have a child to take care of, but you have a responsibility to your own psyche and that's going to be totally off balance." Carolyn discusses her experience as a pro-life counselor.

> [Abortion] does [allow people to avoid their responsibility] because we've seen it. It's not the attitude of everybody, we've had a number of clients that we've seen who have really tried to act, in their minds, as responsibly as far as they're concerned. They're not people with multiple partners, they are using birth control, it just failed. We have seen this a good bit, where the birth control failed. It happens a good bit. But, we have had that client, we had one this week that has already had one baby without being married, and thought she was pregnant, but tested negative . . . and was planning to abort, and the counselor said her attitude was like, "It's no big deal." Abortion would be a backup form of birth control, and often times, these people are not even attempting to use any form of birth control. And, as far as I'm concerned, that is skirting responsibility. We live in a selfish generation. I don't mean to be unkind.

Enoch comments, "Everyone is trying to take the blame off themselves, I mean if you asked everybody; it's not their fault that [an unplanned pregnancy] happened, so everyone is looking for a way out by placing the blame on someone else." Dave has a major problem with this "cavalier" attitude toward abortion.

He recalls a high school classmate whom he says "had three abortions," and says that to her, "[abortion] was nothing, it was an inconvenience, it was a trip to the doctor. She didn't look upon it as a human life, the value of that child's life wasn't apparent to her."

Rebel says abortion "lets the women off the hook, the men can hit and run; they've scored their goal, they're gone and the woman is fixed with the problem. And with abortion it's just a quick way to get her out of the problem." Most of these interviewees feel that "there's no need for pregnancy, when it's unwanted," as Harold states. They see ample opportunity for precautions to be taken and believe that any woman who gets pregnant must have been careless with contraceptive methods, or she would not be in that predicament. Harold continues, "There's no need for them being in that position, because the help is there to give them birth control pills or anything they want, and they can get them without their parents' consent."

Warren has a problem with "cavalier attitudes" among young women, which he feels are reinforced by the medical profession.

> Let's say I'm eighteen years old. I'm a girl and I get pregnant. I don't want a kid. Hell, I'm having a good time. Who needs a kid trotting around after me? You go to a local respected figure. He's a doctor, practices in a hospital in the community, is well-respected, and the doctor says, "I'll take care of it." What's the problem? So they go and do it, and a human being just died. You don't have to think about it dying because your own doctor just did it. And they did it right in the hospital up the street. Because your peers don't find anything wrong with it either, next Monday, by next Monday I'll be all better and no kid. It's a cavalier attitude, absolutely. At a million and half [abortions] a year? What can it be but cavalier?

Suzanne disagrees with most of the other interviewees in saying that "it's true [that abortion lets people off the hook], but I'm not into dictating to other people what their responsibilities are." And Leo sees abortion as indicative of a social malaise. He claims that "there's no responsibility to begin with" in society. "No one has very much responsibility which seems to be about sex, you know? I mean kids are doing it!"

These interviewees feel that people, especially women, will be held accountable for having abortions or performing abortions. Dave relates accountability to the abortion issue by pointing out, "You didn't decide to be born, you didn't decide your parents or your hair color or any of that. Therefore, God cannot hold you accountable for something you had no control over. But, abortion, you can be held accountable for, you have control, you have the choice." In Carolyn's opinion, "We as humans are the only creatures in God's creation capable of sin,

He doesn't hold animals into account, they have no ability to know or commit sin, but human beings are held accountable to Him."

Rebel believes that Henry Foster's nomination for Surgeon General was not confirmed because Foster was being held accountable for having performed abortions. "Maybe he was being punished here on earth by that. But, I don't know [to] what degrees God has to punish people." Harry thinks that "everybody should be accountable [for abortion], something should be done; what, I don't know."

Among these interviewees, some form of punishment is the most appealing mechanism for holding people accountable for abortions. The punishments advocated include condemnation to hell, jail time, and the death penalty. Some interviewees express uncertainty about what kind of punishment should be given. Carolyn says, "I have no idea. I have not even given that any consideration. I'm sure if it would be illegal there would be a law that prohibited it, so there would have to be a penalty . . . a doctor could lose his medical license. I don't know—I haven't given that a whole lot of thought." Johann believes that abortion involves a "spiritual penalty."

> Just sadness afterwards. Sadness and it just really makes you think about it. I probably should say that my ex-girlfriend had one. And this hurt a lot. Well see what happened was we already had a child together, and this is when I was quite young, with her, and then afterwards, when she got pregnant again, and she couldn't handle going through all that again, especially with her parents and all that. She was seventeen. And then after what happened, and then we just broke it off afterwards. I regret it. I don't know if she thinks about it as much as I do. Probably because I still, I wasn't . . . It sucks that we broke up because we were a really good couple together. If that didn't happen I think certain events in life wouldn't have happened either. Then we'd still be together.

Dave says, "I'd probably have to talk with God himself and ask him, 'Well, what do you make [women who have abortions] do, wash the clouds or what?'" Harry comments, "I think they should go get punished for a while, I think we should be well aware that they know what the heck they're doing. Here again, they don't care, a lot of people don't care."

Harold proposes jail sentences and a fairly complex punishment scheme for those who perform or have abortions. First, repeat abortions would result in an automatic tubal ligation for women—"Three strikes and you're out." Punishment would also be determined by the gestation of the pregnancy that was terminated. "The farther along in the pregnancy the stiffer the sentence, a lot of people are sentenced to jail time for less," Harold argues. This would apply to the women as well as the abortion providers. "I know I sound harsh, I'm not really. I'm a very gentle person. I'm talking about [abortion] destroying someone's life, and I wouldn't want to destroy anybody's life, but I think the punishment has gotta start fitting the crime, because it is a crime." Late-term abortions, especially "partial birth abortions," would be subject to the death penalty in Harold's scheme. "If that wouldn't be murder and call for the death penalty, what would you call it?"

Warren feels that abortion providers should be punished by jail time but that pregnant women should not be held accountable because "the woman who is pregnant . . . is not always in full possession [of her mental faculties]."

> I think the mental state of a woman, I don't know how to word this exactly. Here's a woman has a whole lot of kids, financial trouble, a man who's not necessarily stable, maybe drinks, maybe gambles, she gets pregnant, her mental state, she is in no condition to make a rational decision about what she's doing. So, you could make a strong case that most any woman is not in the position to make a judgment like that.

Doctors who perform abortions, on the other hand, should be sentenced to die, according to Warren, Harold, Leo, and Enoch. Leo says:

> They ought to just say, abortion is no longer legal and we'll not have any. And anybody who does one outside the hospital will be brought to trial and put to death for abortion, for illegal abortion. We've come to our senses and know that to do this now is murder. We've made a horrific mistake, God forgive us, if He will, and get on with your life. It was a capital offense at one time. You couldn't commit an abortion, that was considered murder in this country. You see, I can remember treating a girl who came in the hospital from a criminal abortion. And she died, too. . . . They couldn't even transfuse her. Her blood hemolyzed due to the procedure. And the arguments, how stupid. The arguments, well make abortion legal. Here, this is one of the arguments. You're not old enough, probably, to remember this, but we'll make abortion legal so that girls won't have to go out and get, procure, an illegal abortion. Well, that all sounds very nice and it's all very wrong and it's all very unclear thinking and it's all very stupid. Here. We will make abortion legal so that they will not go out any longer and get an un-legal abortion. But why were abortions illegal to begin with?

Dave, Enoch, and Leo feel that abortion is a sin for which people will be sent to hell by God. In Enoch's opinion, "the judgment that's coming" will answer the question of punishment for abortion. People who have or perform abortions can avoid eternal damnation by professing faith in Christ and seeking forgiveness. Enoch believes that one cannot "earn" salvation but must profess belief in Christ, whereupon one would no longer be compelled to sin. Any Christian who disagrees with this, according to Leo, must be "a liar" because "Christians are not free to disbelieve."

Moral Issues

Abortion is not the only social issue that greatly concerns these interviewees. They see abortion as one sign of a moral decay that is afflicting modern society. The most commonly mentioned social condition associated with abortion is the loss of traditional morality in modern society. Warren sees evidence of this loss in the rise of "secular humanism," which he believes promotes the "culture of abortion."

> I think that from the days when man came out of the cave dragging the woman by the hair, batting the kids over the head with a club, that may sound ridiculous, but it did occur. Man struggled up and embraced his civilization. Now in the course of doing that, over a period of twelve thousand years or more, certain activities it became understood were good for society, and certain activities were bad. Don't bash your wife over the head with a club with nails in it. Don't do that. Even without nails in it. Certainly, don't kick your kids in the head. Certain rules governing civilized human beings. Listen to the [classical] music you hear coming through that [radio]. Look to the literature. Look to the moral background against which our culture has developed to what it is today. Now in America, as I look back over a lifetime, sometime in the mid or early sixties, that moral anchor, the moral anchor to the ship adrift, began to be pulled from its moorings. The people began to question the morals of ten thousand years of civilization, and in fact, deny them. A number of so-called intellectual elites, in fact, negated all that had gone before, and said, "These people are wrong. There is no God. There is no penalty. There is no heaven. There is no hell. There is no place to pay. So, enjoy." As a matter of fact, I'm trying to think and my mind is going blank. The basic document starts off with, the secular humanists around the world wrote two documents. One in the 1930s and one, I think 1970. Humanist Manifesto,[1] published in 1973, was the beginning of relativistic morality. From the day man came out of the cave, in fact if you go into the old caves you'll see there was a supreme being somewhere that led man from the cave to the music we got going out there. Then 19 . . . Humanist Manifesto I, let's see what the date of that is on here, too. It was published, I think in the middle of the Depression. 1933, yes, the middle of the Depression. Humanist Manifesto II in 1973. And I'm not going to go into great

detail. I will quote from the [preface]. "We believe that traditional dogmatic authoritarian religions that place revelation, god, virtue, or creed above humans do a disservice to the human species. . . . Anybody that places anything above humans do a disservice. . . . We find insufficient evidence for the existence of a supernatural force. If there is, it is meaningless or irrelevant." Now, to me, that cuts the underpinnings out from under ten thousand years of development and freedom. There is no being superior to man. You've been delivered from God or responsibility for what you do. There is no supernatural being. There is, and religions that preach it do a disservice. Man is the be-all and end-all. Since we don't answer to anybody, why should you care whether they kill a million or a half a million or a hundred million [babies]? So, and of course, and that was signed, and I need not go into the names, believe it or not, these are academics from around the world. And church figures, mostly Universalists, president of Columbia University, and Irving Horowitz, Alfred McLung Lee, and Elizabeth Bryant Lee, those are the movers and shakers in the world of thought, and they permeate college campuses around the world. Now, in 1973 you started educating people in these things, by 1993, they're running the boat. And of course under those principles, abortion is a moral insignificant.

Enoch refers to this social-spiritual condition as a "man-centered world view," which must be combated in order to return society to a "God-centered world view." Enoch hopes to accomplish this as a pastor.

Rebel also criticizes modern society.

[Society should be] getting back to the old-style family morals of respecting your peers, yes ma'am, no ma'am type of situation. If I didn't say "yes ma'am, no ma'am," I got hit. And I've raised my daughter that way. And when I do crime prevention programs in schools, when students say, "yes sir, no sir," it stands out like a beacon light. You don't see that in schools any more. And parents are not with their kids any more. Kids are losing respect for other people and then respect for themselves. And so that's just one of the reasons . . . and it ties into the abortion issue because they have no respect for their own body. And kids nowadays, teachers are scared of the kids. And that's not the system. The system is failing. And any time a student can tell a teacher to go to hell and the teacher can't do nothing about it, the system is failing. God never called me to be a teacher. Because I told the kids, I said, "I would half kill y'all. I'd have a paddle and I've half kill you." It didn't hurt me when I was growing up. I got whippings all the time in school.

Leo attributes the loss of morals in society to the separation of church and state, which he considers an "abomination." Dave looks at the "moral decline" through an historical lens, arguing that "two hundred years ago abortion didn't exist," and that "women who were raped two hundred years ago didn't even think about abortion, they just went off somewhere else and had the kid." Dave attributes this to the "fact that their morals were higher, as what they thought was right and wrong. I mean two hundred years ago for the government to say 'Yeah, it's OK to kill babies' that would have been an outrage, unheard of in 1795."

Other subjects that the interviewees relate to abortion include the Holocaust, infanticide, and child abuse. Carolyn sees infanticide as related to abortion because in the case of infanticide, "imperfect" babies are allowed to die if "they're born with deformities or life-threatening conditions that someone judges their quality of life is such that their life is not going to be worth living. Who makes those decisions? By whose standard of perfection?" Carolyn suggests that it was this desire for perfection that led to the Holocaust.

> Hitler had a standard in Nazi Germany that I never understood, I mean, what was it? The Aryan race, fair-haired and blue-eyed? And he was little dark, squatty, dark-haired . . . and I'm like, "You didn't fit the profile, really, of the people that you were saying were the most acceptable." He began to annihilate people that did not fit that mold, people that he did not consider to be members of the master race, and you know we saw the horrible results of that with the millions of Jewish people that were put to death. I think you're dealing with the same type of mentality, that there are some lives not worthy to be lived and you can have a different basis for that. That's really scary. And to me, anything that devalues human life is a scary thing. And I think abortion does that.

Suzanne relates abortion to high rates of child abuse. In her opinion, abortion "cheapens children, and I suspect that the fairly high rate of child abuse we're seeing in what is otherwise a very wealthy society must have something to do with it."

> If you can choose whether or not to have a child, that child has no intrinsic value. Therefore, even after the child is born it's like a chattel and you can do with it what you want. That's the logical progression. I don't think most people have thought that through, but I think it's sort of there, a way of looking at the universe. I can't explain the rates of child abuse in any other way.

Concern about "family values" is also a commonly expressed theme in these conversations. Carolyn defines family values as "exemplifying conservative issues that have to do with what I consider, that certain people still adhere to in society, that love their country, love their family, believe in the work ethic, honesty, right and wrong, [and] believe in God." Dave feels that family values are missing from contemporary society.

> The problem with family values today is, is you have a father, and in any given situation, suppose you have a father that's not there. The parents are divorced. It leaves [children] with their friends for eighteen to twenty hours a day, who are just like them. No guidance, no leadership whatsoever, other than one leading the group. The family values that were present forty, fifty years ago aren't here today.

Harold believes that family values can best be maintained in rural settings because "you help one another out, to make sure that everybody survives." In urban areas, Harold says, "Survival don't mean anything, death don't mean anything." Suzanne says she applies family values to her own life. She has home-schooled her seven children and five step-children, among them a seventeen-year-old daughter who has just graduated from college. Suzanne feels that home-schooling allows her to apply the concept that "children have intrinsic value" and thus demonstrate her family values to the children.

Abortion Politics and Activism

Interviewees in this group stress the necessity of voting for pro-life candidates and voicing support for pro-life Supreme Court appointees. Some of these interviewees have been active in the pro-life movement, but not in prominent ways. They also have concerns about welfare recipiency and distinct perceptions of women and girls. Many of these interviewees view women in essentialist terms and consider them incapable of making difficult decisions in times of stress. Essentialist perspectives on gender give priority to the biological differences between men and women, stressing that women are "naturally" nurturing and caregiving while men are "naturally" aggressive and dominating. This biological determinism has been challenged by other scholars as discounting the importance of environmental influences in the social construction of gender (Nielsen 1990).

Enoch is very specific about what he looks for in political candidates and takes his criteria from the Bible. "In Deuteronomy 17 God set up a standard for a king[2] who was to be over the Israelites. And then God said that this is what the king would be like and this is what the king would do . . . taking that one application and applying it to today, saying these are the leaders we should have, and this is what they should be like and this is what they should do . . . that, I would say, governs who I vote for. If the person isn't consistent with those things then I don't vote for him." Enoch specifically mentions the verse in Deuteronomy 17 requiring the king to "write down a copy of the law and keep it with him all the days of his life." Enoch is concerned about "the character issue" in reference to contemporary politicians. He says, "Second Timothy, 3: 16 and 17 . . . inspired by God, and is profitable for doctrine and approved for teaching of correction. Therefore, it would be a standard by which man should live. . . . Psalm 119: 9 says how can a man keep his way pure by following Your decrees." [3] This, therefore, prevents Enoch from voting for a candidate who does not share his Judeo-Christian views, including those regarding abortion.

Carolyn would "definitely disqualify a person if they were pro-abortion; it is such an important issue to me and to the future of our country." Rebel "won't vote for [a candidate] if he's in favor of abortion." But for Rebel abortion is a companion issue with the right to own guns. "I don't like the idea of any politician telling me I do not have the right to own a firearm. And so if a politician stands up and says he's in favor of banning [guns], he's automatically lost my vote. I won't vote for him." Warren "would not make [abortion] a litmus test," but it definitely influences his vote. The other social issue that influences his vote is gay rights, which he opposes because "sodomy is wrong, period."

Suzanne views pro-life candidates as independent thinkers. "I would probably vote for somebody who was pro-life more than somebody who's on the rabid pro-choice side. Simply because I would, I guess I regard the pro-choice as sort of current wisdom, and somebody who's pro-life obviously thinks for themselves. It's not an opinion you come at easily."

Despite his deep opposition to abortion, Johann would be more likely to vote pro-choice. "I'd say I want, I'd want to vote for somebody who would actually stand up for and keep to what they say. I think I'd be more apt to vote for a pro-choice than a pro-life. I don't feel it's up to the politicians. I believe it's up to the mother and the parents. And if the person's under eighteen then the consent from the parents."

Dave and Harry have not been participants in the election process. Harold, who does vote, is not influenced by his anti-abortion opinions. In Harold's opinion, "politicians who are pro-life are trying to buy votes, and therefore it's a false statement on their part." Harold voted for Bill Clinton in 1992 because of his own concerns for Social Security and also "I think [Bush] was too old to be there, and I think Dole is too old to be there. Let the young men get in there. Here's Dole, he's been in Congress now, what? thirty, forty years? He's set in his ways, he ain't gonna change the country. And Reagan was a B-rated actor and he didn't change the country any, he put it in debt."

These interviewees express disdain for the pro-choice movement and pro-choice activists. Suzanne finds pro-choice arguments to be overly simplistic.

I just find it repulsive to be that simplistic and only talk about women's rights without any regard for what it does to society as a whole. What you and I talked about earlier, the whole attitude toward children and child abuse. I don't go around throwing tin cans and bottles wherever I please, because that does something to the environment. I don't use sprays that take away the ozone layer. I try to make informed choices that will be good for the planet and everybody on it. And I think of abortion, you can't simplistically just look at this particular woman now, in whatever situation she's in, and what she chooses to do. In everything else, we try to say how will what I do now impact the rest of society. Why is abortion different? I just find that very disgusting.

Dave feels that pro-choice advocates are endorsing abortion because they promote the view that having children is sometimes "inconvenient" and they tend to forget that while women are allowed to do what they want with their bodies, "[women are] neglecting to remember that it's not just their body anymore; they're sharing their body with another once the child is conceived." Carolyn says that if there's any doubt as to when the child becomes a person, "Why take a chance?"

Leo perceives the pro-choice agenda and activists as "very evil." He believes they have misconstrued the intent of the pro-life agendas.

For the pro-abortionists to say that the anti-abortionists are against choice is an absurdity. Except no one sees it. It's been very clever. This person is pro-abortion, this person is anti-abortion. This person is pro-choice? Well what damn fool is anti-choice? How clever, though, to say that these people are against our choices to abort. Therefore they're against every choice concerning everything in existence. It's very clever, very insidious, and very evil. That's a lie!

Warren expresses disapproval of pro-choice activism based on his observation of a demonstration in Dayton, Ohio, while visiting his son at Wright-Patterson Air Force Base in the early 1990s.

It was an abortion protest in front of an abortion mill in Dayton, Ohio. And I was amazed that on this side of the street was the people against abortion. Some were priests, nuns, ministers, and they were kneeling on the street praying. On that side of the street were the people for abortion and between you and I, they were throwing stones, tomatoes, rotten eggs at the anti-abortion people, and spitting on them. Kicking them. That really bothered me. And one of the things about it was the police were standing there looking on. I saw a priest get spit on, right in the kisser, and there was a cop standing there with his arms folded. Now here, let me tell you what else about it. The groups that were shouting and hollering were two feminist organizations and I think I saw, there were signs NOW, NARAL, those groups. And gays. There were gay people there. Homosexuals for abortion. I thought to myself, isn't that strange. Why would homosexuals worry about that? And to be truthful, I still don't know. And then again, reading some of the literature, there's no question about it. The feminists and homosexuals are in the pro-choice camp with both feet. One I understand, at least partly. The other I still don't have any idea. However, I left that event. Oh, one other thing happened. As the thing was in progress, a flatbed truck came by, and there was a guy standing on the back of the truck and he said, "The media is covering an event in Cincinnati. Let's go. . . . I want to convene the rally." And the pro-choice forces left en masse. And the pro-life people stayed there praying, and when the pro-choice people left, they didn't change anything at all. I shouldn't have said, I maybe misconstrued it. A great number of the pro-choice forces left. They responded to this clarion call to go to Cincinnati where the media was, apparently doing something. I don't know what it was. I never did find out. So after having witnessed that also, and thinking about my own thoughts on the subject, I became more knowledgeable and more vigorous in the pro-life camp.

The interviewees express veneration for pro-life activists, except for the violent actions of (in Carolyn's words) "a few" extreme activists. Carolyn sees the vast majority of pro-life activists as "peaceful and prayerful."

I have friends who have protested. But, I think the screaming wild people that are presented are in the minority, and I think that's unfortunate that that's the image that's presented on our national news. The people that I know who have gone to protest in Jackson, are soft-spoken, sweet, caring Christian people who would no more scream at a girl, "You're killing your baby," nor hit her . . . they're not that kind of people, they're there peacefully prayerfully. . . . If they can give out a piece of literature that tells her what she's doing, they'll give it to her, if they can talk to her and tell her what her other choices are, they'll say, "Let me tell you what your other choices are" so that they're not screaming at people.

None of these interviewees express wholehearted support for Paul Hill or other activists whose efforts to stop abortion have resulted in murder. Carolyn, however, comes the closest to supporting Hill.

Personally, do I have any kind of understanding or compassion for Paul Hill? Yes, I think I do. I think he was probably so frustrated with the fact that for years and years we tried to change the laws and have done almost no good at all. Paul Hill was frontline. He stood outside of clinics where babies were being murdered, day in day out day in day out. Thank God He did not call me to do that. That's all I can say, Thank God I was not called to do that. Had He called me, I like to think I would have [gone]."

Carolyn understands the logic and passion behind Paul Hill's actions. "I've heard his logic and I really can't refute it and that bothers me." She also says that part of her understands his "justifiable homicide" argument. "But, could I do it? No. I don't think so." As a result of this violence, Carolyn sees the pro-life movement splitting to a small degree between the "extremists" and those who want to stop abortion through legal channels. However, she predicts that the movement will remain strong and vocal for many years to come, despite the negative images resulting from the actions of a few extremists. Carolyn hopes that Hill will not be executed. Suzanne shares this hope with Carolyn, because "the guy sounds insane to me. So [he should receive] some sort of psychiatric treatment and I guess when somebody's gone off the deep end enough to kill somebody else, I'd be inclined to lock them up and throw away the key, but I don't think I would be inclined toward the death penalty."

With the exception of Johann, the men in this group feel that Paul Hill should be executed because, in Harold's words, "man has to live by the law, there's no way man can live without law." Enoch declares, "It doesn't make sense to kill somebody over [the abortion] issue." Dave thinks that Hill should be executed "because he had the choice to take that doctor's life; no one put a gun in his hand, no one drove him to the clinic, no one made him wait for the doctor to come, and no one told him to pull the trigger." In Dave's opinion, "the woman is the final deciding factor; if the woman does not go to this doctor to have an abortion, he can't kill her child." Therefore, Dave says, Hill should have been trying harder to talk to the women who were seeking abortions. Rebel says that "even though [Dr. Britton] was killing a defenseless child, the law should have been able to handle that type of situation. The law could handle it."

Warren considers the possibility that Hill was insane at the time of the murders. "He's off in outer space! I didn't follow the Hill case carefully but my suspicion is that these people are half-cooked. The law controls activities in that and if he violates the law, he deserves the death penalty, if he was in full control of himself, and he's not a mental case." Warren goes on to say that "now, it's up to society to change the law to make the commission of murder punishable in some way or another, and that murder to include abortion."

Leo recognizes the authority of the law, but says that the judge who would not allow Hill to use the justifiable homicide defense was wrong.

[Hill] does have the right to give his reasons, motives, why he did this. He does have the right to explain himself to the jury, number one, may be merciful. And number two, because the jury might agree with him and overturn the law. The jury could come back and say "innocent" even after the law had been proposed, and in a sense say, we're not accepting the application of this law in this case. The jury can. However, no one has the right to take the law into their own hands. There's a conundrum there. Does he have the right, if this is a human being, to defend the life of this [unborn] human being? The answer to that question is yes. The problem is, there's a law that prohibits it, constituted by rightful authority. One perhaps ought to just let [the law] alone. God allows it for whatever reasons. Maybe we ought to allow it. St. Thomas Aquinas has a beautiful argument, "Why do tyrants rule?" You see, a tyrant may be a duly constituted authority. It may be a king that's duly appointed, a monarch that lapsed into a tyrant. But people who have usurped the throne, who do not have a right to rule, they can be overturned. But St. Thomas says that perhaps one of the reasons that good men should bear the assaults of tyrants is so that their reward in heaven will be greater and the tyrant's punishment in hell will be all the more. These things are left to God. So, even though [Hill] broke the law, the law should never have been in existence. No one has the right to make a law that will allow abortion! No one has the right to have an abortion! No one can take that right upon them. Lies! When you give somebody a false right, that's a lie, isn't it?

Warren voices a common perception of welfare recipiency among these interviewees.

I was watching Bill Moyers on channel 10 here one time, and he was getting down to the welfare system in this country. There was this black man in New York that had seven kids by three different women. And they were just, they showed the scene where he was in the delivery room with this last one, and Bill Moyers asked him how he was going to take care of them kids. And he says, "Well, when I get a good paying job," and everything else. Now there's a guy that should have had his tubes tied after the second one, and them girls too. Because there's seven kids that really don't have no father and they ain't going to have no mother, because [they're] going to be on welfare. You see what I'm saying? It's welfare now. Because the father is not taking care of them. And there was also one girl on there that had seven kids by different fathers. How can society keep accepting that? You can't. And not because they're black. I don't mean because they're black. They would, it'd be the same if they were white. But how can society keep accepting that? You can't.

Enoch considers the issue in religious terms. "[The Bible] says that man who does not work shouldn't eat." Dave is angry because the "general concept is that if a girl gets pregnant and she's thirteen, fourteen, fifteen, sixteen, she does not have to worry about it because the government will help her pay for that child. If they're adult enough to make it, then they're adult enough to take the responsibility of raising it." Johann is bothered by the current state of welfare recipiency because "it's a burden" to society and "people who really need it should have it." Rebel expresses his concern also.

> One thing that bothers me is women that go out and continuously have kids with no fathers. And sometimes they refer to that as welfare, the more kids you've got the more money you've got, and I can't see that. I can't. If a woman has had two children out of wedlock, she shouldn't have any more. Why should we have to pay for the children that are coming up like that? Do I sound crazy to you? Welfare is fine. There are people out there that need it. But there again, don't have six kids just to have the extra money coming in. Don't, I'm not in favor of foreigners coming into this country and staying here a year and they're entitled to more welfare for instance than my brother is. My brother's handicapped. He's twelve years older than I am. He lives by himself. Mom left the house to me when Mom passed away eight years ago and I've taken care of my brother. I went and tried to get him food stamps. "Oh yeah, he can have food stamps. Twenty dollars' worth." I'm sitting there going, "Damn, lady, he's only on Social Security." Excuse me for cussing. Occasionally it happens. I don't cuss as much as I did before I got saved. Every other word was a cuss word. Cussed bad like a sailor.

These interviewees hold essentialist views of women and girls. Carolyn refers to the clients at the Crisis Pregnancy Center as "girls," regardless of their ages. Most of her clients are in fact young women. Carolyn says, "The clients I've seen down here, and there've been thousands since we began, of the girls that I've seen and talked to that have had abortions, I've seen very few that don't have regrets, and some of those regrets are severe. You know, physical problems associated with it are a whole different issue. . . . Occasionally, an abortion will be botched so badly that a girl will have to have an hysterectomy."

Dave implies that it is the woman's responsibility to provide contraceptive measures and prevent pregnancy. He talks about a high school classmate: "Everyone knew that she was sexually active. The point I'm making is, is not that she was sexually active but that she was reckless with it." Rebel feels that it is natural for men to look at "pretty" women, but that women should not dress in ways that make men look.

I walk into WalMart and see a lady with a T-shirt with no bra on. For a second there, depending on her looks, your brain clicks in. That's natural for a man. That's like my dad was telling my mom one day, when dad was looking at a very attractive young lady, she said, well, I forgot what my mom said, but anyway, Daddy said, "Honey, there's nothing wrong with looking at young ladies. God made them pretty. It's just like a fisherman. Fishermen love fishing ponds. He looks at all the fishing ponds he sees. But he knows which one he's legally licensed to fish in." And so, that makes a point. Knowing, there's nothing wrong with looking at ladies. I hate to see them lower, to me they're lowering themselves down to nothing. First thing to waltz in your mind, "That gal's easy to pick up."

Harold talks about a "mother's instinct" to protect her children. "They'll face a charging elephant to protect their kids where a father might try to get out of the way, but a woman wouldn't. That's the way I see it, I don't understand women." As a result of this "instinct," Harold believes, the vast majority of women will feel guilty for having an abortion. As mentioned earlier, Warren believes that pregnant women are incapable of thinking rationally about the pregnancy and they are "not in full possession of the mental faculties," due to the hormonal changes occurring.

Suzanne expresses her view that women have biological urges towards reproduction.

> I don't know whether it's because of some sort of deep-rooted thing in the human psyche or whether it's programming from society at large, that kind of thing. I really don't know. I suspect on a biological basis that the human race wouldn't be here right now if we [women] didn't have some pretty deep-rooted biological urges toward reproducing ourselves. And I suspect that having an abortion goes against those instincts.

During pregnancy, Suzanne says, "I think you're very suggestible either way. I'm not degrading women by saying they're more suggestible than normal, any sort of crisis makes people more suggestible." Therefore, Suzanne feels, decisions made during pregnancy must be considered very carefully.

Death Penalty Opinions

Many interviewees say that they support capital punishment simply because they "believe in it." Believing in the death penalty, for these interviewees, involves having faith that it accomplishes certain important goals. This "belief" in the death penalty includes the convictions that capital punishment is a deterrent to violent crime, that it is less costly than incarcerating someone for life, that it is morally supported by the Bible, and that executions demonstrate the value of human life. Although these interviewees are concerned about making sure that all executed individuals are "completely guilty," they are willing to tolerate a level of error in executions. These interviewees are much less detailed in their death penalty opinions than in their abortion opinions. Therefore, this section of the chapter may seem lopsided when compared with the wealth of opinions on abortion.

Support for the death penalty ranges from Carolyn's statement "I'm struggling with the death penalty, but I think there are some crimes that are so heinous that it's best to just execute them" to Rebel's impassioned advocacy: "I'll throw the switch, I'll inject the needle, I'll pull the trigger. It doesn't matter. I'm a firm believer in capital punishment, now go ahead and trick me up on some other question!"

Carolyn expresses her struggle with the death penalty.

> I have been in favor of the death penalty. Based on Biblical standpoint, my struggle with it comes from people who say, "How can you be pro-life and support the killing, the taking of another person's life?" To me, the distinction is that in abortion you're talking about an innocent human life, a baby that has not done anything wrong, and in capital punishment, theoretically, you're speaking of a person that has murdered, which is taking another person's life, which as far as I'm concerned is as serious a thing as you can do. Let me tell you the problem I have with it . . . that person's spiritual state. That once you end that life you might end any chance of redemption that that person has. If they have not made a commitment or conversion then or whatever . . . I think some people that said this while in jail, they all of a sudden are converted, and to me, if a person truly has done that, I think that person would be the first one to step up and say, "I committed that crime, yes, I will accept the penalty that is imposed on me." They may not like it, but a person who had a true conversion would be willing, would understand, and would be willing to suffer that penalty. But, that probably would be one of the little icky situations for me.

Enoch explains his support of the death penalty in Biblical terms, saying that in "Genesis 9: 6 it says whosoever sheds man's blood, by man shall his blood be shed." He also cites passages from Exodus and Deuteronomy in which the Mosaic laws are being enumerated, 613 minute directives covering dietary and sexual laws of proper behavior and the variety of punishments for such violations. Because "the Bible says that the person who does these things should be killed,"

Enoch supports the death penalty for murder, abortion, and homosexuality. A passage of scripture that many death penalty opponents use to claim the moral rightness of opposing executions is John 8: 3–11, in which Jesus intervenes to stop the stoning of a woman who has committed adultery. Enoch does not think this story implies that Jesus was opposed to the death penalty, because "his position would be the same as God's, it would have to be that he was for the death penalty." Instead, Enoch suggests, Jesus might have been stopping the crowd from stoning her because he was displeased with their "pride or arrogance in stoning her."

Dave became convinced that the death penalty is justified while attending a Catholic high school in Alabama in the early 1980s. In sixth grade, he participated in Scared Straight, a program designed to frighten youth away from criminal activity. He says the "Catholic school decided that 'we can't control you guys after you leave here, so we'll just give you a little incentive to walk a chalk line.'" Dave and his classmates went to the state penitentiary and met death row inmates, including John Evans, who was executed in 1983 (Canan 1989). Dave describes meeting Evans.

> He had religion before. He was raised in a religious family. And he had been talking to a priest the whole time he was in prison. And I believe that he was truly sorry for his sins. He had accepted, by the time we got to meet him, he had accepted that this was what the government said was going to happen to him, because he had killed an innocent man. He had the choice of letting that man live or die. And this was what the government said was his punishment. The electric chair malfunctioned and he was electrocuted three times before he died. And when I met him, and he, like I said, he had accepted it, and basically what he was telling us was, "Don't screw up, kids. I did a bad thing and this is what I've got to pay for. This is what I give in return for me doing what I did, and that is my life. If you don't want to end up here with a shaved head and shaved legs, watch what you do." And it is those people that are reasonable and have the ability of choice that should be held accountable for it. If you didn't have people being held accountable for killing someone, why hold someone accountable for stealing something or destroying public property? You'd have anarchy.

Dave limits his support of capital punishment to those who commit premeditated murder. Rebel, on the other hand, would like to see the death penalty extended to include any violent crime committed with a firearm, including drive-by shootings. He admires "foreign countries [where] you only steal three times. The first time you steal you lose a hand. The second time you steal you lose the other hand. The third time you steal you have to steal by your mouth, so they cut your head off. What's that now? Three strikes and you're out? OK." Rebel thinks that executions should be broadcast on television and possibly held publicly. "I've been told that years back they used to hang them up on the square [in town], and to me, that would be a pretty good deterrent, and showing it on TV, I don't see anything wrong with it." The only problem Rebel has with the death penalty is that people are "waiting too long to [be] execute[d] and there are too many appeals."

Harold does not like the modern methods of execution because he feels they are not painful enough. He explains how he would like to see executions carried out.

> You know how they produce gizzards as delicacies? They cage the birds in this cement box and force feed them until they die in their own waste. I saw that on TV one time and thought that's a pretty awful way to go and immediately thought that would be a good way to execute criminals. They need to feel pain, the way they're killed now, they don't know what suffering is, they don't know what pain is. So, this would make sure they feel pain. After all, think of the pain their victims must have felt.

Warren refers to the "Willie" Horton case as a description of what he considers a heinous crime worthy of the death penalty.

> Willie Horton was let out of prison in Massachusetts on a weekend pass by then-Governor Dukakis. He stole a car, drove to New Jersey, was low on gas, pulled into a gas station late at night. Walked in, and there was a man and his wife at the gas pumps. Told the guy to fill up the tank. Pulled out a gun, tied up the husband, cut his penis off, sat him against the wall, and while he lay bleeding to death, raped the woman. The man died, the woman was raped. Then shot the gas station attendant. Willie Horton deserves to swing. At the end of a rope. That's a heinous crime. But, there's damn few that actually swing, and our appeals process stretches for decades.

Taking the example from the 1988 Presidential campaign, Warren relies on the famous ad to explain what a heinous crime is. Unfortunately, the facts of the case are different from what Warren has recalled. Horton had been furloughed nine times previously and had safely returned back to prison on time after each furlough. This one time, in 1986, Horton was late returning from furlough and fled out of state. He was convicted of assault and rape in Maryland, not murder in New Jersey. The crime to which Warren refers was committed in 1974, for which

Horton was sentenced to life without parole. However, there was no evidence of mutilation of any victim (Feagin and Vera 1995, 114–121).

Harry attributes his support of the death penalty to his "oriental instinct," because "over in China there, they don't play games. If you're found guilty, then you're gone." Suzanne sees the death penalty as a human rights issue, and as a way to educate people. "Somebody who murders someone else has, at the most basic level, cut off that person's human rights, and at some point I think we need to say to people, if you take away human rights of other people, we're going to take away yours. There are consequences." She is "less focused on retribution, and all that stuff. I'm more interested in educating society as a whole. Other people, potential murderers out there, need to see there's a penalty."

Even though Leo does not think the death penalty is "effective" at reducing murder rates, he thinks "the state has within itself the right to put to death criminals." Leo would use the death penalty in all cases of murder, for "rape of women," and for "dope pushers."

Many of these interviewees rely on Scriptures to justify their support for capital punishment. Carolyn says simply, "God himself authorizes it." She finds scriptural support for capital punishment mostly in the Old Testament. Enoch's opinion is heavily influenced by Scriptures, while Dave and Rebel adhere to the philosophy of "an eye for an eye" in their support of the death penalty. Suzanne quotes Scripture, even though she says organized religion is "not my path," and suggests that murderers must "render unto Caesar that which is Caesar's."[4] To Suzanne, this means that the government has the rightful authority to take the lives of those individuals who have committed capital offenses because the convicted murderer no longer has the right to live. Rebel's reliance on Scripture is a bit spotty; he believes that God allows for the death penalty because of the Exodus of Jews from Egypt, when God caused the Pharaoh and his army to be swallowed up by the sea. "He let the water come back [on] them, and I'm going, isn't that great? That's fantastic, all those folks drowned in [that] water." For Rebel, this means that God authorizes killing those who are the enemies, including convicted murderers.

The risk of executing innocent people concerns this group of interviewees. Johann says that "an increasing amount of innocent people being executed would lead me to oppose the death penalty." But the others are willing to tolerate some level of error in capital sentencing. Dave believes that "Yes, a few innocents get caught up in that, and it bothers me that innocent people may be put to death. But, it's a risk worth taking, and wouldn't happen near as much if the legal system were more efficient." He points out that the appeals process is there to help those who are innocent prove they're innocent, "and I know a lot of times someone's going to fall through the cracks, it's the price you pay when you let people, human beings, start to play God." Rebel admits, "Sure, there are going to be people slipping through the system," but this is not a major problem for him.

Warren stresses that it is absolutely essential that the judicial system prove the defendant guilty before the execution takes place. "We must be absolutely, one-hundred-percent sure that they were the guilty party and they acted in full possession." But then he goes on to discuss cases of "supposedly innocent" people he has heard of.

> To be truthful with you, I've heard that challenge laid down before. Name me one person who was executed and was proven innocent. Not thirty years after the fact. And that challenge has never been met, to my knowledge. Now I have heard cases where the guy comes back ten years later and says "Aw, he didn't really do it. Charles did." If you can believe him any more than you did the first time. I don't consider that proof of innocence. That's just more horseshit.

The interviewees are more concerned with the guilty people who "get off on a technicality," as Warren puts it. He believes that "the people responsible for freeing [convicts], prison chiefs, psychiatrists should be held responsible for the crimes that are committed. If I free you and you murder the guy across the street, I should be tried for that murder."

A common misperception among these interviewees is that the death penalty is more cost-effective than imprisoning a convicted felon for life. Belief in cost-effectiveness has an impact on their support for the death penalty. Carolyn explains her reasoning: "There you've got them living a life, maybe not of comfort but they've certainly got to live which their victims weren't, and our tax dollars have to pay to keep them alive, so it's best to just execute them." Dave feels the same way. He says that "as far as put them away in prison for life, you have the problem of who's going to pay for him to live the high life for the next forty to fifty years." Keeping people in prison for life, in Harry's opinion, "is a waste of taxpayers' money, but I don't think they should be kept on death row that long, either." Suzanne is concerned about the "working poor who are paying very high taxes to keep people in [prison]."

Capital punishment is not a sufficiently important political issue to most of these interviewees for them to prioritize it in assessing a candidate's positions. Enoch, however, would disqualify a candidate who opposed the death penalty. Rebel also holds this view and says that rather than build more prisons, "because that's just more tax dollars," the government should use death penalties to reduce the prison population. Warren, who supported Pat Buchanan in the 1996 presidential primaries, comments on Buchanan's statement that if a woman is pregnant as the result of rape, "You should execute the rapist, not the unborn child."

> Well that's pretty close! The rapist is guilty of something anyway, the unborn child is not. I think he probably exaggerated. He thinks there should be a penalty against the rapist but not against the unborn child. And I would agree with that. I think he probably exaggerated when he used the word "execute." Rapists aren't executed in our society, under law. And I think Pat Buchanan knows that fully well. He was exaggerating those positions, but that position is one that I can relate to, yeah.

Many of the interviewees feel that politicians are corrupt and seeking personal gain, not policy change; therefore, voting is an exercise in futility. Harry, Dave, Harold, Suzanne, Johann, and Carolyn are not very interested in political candidates' positions on the death penalty.

Connecting Opinions on Abortion and the Death Penalty

The most common theme that brings these two moral issues together in the minds of this group of interviewees is the distinction between innocent life (the fetus) and guilty life (the convicted murderer). They feel that the fetus has the right to life and the murderer has sacrificed his or her right to life through violent actions. Related to this distinction is the underlying theme that those who are guilty must be punished. Carolyn states it this way:

> To me, the distinction is that in abortion you're talking about an innocent human life, a baby that has not done anything wrong, and in capital punishment, theoretically, you're speaking of a person that has murdered, which is taking another person's life, which as far as I'm concerned is as serious a thing as you can do . . . there, therefore has to be a serious penalty attached to it.

Dave believes that "anyone that would abort a baby is sentencing them to death, my personal belief is that abortion is the death penalty for someone who committed no crime. That's how I sleep at night knowing that I believe in the death penalty and am also against abortion. In my heart, abortion is killing innocent children that never had a chance or a choice whether they wanted to live or not, and the death penalty is putting to death people who have the choice to be there or not."

Warren includes the idea of punishment for the guilty. "The unborn is innocent of any crime and does not deserve the execution at the hands of society. And abortion is execution, make no mistake about it. The guilty party deserves censure, stricture, penalty, depending upon the crime committed."

Punitiveness, the desire for punishment, connects anti-abortion and pro-death penalty opinions in the sense that abortion is seen as the moral equivalent of murder, and murderers must be punished with the loss of life. Carolyn expresses the punitive mentality underlying these opinions.

> Since the murderer committed such a terrible crime, and we value the life of his victim so much, we're going to get the most costly and severe punishment we can in order to demonstrate how much we valued the life of that victim. So, the laws are there to protect law-abiding citizens, and to demonstrate how much we, as a society, value them. And, anti-abortion laws are necessary to protect innocent un-born babies, and capital punishment is necessary to protect good citizens from those who would commit horrible crimes.

Enoch places this punitiveness in the context of Scriptures. "In Isaiah 43: 7[5] it says that 'I created them for my glory,' so everyone is there to glorify God and those who don't are sent to hell." Abortion and murder do not glorify God, in Enoch's opinion, and that makes them both "condemnable sins."

Others use the more secular language of "accountability" to explain their opinions. Dave says that "if you don't have people being held accountable for killing someone, why hold someone accountable for stealing something or destroying public property? I think we all ought to be held accountable for our choices."

Rebel sees the problems of modern society as apocalyptic. "The world now is in worse shape than what it was in Sodom and Gomorrah's days, in my mind. They were doing the same things we're doing now; men with men, women with women, just sexual lust everywhere, what I understand, and that's the way we are now. And if [God] destroyed it then for what was going on, how much worse is it now than what it was then?"

Leo expands on this apocalyptic theme.

> You know, I hope I'm dead and gone when there comes a time to pay the tender his due, because all of us will be suffering for this because we've all remained silent. And you remember the famous saying, "Peace on earth, good will to men?" No, it's not. It's "Peace on earth to men of good will." The good will factor will get a lot of people into heaven. There'll be a lot of people who will never have seen God, never even known, never even have any conceptions that we have, but will be of

such good will that they will . . . "Peace on earth to men of good will." It's the good will factor. It's so important. And we have none of it.

Solutions

According to the people in this group, solutions to the problems surrounding the abortion and death penalty issues hinge on conversion to a God-centered world view, education, and increasing the penalties for offenders. Enoch describes a religious approach.

> This goes back to the 1500s when Descartes said "I think, therefore I am." He placed himself at the center of the universe, saying basically that everything revolves around me . . . so everybody's world view has changed to being man-centered. Everything focuses on the way man thinks, the way man does things, and man's concepts of right and wrong, his judgments and that kind of thing. . . . But, if you go back to uh, Adam and Eve, or before 1500 even before he said that . . . people viewed things not strictly from "God's" point of view, but that they were not the ones who were in . . . uh, everything did not revolve around them . . . and your question was, what's the solution? Changing the world view, back to a God-centered world view so that there is something, or I hesitate to say there's a power out there that's in control, that has a standard of judgment of right and wrong and that those are what you should live by. It should change the person's world view, because the conversion says "I believe that what God has said is true and therefore I will live according to these principles" and it's not the living according to the principles that makes a person righteous, but it's the believing that what God has said is true. So it doesn't necessarily come down to obedience and disobedience, it comes down to if you believe what God has said is true.

With this conversion to a God-centered world view, Enoch believes that people will enjoy the "fruits of the spirit," as outlined in Galatians 5: 22, 23.[6]

Although Rebel and his family are not regular church members, he believes that expanding Christianity throughout society would greatly improve the world because of the "good morals" it would produce. "If you have good morals built into the family, with mom and dad, the child should never stray from what's been taught. If my daughter does, she's going to get a whipping, in that situation." Dave comments on the importance of prayer in school. At the Catholic school he attended, "non-Catholics" were present, and "if they didn't want to pray they didn't have to, but the problem is we're living in a godless society anymore and without God, no one has a moral anchor."

Suzanne would not propose conversion to Christianity as a solution, but she would encourage people to make "higher moral choices" in their lives. "I would just make it mandatory, I guess, for people to stop and listen before they do certain things; in the case of abortion they should have to see the arguments on both sides. I would try to increase choice, not decrease it." For Suzanne, increasing "choice" means providing pregnant women with a more welcoming society for themselves and their babies. This way, abortion will not be seen as an option.

Better education on sexual behavior and contraceptive measures is offered as a feasible solution. Dave says, "I think there needs to be a college course on sex education morals and responsibilities." He compares the rate of teen pregnancy in the United States with the rate in Europe and credits sex education in European countries with reducing the rate of teen pregnancy. Harry takes this a step further by advocating classes on marriage and parenting for all engaged couples. In his opinion this would reduce the rate of divorce and promote domestic harmony, which would ensure that children are raised in stable homes and develop into moral adults who would not seek abortion or get involved in violent crime.

The interviewees also discuss increasing punishment in society and the number of people who would be punished. Rebel explains, "Knowing that if I do something wrong I am going to get penalized, so, why take that road? Why not take the road that mom and dad's been trying to teach me?" He suggests castration as a punishment for rape, and for drunk driving, "take their license away from them, then I would take their car away from them. The state ought to be allowed to do that."

Warren would expand the penalties and make prison conditions less habitable.

Jails. Toughen the laws. You apply them. Somebody commits a crime, he goes to jail. That's all there is to it. Jail has got to be a lot more miserable place than it is. I have no problem with tents in the sun. Doesn't bother me in the least. I have no problem with no TV. I think the food should be rotten. Maybe even rottener! Apparently [convicts] don't mind. If you don't fear the penalty, then every action is relative to you. So I think that society has to enforce and enforce rigorously, and it ought to be just horrible to go to jail. It really should. It should be something that you dread.

Among this group of interviewees there is a consistently punitive mentality toward those who violate the presumed natural order of life—traditional values, morals and behavior. Such a punitive mentality includes justifications based on Scriptures. In this group's opinion, the Bible clearly illustrates the many behaviors that deserve severe punishment such as murder, homosexuality, and abortion. Extending punishments would rebuild society and renew morality in the modern world, which these interviewees see as hopelessly lost and mired in sinful behavior. Improving the condition of the world, therefore, relies on extensive and severe punishments of the people whose behavior is sinful.

CHAPTER SEVEN

Analysis and Conclusions

As discussed in chapters 1 and 2, punitiveness appears to be a major link between people's opinions on abortion and capital punishment. Punitiveness is defined as the desire for punishment in circumstances where people are perceived to be violating a code of ethical behavior. The nature of punitiveness may vary among individuals, but one thing is steady: support for punishment as an appropriate response to offending behavior. In this chapter, I review my findings in the context of previous research on abortion and the death penalty, briefly outline the current empirical understanding of punitiveness, analyze the punitive attitudes among the respondents in this study, and offer some concluding comments.

Kristin Luker argued that the abortion debate in the late 1970s and early 1980s was "so passionate and hard-fought *because it is a referendum on the place and meaning of motherhood*" (1984, 193; emphasis in original). The argument stems from her examination of the "world views" of abortion activists' conception of the "proper" role for women as mothers. The anti-abortion world view involves a deep reverence for motherhood and a religious piety that supercedes all other obligation in women's lives. The pro-choice world view involves a deep commitment to gender equality and secular ambition to succeed in the male-dominated public arena. The women activists interviewed for Luker's study recounted their own life experiences in an attempt to fully explore their commitments to the cause of abortion. Based on these life experiences, Luker argues, that "they have made *life commitments that now limit their ability to change their minds*" (1984, 199; emphasis in original) for both the anti-abortion and pro-choice women. Essentially, her argument is that when these women made decisions to either have careers or become homemakers, they developed a rationale to justify their own choices. This inevitably included opinions about abortion legality to such a degree that women who chose careers developed a pro-choice identity and women who chose homemaking developed a pro-life identity. The political identity served to vindicate themselves for their lifestyle choices in a world that appears to be hostile to such choices among women. The pro-life homemakers felt marginalized and devalued in a world where women were being encouraged to "be like men." The pro-choice career women felt marginalized and devalued in the work world where women are penalized for not being like men.

Unfortunately, Luker's argument oversimplifies views regarding abortion. It is important to bear in mind the differences between the data Luker presents and the data presented in this book. First, Luker's sample was taken from women activists in the abortion movement, mostly in California. The sample for this book was taken from the general public, not necessarily activists and not limited to women, from Mississippi and Maine. Second, Luker's interviews focused on her interviewees' activism, while the data presented in this book focused on the structure of interviewees' opinions. In the data presented in this book, the opinions demonstrate that the pro-life view hinges on personal convictions about the sanctity of fetal life and the belief that abortion is equivalent to murder. While the pro-life interviewees in this book, especially those in chapter 6, expressed some concern about the role of motherhood, they were primarily concerned with the devaluation of human life.

Furthermore, the pro-life opinions expressed by my interviewees are not monolithic. There are divisions between the two groups of those identified as pro-life. The first group, pro-life and anti–death penalty, approached the issue based strictly on the sanctity of all human life. They are not necessarily opposed to women participating in the paid labor market and tend to be in favor of contraception. As Bob stated, "I'm pro-contraception, just don't start [a pregnancy], but after you do, don't kill that child." Louise, a Catholic woman, was in favor of available contraception recognizing that non-marital sexual intercourse is a reality of modern life. Only Glenn disagreed, feeling that the "contraceptive mentality" promoted a "culture of abortion." Also, this group believes that while abortion should be illegal, making it so involves some other problems, namely the dangers of illegal abortions. None in this group desire a return to the days when women obtained dangerous abortions in the back-alley; they prefer that social change occur to transform the minds and hearts of women who seek abortions and make abortion unthinkable. Most in this group are also willing to tolerate abortions in some very limited circumstances, such as rape, incest, severe fetal defect, and when the pregnancy endangers the pregnant woman's life.

In contrast, the pro-life and pro–death penalty group had another view of abortion. They prefer to see it as illegal in nearly all circumstances. The one exception these interviewees would make for abortion is when the pregnancy poses a serious threat to the woman's health, such as with ectopic pregnancies or a "malignant uterus," as Leo stated. In their minds abortion is the deliberate act of killing another human being and should be legally defined as murder, with a severe (perhaps capital) punishment for those who have or perform abortions. This theme of punitive condemnation is targeted at those who engage in "scurrilous" activities, such as abortion, and whose actions have undermined traditional social order. In the opinions of this group, motherhood is *the proper role* for women, and women who deliberately reject that role through abortion avert God's will and will suffer spiritual condemnation. So, for this group, abortion is not so much about the politics of motherhood, as Luker argues, but rather it is about the politics of God's will.

Neither are the pro-choice views monolithic. The pro-choice and anti–death penalty group is primarily concerned with personal privacy and interested in keeping the government out of personal decisions, such as abortion. In Madeline's words, the pro-choice anti–death penalty position is a matter of "jurisdiction" and how far the state will intervene in the private lives of citizens. Even though some in this group have personal qualms about abortion (it's "kind of an evil" in Sara's opinion), they are unwilling to permit the state to restrict decisions of personal autonomy such as reproductive choices. The pro-choice opinions expressed by this group include a reverence for motherhood balanced with their advocacy for women to participate in the public world of careers. Their reverence for motherhood is framed within the belief that only women who *desire* motherhood should have children, thus ensuring a better quality of life for their children. To them, *forcing* motherhood on women by restricting legal access to abortion services would be putting children in jeopardy of being poorly reared and possibly abused. Also, this group expressed concern that a loss of community has contributed to a social decay wherein politicians are debating how to limit welfare assistance to the poor. Pointing out the irony that the anti-abortion politicians are the very same legislators advocating for severe reductions in welfare spending, these interviewees see a rising mean-spiritedness targeted at those least powerful in society. It is precisely this mean-spiritedness that this group wants to change by allowing women to make their own reproductive choices while at the same time providing humane assistance to the marginalized and poor. They view their perspectives as a communitarian ethic, a human obligation to help—not harm or limit—others.

The pro-choice and pro–death penalty group shared different concerns about abortion. Rather than being primarily concerned about privacy, they are mostly concerned about the responsibilities of motherhood. They view motherhood as the most important obligation a woman can have and believe motherhood should be a choice. However, once a woman chooses to become a mother, this group believes there is a requirement to be financially self-sufficient. If a woman feels that she cannot take on the responsibilities involved with having a child, she should not be forced to have it, according to this group, because then the child will become a welfare dependent and a drain on their tax dollars. There is a deep resentment among this group towards people who abuse the welfare system. Such abuse may be in the form of "having more kids to get more money," as Johnnie said; "driving [new] cars and looking for a free Thanksgiving dinner," as Maria said; or "living on welfare for years without trying to get a job," as Rick said. Welfare abuse is seen as irresponsible for the children being brought into the world, and people must be held "accountable" for this irresponsibility. So, for this group, having an abortion is seen as the responsible decision in many circumstances.

Luker's argument that the abortion debate hinges on the conceptions of motherhood people hold is partly supported by the data presented in this book. The ideals of motherhood employed by the interviewees in my study are varied depending on which group they fit into. Curiously, examining death penalty opinions at the same time as abortion opinions has illuminated this diversity within pro-choice and pro-life beliefs. Therefore, the abortion debate appears to be a referendum on perceptions of fetal life, views of motherhood, and ideals about responsibility and punishment.

Faye Ginsburg argues that in "the pro-life view of the world, abortion destroys the bases of gender difference critical to biological, cultural, and social reproduction" (1989, 216) and that the pro-choice view equalizes such gender difference. Central to her thesis is that men share a specific type of responsibility for pregnancy and child-rearing depending on which perspective on abortion one adopts. In the pro-life perspective, "men are using abortion as a way out of their problems" (Jones, cited in Ginsburg 1989, 216). This is a theme echoed by the anti-abortion groups in this study, particularly among the pro-life and pro–death penalty interviewees. Dave and Rebel referred to abortion as a "quick fix" for both the men and women involved, but their views were that men could more easily "hit and run" (as Rebel expressed it) than women. Ultimately, for women, there is no escaping the biological reality of the womb, including abortion. Another view expressed by those in the pro-life and anti–death penalty group is that abortion does not allow women to escape their responsibilities; rather, it changes the nature of their responsibility. "They can either have a live child, or a dead child," according to Glenn. Either way, women bear the majority of the consequences for unplanned pregnancies. In this view, a man should be part of the decision-making process and, as Connor expressed, have "veto power" over the abortion. This would require honest communication between the two parties involved and thereby reduce the number of abortions. Allowing men to have such "control over the womb" (Ginsburg 1989, 213) further disenfranchises women's autonomy, removing the embryo from pregnant women's "jurisdiction" but providing it with a distinct existence apart from the womb in which it grows— thus leading to the "disembodiment of gender from the bodies that ultimately bear the consequences and contradictions" (Ginsburg 1989, 218) of the abortion debate.

The pro-life interviewees in this study would disagree with that analysis, however, because to them abortion is not about "control of the womb" so much as it is about "control of the baby." For most of them, the "baby" is the paramount concern, and protecting that life can only be accomplished by denying women the right to choose abortion in the vast majority of situations. Casting the dilemma in the context of the "womb" literally disembodies the life of the fetus. So, the fault lines are drawn: while pro-choice people remain focused on the womb and pro-life people insist that the focus must be on the fetus, the debate over abortion remains at an impasse.

Fifteen years ago, Ellsworth and Ross published a classic study in death penalty opinion in which they described how death penalty opinions are based on emotions, beliefs and values rather than facts (1983). Central to their research was data demonstrating that even without evidence of a deterrent effect in capital punishment, supporters would continue to favor the death penalty. The most widely endorsed view among their pro–death penalty respondents was that "society benefits" when murderers are executed. Another significant theme among the death penalty supporters was their belief that "society has a right to get revenge" for the murders committed (Ellsworth and Ross 1983, 151), referring to this as the retribution motive. The death penalty opponents, however, strongly endorsed the view that it is "immoral for society to take a life regardless of the crime the individual has committed" (Ellsworth and Ross 1983, 154). There was little indication that respondents in their study were well-informed on the factual issues related to capital punishment in the United States. The evidence led them to conclude that "people's attitudes about the death penalty are emotionally powerful and immediate, and that their rational explanations are derivations from, rather than sources of, these attitudes" (Ellsworth and Ross 1983, 155). In reviewing the research that had been published since the 1983 study, Ellsworth and Gross (1994) further illuminated that death penalty opinions remain fundamentally emotional, not rational. "Most people care a great deal about the death penalty but know little about it, and have no particular desire to know. This is not surprising, as their attitudes are not based on knowledge" (Ellsworth and Gross 1994, 40).

Other research has examined the relationship between factual knowledge of the death penalty and attitudes toward it (Bohm 1991, Bohm and Vogel 1994) and found that the "Marshall Hypothesis" is not supported. Justice Thurgood Marshall predicted that as people became more aware of the facts related to capital punishment, they would reject it (Bohm 1991). Clearly, the facts as Marshall identified them are on the side of death penalty opponents in that capital punishment serves no discernible deterrent effect, remains racially biased and arbitrary, and is exceptionally costly, as has been demonstrated by scholarly investigations (Ellsworth and Ross 1983, Ellsworth and Gross 1994). However, the research findings on factual knowledge and relation to death penalty opinions have been mixed (McGarrell and Sandys 1996).

The interviewees in this present study confirm and expand this empirical understanding of death penalty opinions. With respect to factual knowledge about the death penalty, the foes of capital punishment were generally more well-informed than the supporters. However, distinctions must be made regarding each group of death penalty opponents. The pro-choice and anti–death penalty interviewees oppose capital punishment because they see it as a poorly implemented state policy that has led to racial bias and error. While they understand the emotional desire for revenge (recall Madeline's statement about the child-murderer), they also believe that society (and therefore the government) should rise above such "barbaric" practices and emotions. This group also felt that one of the purposes of the government is to protect citizens, not to kill citizens, including convicted murderers. Another purpose of government is to alleviate the suffering of the economically marginalized through better social services and social programs; as Felicia declared, she is an "underdog rooter." Finally, their anti–death penalty opinions were founded on the belief that the world is already harsh enough without adding more brutality (i.e., the death penalty) to society.

The pro-life and anti–death penalty group, however, had a different set of values associated with their opposition to capital punishment. Those interviewees oppose the death penalty because they value the sanctity of life and believe that it is morally wrong to deliberately end human life. They are less concerned with the "facts" of the death penalty indicating error or racial bias; as Glenn stated, the reality of innocent people being sentenced to death does not influence his opposition to capital punishment. He and the others oppose even a "flawless" system of death sentencing. The factual problems are further justifications for their established opposition to death sentencing. The sanctity of life is among their most preciously guarded values, and they attribute many contemporary social ills (abortion, teen pregnancy, wars, and harsher welfare policies) to the abdication of this value. Following their religious convictions, this group is living intentionally for God's will as they perceive it—to be able to "meet my maker," as Connor stated. Their religious faith has profound influence on their opinions.

The death penalty proponents in my study illuminate an interesting distinction between retribution and vengeance that must be examined in light of their abortion opinions as well. Kenneth Haas (1994) described at length the dissimilarities between retribution and vengeance. Until recently, most death penalty scholars have collapsed the two concepts into one broad category of "retributive justice" and thus obscured their differences. Retributive justice has typically been seen as the punishment being proportionate and equivalent to the offense committed, and that a murderer ought to pay with his or her own life for the life that was taken. Haas explains that our "modern retributive theory calls for a system of objectively fair punishments that are proportional, not identical, to the offense committed" (1994, 132). Therefore, retribution involves a fairness and proportionality in sentencing. Vengeance, on the other hand, is an "unmeasured infliction of punishment on the offender" in retaliation at the behest of the victim or victim's survivors. Paraphrasing Emile Durkheim, Haas states that "the public's passion for vengeance is an extraordinarily powerful force and it will probably always play a major role in the punishment of criminals" (1994, 133). Therefore, Haas observes that public officials "understand that the greatest political rewards accrue to those who master the rhetoric of vengeance" (1994, 136).

In this study, the pro-choice and pro-death penalty interviewees lean more toward the retributive motive for supporting capital punishment, whereas the pro-life death penalty supporters lean more toward the vengeance motive. The pro-choice death penalty supporters adhere to the retributive value that death is a just punishment for heinous crimes. Some in this group, such as Autumn, are willing to extend the death penalty to crimes they see as heinous (drunk driving fatalities, drug sellers who "deal in death," etc.). Others simply leave the death penalty to the worst murderers, but not all murderers. Associated with this desire for proportional sentencing is a recognition that the criminal justice system is unfairly prosecuting some, unduly releasing others, and not sentencing harshly enough still more. Courtney advocates "castration" for rapists, but not death. A sense of fairness pervades this group's death penalty support, as it does the remainder of their opinions, but once the boundaries of responsibility have been violated the punishment deserved should be swift, harsh and certain. The factual issues of capital punishment do not sway their opinions. This group is not terribly concerned about the fairness to convicted criminals but is passionately concerned about the rights of victims and the well-being of those who survive violent crime. In fact, Rick said that he would prefer to see a few innocent people "fall through the cracks" in order to punish more of the guilty who "mostly get off on a technicality in the current system." Even though this might violate his sense of fairness, Rick sees it as necessary to ensure just and proportional punishments for the guilty.

The pro-life death penalty supporters, however, share vengeful motives in their advocacy of death penalties. In their opinions the offender deserves the death penalty because of what he or she did to the victim[s]. Viewing the fetus as a victim of "premeditated murder" leads many in this group to advocate extending the death penalty to abortion. They desire to see offenders punished severely as a means of retaliation for the assault leveled against individuals. The death penalty should be extended to offenses other than murder, such as rape. Clearly, this is beyond the proportionality desired by the previous group. Influencing this quest for vengeance are the religious beliefs of the interviewees in this group. Enoch suggests that he would favor the death penalty for homosexuality because he sees it as a grave assault against God's will. Most in this group adhere to a conservative interpretation of the Bible and believe that God has granted men dominion over women, the earth, and other life forms. Part of that dominion includes the authority to sentence offenders to death for egregious offenses. This group is not swayed by the factual knowledge of capital punishment and in many cases deliberately dismissed such knowledge if it challenged their established opinions. Warren, when asked about the risk of executing innocents, said he's heard that "challenge laid down before" but the exculpatory evidence has never been sufficient to convince him of innocence in any high profile cases, preferring to dismiss them as "just more horseshit."

This "plurality of ignorance" (McGarrell and Sandys 1996) leads pro-life death penalty supporters to search out information to confirm their opinions rather than allow information to sway their opinions. Such a state of pluralistic ignorance also cripples the communication process regarding the death penalty; the media bias toward coverage of the most brutal violent crime fuels the passion for retribution and vengeance and adds fodder to the generalized disdain toward people whose views differ. Because the majority of the public at least tacitly supports capital punishment and the politicians continue to rely on simplistic polling results that demonstrate this support, the future of a reasoned dialogue on capital punishment is seriously in jeopardy.

Garland's Cultural Theory of Punishment

In *Punishment and Modern Society: A Study in Social Theory*, David Garland offers a comprehensive review of theories used to explain legal sanctions in modern western societies. In analyzing these theories, he suggests that not enough theoretical attention has been given to the cultural forces giving rise to penal institutions, but significant scholarship has examined the structural forces of penality. His book reviews the cultural roots of punishment. Garland refers to culture as:

> all those conceptions and values, categories and distinctions, frameworks of ideas and systems of belief which human beings use to construe their world and render it orderly and meaningful. It thus covers a whole range of mental phenomena, high and low, elaborated and inarticulate, so that philosophies, sciences and theologies are included alongside traditional cosmologies, *folk prejudices and 'plain common sense'* (emphasis added). (1990, 195)

"Folk prejudices and 'plain common sense'" become what Garland refers to as *mentalities* and *sensibilities* about punishment. Garland defines punitive mentalities as "ways of thinking" about punishment and punitive sensibilities as "ways of feeling" about punishment, arguing that they are very closely linked to each other because punishment can be both a utilitarian and an emotional activity. Mentalities and sensibilities of punishment are largely influenced by our cultural frameworks of understanding the world around us, particularly religious traditions (see Garland 1990, 193–211). If we subscribe to fundamentalist religious beliefs, we are more likely to think and feel that certain behaviors are sins against God (divorce, abortion, single parenting, homosexuality, etc.) and also to believe that God ought to punish those who engage in such activities (Falwell 1981) and punish societies as a whole for allowing such activities to occur.

According to Garland, punishment, punitive mentalities, and punitive sensibilities are forces that reproduce and possibly expand our cultural notions of the "other" (i.e., criminals, murderers, sinners, headstrong children, etc.), against whom images of goodness and normality are established (see Garland 1990, 249–276 for complete discussion). Punitive mentalities and sensibilities obtain their power from a culture that condemns certain acts. Punishment is a powerful form of social control that serves at once to correct the misbehavior of the individual, save him or her from continued misfortune, and communicate to others that such misbehavior is unacceptable.

Defining Punishment

Garland defines punishment as "a legal process whereby violators of the criminal law are condemned and sanctioned in accordance with specific legal categories and procedures" (1990, 17). However, I refer to punishment as a social process whereby violators of the social contract or moral order are made to experience physical, social, psychological, or economic pain or deprivation in accordance with specific social categories and procedures. This definition includes non-violent punishment as well as corporal and capital punishment. Punishment is one means by which boundaries of appropriate behavior are reinforced (Erikson 1966), and one means of excluding offenders from mainstream society, either through legal channels or informal social channels. A key element in my definition of punishment is that offenders are treated in accordance with specific social categories. Women are punished based on the cultural framework of what it means to be feminine, and minorities are punished based on the cultural perceptions of their specific ethnic categories (see Garland 1990, 193–203).

Garland (1990) suggests that the understanding of punishment must be extended to look past the actual sanctions toward the cultural forces that impel such sanctions. He identifies religion as one of the formative social institutions that has an important impact on the use of punishment. Even though we live in an increasingly secular society, he argues, the residual effects of religious tradition become manifest in the modern moral order in terms of the mentalities of justice (1990, 203–209). Garland argues that punitiveness is a mentality that provides cultural, emotional, and rational support to acts of punishment. Certain religious beliefs (e.g. fundamentalist, as discussed by Marty and Appleby 1991) are important justifications for specific forms of punishment, and these justifications take shape in punitive attitudes. Punishment's strength lies in the broad cultural support for the punitive reaction to perceived transgressions in society.

Theory of Punitiveness

Punitiveness arises, in part, from a belief in and reliance upon authoritarian values in several spheres of life (Adorno et al. 1982). It is a dual-faceted phenomenon with cultural foundations in the Judeo-Christian tradition.

Legal Punitiveness

Since Blackstone's early examination of the foundations of law, sociologists have suggested that by enacting laws, the government encodes the dominant values of the society and makes them enforceable through the authority of the state (Ranulf 1938). In advanced democratic societies the law and the state become the mediators of disputes between people, and the judges when violations of the moral/legal code have occurred. When norms and values are encoded into law, the state retains the right to punish violators on behalf of the citizens. In most democratic societies, citizens want the state to punish offenders on their behalf, at least to some extent.

Punishment is a form of communication in society. The meaning attached to this style of communication is complicated and dramatic. Punishment varies based on the perceived offense, suspected offender, and context of the offense. The collective outrage and anger that some people feel regarding deviance and criminals is transferred into a call for action. The punishment is intended to communicate dissatisfaction, not from individuals within the societal structure— the jury, the judge, the prosecutor—but from the society as a whole. In this way, punishment becomes exemplary; the punished person is made an example to the rest of the society as to just how strictly certain laws will be enforced. Theoretically, this results in the specific deterrence of the offending individual, as well as the general deterrence of the rest of the population (Gibbs 1978).

In order for this message to be effectively communicated in a democratic system, the messengers must tailor it to the popular feelings of the general public. As Tocqueville commented more than a hundred and fifty years ago, Americans are a practical people who like to know that there is more of a purpose to an action than a singular impact (Heffner 1984). Punitive communication is camouflaged under the guise of a desire for security in life. A deeper examination reveals the foundation of resentment that is the emotional basis of punishment (Garland 1990, 62). Law and utilitarian justifications clothe this resentment and hostility in a robe of noble goals. Resentment is a terribly powerful emotional force that moves people to do something about the immoralities they perceive.

Extra-Legal Punitiveness

This facet of punitiveness involves overlapping social forces, such as religion and notions of family authority. Lambert, Triandis, and Wolf (1959) show that cultures with aggressive and malevolent deities are more likely to use punitive measures in child discipline. In the western tradition, religious punitiveness entails two basic features: punishment in the name of God and punishment by God. In the Old Testament, parents (especially fathers) are imbued with divine authority to act in the name of God and to punish their errant children. As children are required to honor their parents, the devout are mandated to honor God above all others. Failure to do so invokes the wrath of God. Regarding punishment for idol worship, the Second Commandment reads:

> You must not bow down to them in worship; for I, the Lord your God, am a jealous God, punishing the children for the sins of the parents to the third and fourth generation of those who reject me. (Exodus 20: 4–5: Revised English Version)

When the Hebraic law is revealed to Moses by God, punitiveness is apparent as the justification for which death must be the punishment:

Whoever strikes another man and kills him must be put to death (Exodus 21: 12). Whoever strikes his father or mother must be put to death. Whoever kidnaps an Israelite must be put to death. Whoever reviles his father or mother must be put to death (Exodus 21: 15–17). When, in the course of brawl, a man knocks against a pregnant woman so that she has a miscarriage but suffers no further injury, the offender must pay whatever fine the woman's husband demands after assessment. But where injury ensues, you are to give life for life, eye for eye, tooth for tooth, hand for hand, burn for burn, bruise for bruise, wound for wound. (Exodus 21: 22–25)

God declares that if anyone mistreats a widow or a fatherless child and then appeals to God, "My anger will be roused and I shall kill you with the sword" (Exodus 22: 24). Such scriptural passages have been interpreted to mean that God will allow other people to act on His behalf and punish wrongdoers by death, and that He will also mete out this punishment Himself. Fundamentalist Christians understand this to be a mandate for the death penalty and other forms of punishment in modern society (Falwell 1981; Ammerman 1987; Greven 1990).

The Old Testament[1] is often used to justify corporal punishment of children by parents. Greven offers a list of scriptural references that are cited to support the use of "the rod" in rearing children (1990, 48). The common colloquialism "spare the rod and spoil the child" does not appear in the Bible, but is taken by some people as a basic point of proper religious parenting (Greven 1990). Straus (1994) reports the percentage of children who are corporally punished by their parents: more than 90 percent of children between the ages of two and six, 52 percent of thirteen-year-olds, and 30 percent of sixteen-year-olds. Corporal punishment of children is not only justified but also mandated, according to biblical literalists (Ellison and Sherkat 1993; Grasmick et al. 1992; Grasmick and McGill 1994; Ellis and Petersen 1992; Straus 1994).

Previous Research on Punitiveness

Sociologists and social psychologists have examined the issue of punitiveness for decades. Research by Adorno et al. (1950 [1982]) in the 1940s examines the many components of the Authoritarian Personality. In considering such attitudinal dispositions of authoritarians as anti-Semitism and ethnocentrism, Adorno and his colleagues found that punitiveness and aggressiveness are two of the consequences of authoritarianism. The scales constructed for measuring authoritarian attitudes include several punitive items (see Adorno et al. 1982, 105–108).

The research by Adorno et al. showed that high scorers on the ethnocentrism and anti-Semitism scales tended to see the world in dualistic terms. They saw themselves as members of the "Ingroup," and saw Jews, minorities, and women as part of the "Outgroup." They felt it necessary for the boundaries between Ingroup and Outgroup to be rigidly maintained so as to preserve the social order. High scorers were hostile toward members of the Outgroup and favored taking action to subdue them. High scorers also tended to support the dominance of Christianity as the only legitimate religion upon which state laws should be based. They tended to view God in Old Testament "hell-fire and brimstone" terms.

"[A]uthoritarian aggression [has] to do with the moral aspects of life—with standards of conduct, with the authorities who enforce these standards, with offenders against them who deserve to be punished" (Adorno et al. 1950 [1982], 162–163). Adorno and his colleagues (1950) were interested in the psychological foundations of prejudice that grew to genocidal proportions during the 1940s in Nazi Germany. In the preface to the abridged edition of *The Authoritarian Personality*, Levinson and Sanford observe that the "decade of the 1980s is in some ways similar to that of the 1940s, and the phenomena of authoritarianism may again urgently invite study, understanding and social action" (1982, v).

Eysenck's research also focused on authoritarian and punitive attitudes as correlates of political positions. The inventory of social attitudes employed in his research contained several punitive statements that respondents were asked to approve or disapprove (1954, 122–123). Using factor analysis,[2] Eysenck found two factors: factor 1 was typically liberal, or tender-minded, and factor 2 was typically conservative, or tough-minded, punitive, and characterized by the beliefs that

> compulsory religious education is desirable, that the Japanese are cruel by nature, that we should go back to religion, that Jews are too powerful in [America], that flogging should be retained as a deterrent, that war is inherent in human nature, that conscientious objectors are traitors, that birth control should be made illegal, and that coloured people are inferior. (1954, 127)

Plotting these views on two dimensions illustrates the connection between conservatism and punitiveness. The two dimensions used by Eysenck are tender- to tough-mindedness and radical to conservative political views. The findings reveal that tough-minded conservatives are more punitive toward criminals and tender-minded conservatives are more concerned with religious issues. Tough-minded and punitive parenting, most likely found among the conservative respondents, resulted in prejudiced children (Eysenck 1954). Conservative and tough-minded parents tended to agree that being strict with their children was good, that children should always be obedient and grateful, that parents should not show affection toward each other in front of their children, and that parents should heed the maxim "Spare the rod and spoil the child" (1954, 194). Radical and tender-minded parents disagreed with the previous statements. Tough-mindedness was significantly correlated with aggression and dominance.

As previously discussed, religion is one of the key correlates of the desire to punish wrongdoers. Some researchers used religious items when measuring punitiveness. Ellison and Sherkat (1993) and Cook et al. (1992) used a General Social Survey statement to measure punitive attitudes: "Those who violate God's rules must be punished." This is strongly worded in that it states violators *must* be punished, not *should* be punished. As such, it taps into rigid punitiveness. More than 60 percent of GSS respondents either agreed or strongly agreed with this statement. Many other contemporary scholars have documented the close relationship between conservative religious beliefs and punitiveness (Grasmick et al. 1992; Grasmick and McGill 1994; Cohn, Barkan and Halteman 1991; Straus et al. 1980; Straus 1991, 1992, 1994; Wilson and Brazendale 1973; Dorman 1976; Sidanius et al. 1983, 1987; Ray and Ray 1982; Ray 1985; Raden 1981; Wanner and Caputo 1987; D'Anjou et al. 1978).

Punitiveness Among the Interviewees

Among participants in this study, opinions about abortion and capital punishment were strongly influenced by the desire, or lack of desire, for punishment. Therefore, the analysis presented here focuses on punitiveness among the different groups of participants. These interviewees are predominantly interested in improving the conditions of the world, and their perspectives on punishment reflect their views of how best to achieve this goal.

PRO-CHOICE AND ANTI–DEATH PENALTY. The pro-choice and anti–death penalty interviewees voice their concern that the government should not have the authority to punish women and doctors for having or performing abortions, nor should it have the authority to execute citizens. In a very real sense, then, these interviewees are "anti-punitive," as Emma declares.

> Punishment? I don't know, it seems to me that punishment simply breaks the spirit, and then what do you have? And talking about punishment and discipline, and I think that punishment has to do with control.

This anti-punitiveness is reflected in convictions that the current legal system is unfair to ethnic minorities and women. These interviewees fear that illegal abortion and expanded capital punishment will result in greater discrimination against women and minorities. They also fear that the propensity for partisan agendas will result in politically motivated "witch hunts" against any group of people who disagree with the conservative right.

Also supporting this anti-punitive stance is a deep concern for the under-privileged. As Felicia says, "Maybe I'm an underdog rooter." By putting them-selves in the shoes of those who are subjected to anti-abortion and pro−death penalty laws, these interviewees believe that civil rights are violated. The law, they feel, ought to be used to extend and protect civil rights, not to expand the punitive authority of the state. As Leigh says, the government should not be allowed to "judge people so harshly" simply because those people are "different" from the lawmakers, the majority of whom are white males.

Religion plays a relatively minor role in the formation of anti-punitive atti-tudes. Mildred, Felicia, Wayne, Leigh, and Sara all view God as "loving and compassionate," not judgmental and punitive. This image of God emerges from reading the New Testament, where Jesus represents unconditional love and ac-ceptance of God, and rejecting the Old Testament "eye for an eye" standard. Felicia summarizes: "My friends who say they're for capital punishment, they'll say 'an eye for an eye.' I don't believe that. If you steal my purse I'm not going to steal your purse. Two wrongs don't make a right."

PRO-CHOICE AND PRO−DEATH PENALTY. Interviewees in the pro-choice and pro−death penalty group have mixed feelings about punishment. They be-lieve that women should have the freedom to choose abortion as a legal option. On the other hand, they think that people must be held accountable for their decisions to have children. That accountability needs to be enforced through punishment, according to most in this group. This punitive mentality is espe-cially apparent in views about welfare recipiency and criminals. Johnnie and Rick are harsh in their condemnation of single mothers on welfare. Johnnie refers to them as "whores" with "bastard children," and Rick says they should be "taken outside and shot." Their resentment and subsequent punitiveness is fueled by their perception that their "tax dollars" are used to support "the opposite" of what their moral beliefs dictate. Maria, Courtney and Autumn express a similar pu-nitive mentality but make a distinction between those who need welfare assis-tance and those who exploit it. All of the interviewees in this group see those who exploit the welfare system as "out of control" and in need of punitive sanc-tions to hold them accountable for their actions.

Of course, supporting the death penalty is an indication of punitive mentali-ties among the pro-choice and pro−death penalty group. As discussed in chap-ter 4, this group's support for capital punishment is largely justified by a retribu-tive philosophy. Underlying this support for expanded capital punishment is a deep resentment that convicted criminals who are incarcerated "live better" than the interviewees do themselves. As Rick says: "This easy life these criminals have, it's easy in the court system, and it's easy for these criminals to get off because of these liberal loopholes." Courtney has the same complaint.

> [A convicted criminal eats] better than I do, he has an opportunity to have a better education than I do. I can't afford to be in school right now. No figment government [program] out there is going to pay for anything I have or want. And I know I could do a hell of a lot with it if somebody would give it to me. But that's not going to happen unless I shoot somebody. Maybe they'll give it to me then. And that makes me so mad I want to get up and pace around. It just makes me so mad I can't stand it.

The punitive mentality confirms these interviewees' desire to "hold people accountable" for their actions. They feel that such accountability can best be accomplished through punishment of those whose behavior is deemed irresponsible, such as single mothers on welfare, rapists, drunk drivers, murderers, child abusers, etc. Therefore, people should have the freedom of choice when it comes to abortion but should be aware that they will be held accountable for their choices if they fail to fulfill their obligations.

With the exception of Rick and Johnnie, religion is not a foundation of the interviewees' punitive mentalities. Maria, Autumn, and Courtney place importance on their religious beliefs but are not terribly active in their faith. Johnnie believes that God will punish all those who violate His laws, and counts herself as "God's own." Rick believes that God will hold people accountable by Divine punishment. He says, "It all comes down to a Supreme Being, and His Son died for our sins, and if you have faith and believe in Him, and you fear the wrath of the Heavenly Father and try to play by the rules, it'll all work out, hopefully."

PRO-LIFE AND ANTI-DEATH PENALTY. Within the anti-abortion and anti-death penalty group there is a rejection of punitiveness influenced by religious beliefs. For instance, Jeanie says that punishment is "for God to decide, it's not for me to decide." However, these interviewees talk about "consequences" of human behavior and moral choices. In reference to abortion, those consequences include physical danger, psychological trauma, and depression.

The non-punitive mentality of this group is reflected in a deep sense of connection as a human family. Louise and Connor are most articulate in expressing this. Louise criticizes the dualistic mentality so prevalent in contemporary society, preferring to see humans as "all in this boat together." Connor expresses his rejection of punitiveness by reminding himself that "we're a family" and that we need to rely on each other and be connected to each other from the moment of conception to natural death.

Another feature of this non-punitive mentality is the realization that changing the law to make abortion illegal is not going to stop abortion. Allowing for legal punishment, then, will not change the "unfortunate fact that 1.5 million women desire to end their own children's lives annually," as Glenn comments. What is required, according to these interviewees, is cultural change, which would allow people's "hearts and minds" to reject killing in every form.

The interviewees' non-punitive mentality is based on the idea that God is loving and forgiving, but at the same time holds people to certain rules of conduct. These rules of conduct might be better enforced through the laws of modern society, but ultimately the punishment for breaches of the rules must remain in God's hands. It is not for other humans to decide how any individual will be held accountable because only God knows the secrets of all people's hearts.

PRO-LIFE AND PRO–DEATH PENALTY. The interviewees in the anti-abortion and pro–death penalty group express the most highly punitive mentality among all the interviewees in this study. Their punitiveness stems from their conviction that abortion is murder and that all murderers should be severely punished, and preferably executed. Eight of the ten interviewees in this group believe that abortion should be illegal and punishable. Suzanne and Johann think that there is a spiritual penalty for having an abortion, but are not sure what the legal system ought to do. The others in this group, however, are convinced that some form of punishment is necessary for doctors who perform abortions, and perhaps for the women who have abortions. Suggested punishments range from short prison sentences to executions.

The emotions that fuel this punitive mentality regarding abortion are deeply rooted anger at the legal system that permits this "holocaust," at the people who profit from it, and at the women who seek it. Among this group of interviewees, the passion of their convictions is greatest; interviewees in the other groups are accepting of the fact that there are people who honestly disagree with them. However, in the pro-life and pro–death penalty group, expression of other opinions is met with disdain and hostility, as evidenced by many of Leo's comments.

Support for capital punishment is a mechanism by which these interviewees declare themselves "different from" and "superior to" those individuals in society who are defying their strict moral code. Nearly all of these interviewees view the world in dualistic terms; behavior is either good or bad, people are either deviant or normal. There is very little room for gray areas in moral questions, as shown by the interviewees' lack of tolerance for abortion in such difficult situations as rape, incest, or fetal defect.

Religion plays a tremendously important role in formulating the punitive mentality within this group. Most interviewees rely on the Old Testament to support their desire for punishment, with an occasional reference to the New Testament. The members of this group feel that the laws of God handed to Moses and recorded in the book of Exodus provide strong support for punitiveness, as do the Levitical laws. The passage most often mentioned in this group is Exodus 21:25, the "eye for an eye" statement, which has become such an important feature of the contemporary punitive mentality that even those who reject or are distant from the Judeo-Christian tradition continue to rely on it in justifying their support for capital punishment.

Final Thoughts

At the time of this writing, four major events have just occurred: the twentieth anniversary of the first post-*Furman* execution, the twenty-fourth anniversary of *Roe v. Wade*, the inauguration of President Bill Clinton for a second term, and the national observance of Martin Luther King's birthday. The significance of the King holiday resonates in the memories of those who have fought for civil rights for more than three decades. The late Thurgood Marshall was a staunch opponent of capital punishment and believed it to be inhumane. His colleague William Brennan shared this view (Mello 1996). The current composition of the United States Supreme Court, however, approaches death penalty cases with the assumption that the constitutionality of capital punishment is a matter of settled law. The slim abortion rights majority, on the other hand, decides on the constitutionality of specific legal restrictions on access to abortion. The second Clinton administration is likely to face the task of replacing several justices on the Supreme Court in the next four years. Given that Clinton has based his political campaigns, at least in part, on abortion rights and support for capital punishment, it seems the status quo will hold, and the public will remain in bitter dispute over these issues well into the next century.

Notes

Introduction

1. The advertisement read: "Researcher seeks people to interview about abortion and the death penalty. Financial compensation is offered. Please call Dr. Cook at 324-7891."

Chapter One

1. Source: National Coalition to Abolish the Death Penalty, 918 F Street, NW, Suite 601, Washington, D.C. 20004, "NCADP Stat Sheet: 1996 Wrap Up," December 31, 1996.
2. At the time, NARAL was named the National Association for the Repeal of Abortion Laws (Epstein and Kobylka 1992, 150).
3. See the NARAL home page for Michelman's statement: http://www.naral.org/community/kate.html
4. *Gainesville Sun,* Judge Refuses to Postpone Abortion Trial, April 21, 1993, p. 4B.
5. *New York Times,* Death of a Doctor Refuels a Debate, March 13, 1993, p. 6.
6. See also *New York Times,* Doctor Is Slain During Protest Over Abortions, March 11, 1993, p. A1, where Burt is also quoted: "While Gunn's death is unfortunate, it's also true that quite a number of babies' lives will be saved."
7. *New York Times,* August 22, 1993, p. 29.
8. *New York Times,* July 30, 1994, p. A1.

9. *Cable News Network,* Morning News, November 29, 1996.

10. *Boston Globe,* Salvi Found Dead in Prison Cell, November 30, 1996, p. A1.

11. *Boston Globe,* Rambling Letters to Wounded Guard Speak of Threat to Caucasians, November 30, 1996, p. B5.

12. See also Beirne (1991, 1993) for a more contemporary reading of Beccaria.

13. The scriptures are Matthew 5: 38–39, "You have heard that it was said, 'an eye for an eye and a tooth for a tooth,' but I say to you do not resist an evildoer. But, if anyone strikes you on the right cheek, turn the other also"; and John 8: 4–7, "They said to him, 'teacher, this woman was caught in the very act of committing adultery. Now in the law Moses commanded us to stone such women, now what do you say?' They said this to test him, so that they might have some charge to bring against him. Jesus bent down and wrote with his finger on the ground. When they kept on questioning him he straightened up and said to them, 'Let anyone among you who is without sin be the first to throw a stone at her.'"

Chapter Two

1. *New York Times,* Archbishop of Boston Cites Abortion as "Critical" Issue, September 6, 1984, p. B13.

2. *New York Times,* Troublesome Abortion Issue: Theological Roots Are Spread Wide and Deep, September 8, 1984, p. 8. And *New York Times,* Cardinal Presses Fight on Abortion, September 28, 1984, p. A22.

3. *New York Times,* Women Scored Gains, Ferraro Says, November 8, 1984, p. A22.

4. *New York Times,* Rep. Ferraro Asks Bush For Debates in Fall Campaign, July 14, 1984, p. A1.

5. *New York Times,* Poll Shows Few Votes Changed by Abortion Issue, October 8, 1984, p. B8.

6. *New York Times,* Mandate Claimed, November 7, 1984, p. A1.

7. Ledewitz, Bruce S., Who Did In the Democrats? *New York Times,* November 8, 1984, p. A31.

8. *New York Times,* Bush Under Scrutiny: Lapses Recall Differences with Reagan, September 18, 1984, p. B7. See also: *New York Times,* Bush, in the South, Becomes Embroiled in Abortion Issue, September 12, 1984, p. B9; *New York Times,* Bush Says He Doesn't Remember 1980 Support of Aid for Abortion, September 13, 1984, p. B16; *New York Times,* Abortion Issue Threatens to Become Profoundly Divisive, October 14, 1984, p. E3.

9. *New York Times,* Economy the Key Issue, November 7, 1984, p. A1.

10. *New York Times,* Both Sides Spend in Abortion Fight, November 5, 1984, p. B19.

11. *New York Times,* 2 Groups List Candidates' Views on Abortion, June 4, 1987, p. A24.

12. *New York Times,* Republican Hopefuls Court Abortion Foes in Iowa, September 13, 1987, p. 34.

13. *New York Times,* Bush, In Iowa, Clarifies Stand on Legal Abortions, October 7, 1987, p. B9.

14. *New York Times,* Bush on Offensive Against Two Rivals, January 19, 1988, p. B6.

15. *New York Times,* Groundwork and Guesswork Mark the End of Iowa Caucus Campaign, February 8, 1988, p. A14.

16. *New York Times,* Bush Does an About-Face After Iowa, February 11, 1988, p. A32.

17. Peter Passell, The Economic Scene: The Implications of Iowa Results, *New York Times*, February 12, 1988, p. D2.

18. *New York Times*, Execution Backed in Drug Slaying: Bush Urges Swift Penalties, Citing Murder of Officer, April 14, 1988, p. D27.

19. *New York Times*, The Nation: Illegal Drugs Are an Issue No Politician Can Resist, May 22, 1988, p. 4.

20. *New York Times*, Republicans Seeking Broad Platform, August 8, 1988, p. B6.

21. *New York Times*, Republicans Seeking Broad Platform, August 8, 1988, p. B6 and *New York Times*, G.O.P. Stands Firm Against Abortion, August 11, 1988, p. D19.

22. *New York Times*, G.O.P. Adjusts Some Old Ideas to New Decade, August 10, 1988, p. A1.

23. Tom Wicker, Who Won, If at All? *New York Times*, February 11, 1988, p. A35.

24. *New York Times*, Transcript of the Speech by Dukakis Accepting the Nomination, July 22, 1988, p. A10.

25. *New York Times*, Dukakis Speech Marred by Clash Over Abortion: Protesters and Audience Scuffle in Illinois Visit, September 7, 1988, p. A28.

26. *New York Times*, In the South, Dukakis Faces an Uphill Climb, October 3, 1988, p. A23.

27. *New York Times*, Bush, in Michigan, Travels Two Roads on the Campaign Trail, October 20, 1988, p. B10.

28. *New York Times*, Foes Accuse Bush Campaign of Inflaming Racial Tension, October 24, 1988, p. A1.

29. *New York Times*, A 30-Second Ad on Crime, November 3, 1988, p. B20.

30. Estrich has published the book *Real Rape*, in which she discusses her experience as a rape survivor.

31. *New York Times*, Foes Accuse Bush Campaign of Inflaming Racial Tension, October 24, 1988, p. A1.

32. *New York Times*, Bush, His Disavowed Backers and a Very Potent Attack Ad, November 3, 1988, p. A1.

33. *New York Times*, Fired-Up Dukakis Again Asserts the Right of Choice on Abortion, November 1, 1988, p. A27.

34. *New York Times*, Debate transcript, September 26, 1988, p. A17.

35. *New York Times*, Editorial: Mr. Bush Thinks About Abortion, September 29, 1988, p. A26.

36. *New York Times*, Debate transcript, October 14, 1988, p. A14.

37. *New York Times*, Emotional Issues Are the 1988 Battleground, November 4, 1988, p. A1.

38. *New York Times*, Election Results, November 10, 1988, p. A1.

39. *New York Times*, The G.O.P. Advantage: Peace, Prosperity and a Disaffected South Were Among the Hurdles Faced by Dukakis, November 9, 1988, p. A1.

40. *New York Times*, Election Results: State by State, November 10, 1988, p. B10.

41. *New York Times*, Democratic Strength Shifts to West, November 13, 1988, p. A32.

42. *New York Times*, Bush Names Baker as Secretary of State, Hails 40-State Support . . . , November 10, 1988, p. A1.

43. *New York Times*, Reagan Administration Renews Assault on 1973 Abortion Ruling, November 11, 1988, p. A20.

44. *New York Times*, Abortion Foes See Momentum for Their Drive, November 14, 1988, p. B10.

45. *New York Times*, Abortion Foes Hail Gains in Reagan Era, December 24, 1988, p. A8.

46. *New York Times*, Iowans Caucus without Suspense, January 13, 1992, p. A13.

47. *New York Times*, Arkansas Execution Raises Questions on Governor's Politics, January 25, 1992, p. A8.

48. *New York Times*, Clinton Weighs Clemency for Killer Scheduled to Die, May 7, 1992, p. A24.

49. *New York Times*, Clinton Task: Making Message Heard, February 21, 1992, p. A14.

50. *New York Times*, Bush Considering Shift in Tactics to Fight Buchanan, February 20, 1992, p. A1.

51. *New York Times*, Republican Duel: A Party Wounded, February 29, 1992, p. A1.

52. *New York Times*, March Reflects the Growing Political Clout of a Movement, April 6, 1992, p. B8.

53. *New York Times*, A Way Out for Republicans on Abortion, April 23, 1992, p. A25.

54. *New York Times*, Abortion-Rights Positions Favored in Both Parties, June 3, 1992, p. A17.

55. *New York Times*, On Both Sides of Abortion, Protestors Gird for the Convention, July 7, 1992, p. B3.

56. *New York Times*, Abortion Foes See Pivotal Voting Role, June 13, 1992, p. A9.

57. *New York Times*, Quayle Attacks a "Cultural Elite," Saying It Mocks Nation's Values, June 10, 1992, p. A1.

58. *New York Times*, Quayle Insists Abortion Remarks Don't Signal Change in His View, July 24, 1992, p. A1.

59. *New York Times*, Bush, Asked in Personal Context, Takes a Softer Stand on Abortion, August 12, 1992, p. A1.

60. *New York Times*, New Angle in the Jabs at Clinton, August 25, 1992, p. A18.

61. *New York Times*, Savoring July's Euphoria, July 14, 1992, p. A1.

62. *New York Times*, Democratic Ticket Heads into Fertile Territory, July 19, 1992, p. 20.

63. *New York Times*, First Lady on Abortion: Not a Platform Issue, August 14, 1992, p. A1.

64. *New York Times*, Party Takes More Conservative Stance Than Bush, August 14, 1992, p. A16.

65. *New York Times*, G.O.P.'s Platform Reveals Conservatives' Dominance, August 15, 1992, p. A6.

66. *New York Times*, G.O.P. Avoids an Open Debate on Abortion, August 18, 1992, p. A10.

67. *New York Times*, "Family Values" and Women: Is G.O.P. a House Divided? August 21, 1992, p. A1.

68. Anthony Lewis, Merchants of Hate, *New York Times*, August 21, 1992, p. A25.

69. *New York Times*, Bush Pulls Close in Poll, but Not with Women, August 22, 1992, p. A1.

70. *New York Times*, Transcript of First TV Debate, October 12, 1992, p. A14.

71. *New York Times*, Excerpts from the Debate, October 14, 1992, p. A20.

72. *New York Times*, Transcript of 3d TV Debate, October 20, 1992, p. A20.

73. *New York Times*, The Year of the Yawn, November 3, 1996, sec. 4, p. 1.

74. *New York Times*, Now, This Message from Our Tormentor, March 17, 1996, sec. 4, p. 3.

75. *New York Times*, Polls Find Far Right Doesn't Define G.O.P. Vote, March 31, 1996, p. A24.

76. *New York Times*, California's Governor Joins G.O.P. Abortion-Plank Foes, April 30, 1996, p. A1.

77. *New York Times*, Dole Forces Lose Texas Delegates over Abortion, but a Senator Wins, June 23, 1996, p. A1.

78. *New York Times,* Dole's Daughter Favors Choice on Abortion, September 24, 1996, p. A20.

79. *New York Times,* Dole Sends Message of Inclusion to Abortion-Rights Republicans, July 22, 1996, p. A1.

80. *New York Times,* In Republican State, Dole Finds Himself Lagging Behind, August 8, 1996, p. B9.

81. *New York Times,* In Abortion War, High-Tech Arms, August 9, 1996, p. A20.

82. *New York Times,* Democrats' Left Wing Keeps Its Power Dry: Party Liberals Find L-Word Out of Style, August 24, 1996, p. A11.

83. *New York Times,* Excerpts from Platform Adopted at Democratic National Convention, August 28, 1996, p. A16.

84. *Christian Science Monitor,* GOP Abortion Foes Draw Battle Lines on One Procedure, June 28, 1995, p. 3.

85. Maggie Gallagher, Drawing the Line: Is there any choice, with regard to abortion, that is so shocking to conscience we cannot permit it to be made? *Atlanta Constitution,* June 27, 1995, p. A11; Douglas Johnson, Ban Partial-Birth Abortions, *Washington Post,* July 16, 1995, p. C7; *Los Angeles Times,* A Gruesome Piece of Legislation: The House—shown bloody photos—votes to outlaw a form of abortion, November 3, 1995, p. B8; Robin Abcarian, Lifesaving Option or Criminal Conduct? *Los Angeles Times,* November 26, 1995, p. E1; Allan Rosenfield, Congress Plays Doctor, *New York Times,* April 1, 1996, p. A17.

86. *Los Angeles Times,* Abortion Bill Reveals Fight for the Unconvinced, March 13, 1996, p. A1.

87. *New York Times,* Christian Coalition Offers Dole Both Cheers and Sharp Prodding, September 15, 1996, p. A38.

88. *New York Times,* Dole Gets Christian Coalition's Trust and Prodding, September 16, 1996, p. A1.

89. *New York Times,* House Approves Bill to Overturn Veto on Abortion, September 20, 1996, p. A1.

90. C. Everett Koop, Why Defend Partial-Birth Abortion? *New York Times,* September 26, 1996, p. A27.

91. *New York Times,* Uphold Abortion Veto, September 26, 1996, p. A26.

92. *New York Times,* Senate Fails to Override Veto of Ban on Type of Abortion, September 27, 1996, p. A20.

93. *New York Times,* U.S. Reports Drop in Rate of Births to Unwed Mothers, October 5, 1996, p. 1.

94. *New York Times,* Political Battle of the Sexes Is Sharper Than Ever, October 6, 1996, p. 1.

95. *Portland (Me.) Press Herald,* Police Group Endorses Clinton, September 16, 1996, p. 5A.

96. *New York Times,* A Large Drop in Violent Crime Is Reported, September 18, 1996, p. A14.

97. *Portland (Me.) Press Herald,* Polishing Crime-fighting Images, September 17, 1996, p. 2A.

98. *New York Times,* Dole Uses Clinton Health Plan to Portray Him as a Liberal, September 24, 1996, p. A20.

99. *New York Times,* Dole Carries Crime Theme to a Tent Jail, September 19, 1996, p. A19.

100. *New York Times,* Before Being Sentenced to Die, Child Killer Hurls Accusation, September 27, 1996, p. A16.

101. *New York Times,* Focus Shifts to Contests in the House, October 20, 1996, p. 1.

102. *New York Times,* Dole Camp Looks to Coming Debates as a Last Chance, October 6, 1996, p. 1.

103. *New York Times,* A Transcript of the First Televised Debate between Clinton and Dole, October 8, 1996, p. B8.

104. *New York Times,* On Volatile Social and Cultural Issues, Silence, October 9, 1996, p. A1.

105. *New York Times,* Dole Hints about a "Surprise" for Clinton at the Next Debate, October 10, 1996, p. B12.

106. *New York Times,* Excerpts from the Second Televised Debate between Clinton and Dole, October 18, 1996, p. A28.

107. *New York Times,* G.O.P. Leaders Doubtful that Dole Can Close Gap, October 20, 1996, p. 1.

108. *New York Times,* Excerpts from Debate Between Vice President Gore and Jack Kemp, October 11, 1996, p. A28.

109. *New York Times,* No Bark, No Bites. By Christopher Buckley, October 11, 1996, p. A39.

110. George Will, Kemp Misses Chance at Debate, *Portland (Me.) Press Herald,* October 14, 1996, p. 9A.

111. *New York Times,* Christian Coalition Mailing Prompts Apology to Blacks, October 12, 1996, p. 10.

112. *New York Times,* Campaigns Fail to Stir Passion among Voters, November 4, 1996, p. A1.

113. *New York Times,* Half the Electorate, Perhaps Satisfied or Bored, Sat Out Voting, November 7, 1996, p. B6.

114. *New York Times,* Portrait of the Electorate, November 10, 1996, p. 28.

115. *New York Times,* Christian Group Vows to Exert More Influence on the G.O.P., November 7, 1996, p. B8.

116. See Luker 1984; Cook, Jelen and Wilcox 1992; Arney and Trescher 1976; Chafetz and Ebaugh 1983; Claggett and Shafer 1991; Clayton and Tolone 1973; de Boer 1977; Davis 1980; Granberg 1978; Granberg and Granberg 1980; Huff and Scott 1975; Jelen 1988; Johnson and Tamney 1988; McCutcheon 1987; McIntosh and Alston 1977; Petchesky 1990; Scott 1989; Tamney et al. 1992.

117. There is very little evidence relating to those of non-Christian religious affiliation.

Chapter Three

1. A deist adheres to the "religion of reason," which Voltaire queried "Would it not be that which taught much morality and very little dogma? . . . and which dared not menace with eternal punishment anyone possessing common sense? Would it not be that which did not uphold its belief with executioners, and did not inundate the earth with blood on account of unintelligible sophism?" (Armstrong 1993, 310).

2. David Duke is a former Louisiana state legislator who founded the National Association for the Advancement of White People. Duke rose to national prominence in the early 1990s when he made an unsuccessful bid for the U.S. Senate.

Chapter Six

1. The Humanist Manifesto I, published in 1933, and the Humanist Manifesto II, published in 1973, discuss a variety of social issues and offer a declaration by secular humanists about the futility of religion. More information about the Humanist Manifesto is available on the internet at www.codesh.org/manifest i.html and www.codesh.org/manifest ii.html.

2. Deuteronomy 17: 14–20. "When you have come into the land that the Lord your God is giving you, and have taken possession of it and settled in it, and you say, 'I will set a king over me, like all the nations that are around me,' you may indeed set over you a king whom the Lord your God will choose. One of your own community you may set as king over you; you are not permitted to put a foreigner over you, who is not of your own community. Even so, he must not acquire many horses for himself, or return the people to Egypt in order to acquire more horses, since the Lord has said to you 'you must never return that way again.' And he must not acquire many wives for himself, or else his heart will turn away; also silver and gold he must not acquire in great quantity for himself. When he has taken the throne of his kingdom he shall have a copy of this law written for him in the presence of the Levitical priests. It shall remain with him and he shall read in it all the days of his life, so that he may learn to fear the Lord his God, diligently observing all the words of this law and these statutes, neither exalting himself above other members of the community nor turning aside from the commandment, either to the right or to the left, so that he and his descendants may reign long over his kingdom in Israel" (New Revised Standard Version).

3. 2nd Timothy 3: 16–17. "All scripture is inspired by God and is useful for teaching, for reproof, for correction, and for training in righteousness, so that everyone who belongs to God may be proficient, equipped for every good work" (New Revised Standard Version). Psalm 119: 7–10. "I will praise you with an upright heart, when I learn your righteous ordinances. I will observe your statutes; do not utterly forsake me. How can young people keep their way pure? By guarding it according to your word. With my whole heart I seek you, do not let me stray from your commandments" (New Revised Standard Version).

4. The actual quote is from the Gospel according to Matthew 22: 21. "Render therefore unto Caesar the things which are Caesar's: and unto God the things that are God's" (King James Version).

5. Isaiah 43: 7 reads, "Even every one that is called by my name: for I have created him for my glory, I have formed him, yea, I have made him" (King James Version).

6. Galatians 5: 22, 23 reads, "By contrast the fruit of the spirit is love, joy, peace, patience, kindness, generosity, faithfulness, gentleness and self-control. There is no law against such things" (New Revised Standard Version).

Chapter Seven

1. Greven asserts that many fundamentalist Christians prefer the laws and obligations of the Old Testament and disregard that "Jesus never advocated any such punishment. Nowhere in the New Testament does Jesus approve of the infliction of pain upon children by the

rod or any other such implement, nor is he ever reported to have recommended any kind of physical discipline of children to any parent" (51).

2. Factor analysis is a data reduction technique based on statistically identifying the "underlying dimensions that account for patterns of variations among the observed variables" (Hamilton 1992, 249). Reducing many variables, based on such patterns, into one or two variables provides the statistical analyst with a more parsimonious estimation of the phenomena being examined.

References

Abramowitz, Alan I. 1994. "Issue Evolution Reconsidered: Racial Attitudes and Partisanship in the U.S. Electorate." *American Journal of Political Science* 38:1–24.

———. 1995. "It's Abortion, Stupid: Policy Voting in the 1992 Presidential Election." *The Journal of Politics* 57:176–186.

Adorno, T. W., Else Frenkel-Brunswik, Daniel J. Levinson, and R. Nevitt Sanford. 1982 [1950]. *The Authoritarian Personality.* New York: W. W. Norton.

Aguirre, Adalberto, and David V. Baker. 1995. "Racial Prejudice and the Death Penalty." *Social Justice* 20:150–154.

Ammerman, Nancy T. 1987. *Bible Believers: Fundamentalists in the Modern World.* New Brunswick: Rutgers University Press.

Archer, Dane, and Rosemary Gartner. 1984. *Violence and Crime in a Cross-National Perspective.* New Haven: Yale University Press.

Armstrong, Karen. 1993. *A History of God: The 4,000 Year Quest of Judaism, Christianity and Islam.* New York: Alfred A. Knopf.

Arney, William Ray, and William H. Trescher. 1976. "Trends in Attitudes Toward Abortion, 1972–1975." *Family Planning Perspectives* 8:117–124.

Austin, William. 1979. "The Concept of Desert and Its Influence on Simulated Decision Makers' Sentencing Decisions." *Law and Human Behavior* 3:163–187.

Baldus, David C., George G. Woodworth, and Charles A. Pulaski, Jr. 1990. *Equal Justice and the Death Penalty: A Legal and Empirical Analysis.* Boston: Northeastern University Press.

Ball-Rokeach, S. J., Gerard J. Power, K. Kendall Guthrie, and H. Ross Waring. 1990. "Value-Framing Abortion in the United States: An Application of Media System Dependency Theory." *International Journal of Public Opinion Research* 2:249–273.

Bedau, Hugo A. 1975. "Physical Interventions to Alter Behavior in a Punitive Environment: Some Moral Reflections on New Technology." *American Behavioral Scientist* 18:657–678.

———. 1982. *The Death Penalty in America.* 3d ed. New York: Oxford University Press.

Beirne, Piers. 1991. "Inventing Criminology: The 'Science of Man' in Cesare Beccaria's *Dei Delitte e delle Pene* (1764)." *Criminology* 29:777–820.

———. 1993. *Inventing Criminology: Essays on the Rise of* Homo Criminalis. Albany: State University of New York Press.

Berger, Peter L. 1963. *Invitation to Sociology: A Humanistic Perspective.* Garden City, N.Y.: Anchor Books.

Berns, Walter. 1982. "The Morality of Anger." In *The Death Penalty in America,* 3d ed., edited by Hugo Adam Bedau. New York: Oxford University Press.

Bishop, George F., Robert W. Oldenick, and Alfred J. Tuchfarber. 1985. "The Importance of Replicating a Failure to Replicate: Order Effects on Abortion Items." *Public Opinion Quarterly* 49:105–114.

Blanchard, Dallas. 1994. *The Anti-Abortion Movement and the Rise of the Religious Right: From Polite to Fiery Protest.* New York: Twayne Publishers.

Blanchard, Dallas, and Terry Prewitt. 1993. *Religious Violence and Abortion: The Gideon Project.* Gainesville: University of Florida Press.

Bohm, Robert. 1991. "American Death Penalty Opinion, 1936–1986: A Critical Examination of the Gallup Polls." In *The Death Penalty in America: Current Research,* edited by Robert M. Bohm. Cincinnati: Anderson.

———. 1992. "Toward an Understanding of Death Penalty Opinion Change in the United States: The Pivotal Years, 1966 and 1976." *Humanity and Society* 16:524–542.

Bohm, Robert, Louise Clark, and Adrian Aveni. 1991. "Knowledge and Death Penalty Opinion: A Test of the Marshall Hypotheses." *Journal of Research in Crime and Delinquency* 28:360–387.

Bohm, Robert, and Ronald Vogel. 1994. "A Comparison of Facts Associated with Uninformed and Informed Death Penalty Opinions." *Journal of Criminal Justice* 22:125–143.

Bowers, William J. 1974. *Executions in America.* Lexington, Mass.: D. C. Heath.

Bowers, William J., and Glenn L. Pierce. 1975. "The Illusion of Deterrence in Isaac Erlich's Research on Capital Punishment." *Yale Law Journal* 85:187–208.

———. 1980. "Deterrence or Brutalization: What Is the Effect of Executions?" *Crime and Delinquency* 26:453–484.

Bowers, William J., and Margaret Vandiver. 1991. "Executive Summary of a Nebraska State Survey Conducted April 26–28, 1991." Unpublished manuscript. Boston: Northeastern University.

Breslau, Naomi. 1987. "Abortion of Defective Fetuses: Attitudes of Mothers of Congenitally Impaired Children." *Journal of Marriage and the Family* 49:839–845.

Bynum, Victoria. 1992. *Unruly Women: The Politics of Social and Sexual Control in the Old South.* Chapel Hill: University of North Carolina Press.

Canan, Russell. 1989. "Burning at the Wire: The Execution of John Evans." in *Facing the Death Penalty: Essay on a Cruel and Unusual Punishment,* edited by Michael L. Radelet. Philadelphia: Temple University Press.

Caringella-MacDonald, Susan. 1990. "State Crises and the Crackdown on Crime Under Reagan." *Contemporary Crises* 14:91–118.

Chafetz, Janet Saltzman, and Helen Rose Fuchs Ebaugh. 1983. "Growing Conservatism in the

United States? An Examination of Trends in Political Opinion between 1972 and 1980." *Sociological Perspectives* 26:275–297.

Chilman, Catherine S. 1988. "The Background of the Present Abortion Controversy." *Affilia* 3:41–54.

Claggett, William J. M., and Byron E. Shafer. 1991. "Life and Death as Public Policy: Capital Punishment and Abortion in American Political Opinion." *International Journal of Public Opinion Research* 3:32–52.

Clayton, Richard R., and William L. Tolone. 1973. "Religiosity and Attitudes Toward Induced Abortion: An Elaboration of the Relationship." *Sociological Analysis* 34:26–39.

Cochran, John K., Mitchell B. Chamlin, and Mark Seth. 1994. "Deterrence or Brutalization? An Impact Assessment of Oklahoma's Return to Capital Punishment." *Criminology* 32:107–134.

Cohn, Steven F., Steven E. Barkan, and William A. Halteman. 1991. "Punitive Attitudes Toward Criminals: Racial Consensus or Racial Conflict?" *Social Problems* 38:287–296.

Cole, George F. 1995. *The American System of Criminal Justice.* 7th ed. Belmont, Calif.: Wadsworth.

Colomy, Paul. 1988. "Donald R. Cressey: A Personal and Intellectual Remembrance." *Crime and Delinquency* 34:242–262.

Combs, Michael W., and John C. Comer. 1982. "Race and Capital Punishment: A Longitudinal Analysis." *Phylon* 43:350–359.

Conger, Rand D., Robert L. Burgess, and Carol Barrett. 1979. "Child Abuse Related to Life Change and Perceptions of Illness: Some Preliminary Findings." *The Family Coordinator* 28:73–78.

Cook, Elizabeth A., Ted G. Jelen, and Clyde Wilcox. 1992. *Between Two Absolutes: Public Opinion and the Politics of Abortion.* Boulder: Westview Press.

Cook, Kimberly J. 1993. "Pro-Death Politics: Debunking the 'Pro-Life' Agenda." In *Political Crime in Contemporary America: A Critical Approach,* edited by Kenneth D. Tunnell. New York: Garland Press.

———. forthcoming. "A Passion for Punishment: Abortion Opponents Who Favor the Death Penalty." *Justice Quarterly.*

Cooper, David D. 1974. *The Lesson of the Scaffold.* Athens: Ohio University Press.

Correia, Edward O. 1991. "The Uneasy Case for a National Law on Abortion." *American Prospect* 5:84–90.

D'Anjou, L. M., C. Cozijn, L. V. D. Toorn, and C. M. R. Verkoeyen. 1978. "Demanding More Severe Punishment: Outline of a Theory." *British Journal of Criminology* 18:326–347.

Davis, James A. 1980. "Conservative Weather in a Liberalizing Climate: Change in Selected NORC General Social Survey Items, 1972–78." *Social Forces* 58:1129–1156.

Davis, James A., and Tom W. Smith. 1991. *The General Social Surveys 1972–1991: Cumulative Codebook.* Chicago: National Opinion Research Center.

———. 1992. *The N.O.R.C. General Social Survey: A User's Guide.* Newbury Park, Calif.: Sage.

Davis, Nanette. 1985. *From Crime to Choice: The Transformation of Abortion in America.* Westport, Conn.: Greenwood Press.

Davis, Susan E. 1988. *Women under Attack: Victories, Backlash and the Fight for Reproductive Freedom,* study supported by the Committee for Abortion Rights and Against Sterilization Abuse, Boston: South End Press.

de Boer, Connie. 1977. "The Polls: Abortion." *Public Opinion Quarterly* 41:553–564.

de Parrie, Paul. 1993. "Situational Outrage." *Life Advocate*. May: 43.

Dorman, James E. 1976. "ROTC Cadet Attitudes: A Product of Socialization or Self-Selection?" *Journal of Political and Military Sociology* 4:203–216.

Durham, Alexis, H. Preston Elrod, and Patrick T. Kinkade. 1996. "Public Support for the Death Penalty: Beyond Gallup." *Justice Quarterly* 13:705–736.

Ebaugh, Helen Rose Fuchs, and C. Allen Haney. 1985. "Abortion Attitudes in the United States: Continuities and Discontinuities." In *Perspectives on Abortion*, edited by Paul Sachdev. Metuchen, N.J.: Scarecrow Press.

Ellis, Godfrey J., and Larry R. Petersen. 1992. "Socialization Values and Parental Control Techniques: A Cross-Cultural Analysis of Child Rearing." *Journal of Comparative Family Studies* 23:39–54.

Ellison, Christopher G., and Darren E. Sherkat. 1993. "Conservative Protestantism and Support for Corporal Punishment." *American Sociological Review* 58:131–144.

Ellsworth, Phoebe C., and Samuel R. Gross. 1994. "Hardening of the Attitudes: American's Views on the Death Penalty." *Journal of Social Issues* 50:19–52.

Ellsworth, Phoebe C., and Lee Ross. 1983. "Public Opinion and Capital Punishment: A Close Examination of the Views of Abolitionists and Retentionists." *Crime and Delinquency* 29:116–169.

Epstein, Lee, and Joseph F. Kobylka. 1992. *The Supreme Court and Legal Change: Abortion and the Death Penalty*. Chapel Hill: University of North Carolina Press.

Erikson, Kai T. 1966. *Wayward Puritans: A Study in the Sociology of Deviance*. New York: Macmillan.

Erlich, Isaac. 1975. "The Deterrent Effect of Capital Punishment: A Question of Life and Death." *American Economic Review* 65:397–417.

Espy, Watt. 1980. "The Death Penalty in America: What the Record Shows." *Christianity and Crisis* 23:191–95.

———. 1988. "Facing the Death Penalty." In *Facing the Death Penalty*, edited by Michael L. Radelet. Philadelphia: Temple University Press.

Estrich, Susan. 1987. *Real Rape*. Cambridge, Mass.: Harvard University Press.

Eysenck, H. J. 1954. *The Psychology of Politics*. London: Routledge & Kegan Paul.

Faith, Karlene. 1993. *Unruly Women: The Politics of Confinement and Resistance*. Vancouver: Press Gang Publishers.

Falwell, Jerry. 1981. *The Fundamentalist Phenomenon: The Resurgence of Conservative Christianity*. New York: Doubleday.

Feagin, Joe R., and Hernan Vera. 1995. *White Racism: The Basics*. New York: Routledge.

Figuera-McDonough, Josefina. 1990. "Abortion: Ambiguous Criteria and Confusing Policies." *Affilia* 5:27–54.

Finch, Janet. 1984. "'It's Great to Have Someone to Talk to': The Ethics and Politics of Interviewing Women." In *Social Researching: Politics, Problems, Practice*, edited by Colin Bell and Helen Roberts. Boston: Routledge & Kegan Paul.

Foucault, Michel. 1979. *Discipline and Punish: The Birth of the Prison*. New York: Vintage Books.

Fox, James A., Michael L. Radelet, and Julie L. Bonsteel. 1990. "Death Penalty Opinion in the Post-*Furman* Years." *New York University Review of Law and Social Change* 18:499–528.

Gallup, George. 1986. "The Death Penalty: 7 in 10 Favor Death Penalty for Murder." *Gallup Report* 244 and 245, January/February: 10–16.

———. 1989. "Death Penalty: Public Support for Death Penalty Is Highest in Gallup Annals." *Gallup Report* 280, January: 27–29.

Garey, Margot. 1985. "The Cost of Taking a Life: Dollars and Sense of the Death Penalty." *University of California–Davis Law Review* 18:1221–1273.

Garland, David. 1985. *Punishment and Welfare: A History of Penal Strategies.* Brookfield, Vt.: Gower Publishing.

———. 1990. *Punishment and Modern Society: A Study in Social Theory.* Chicago: University of Chicago Press.

Gelles, Richard, and Murray A. Straus. 1976. "Family Experience and Public Support of the Death Penalty." In *Capital Punishment in the United States,* edited by Hugo Adam Bedau and Chester M. Pierce. New York: AMS Press.

Gibbs, Jack P. 1978. "The Death Penalty, Retribution and Penal Policy." *Journal of Criminal Law and Criminology* 69:291–299.

Ginsburg, Faye. 1989. *Contested Lives: The Abortion Debate in an American Community.* Berkeley, Calif.: University of California Press.

Glaser, Barney G., and Anselm L. Strauss. 1967. *The Discovery of Grounded Theory: Strategies for Qualitative Research.* New York: Aldine.

Goldstein, Jeffrey H., Ralph L. Rosnow, Tamas Raday, Irwin Silverman, and George D. Gaskell. 1975. "Punitiveness in Response to Films Varying in Content: A Cross-National Field Study of Aggression." *European Journal of Social Psychology* 5:149–165.

Gordon, Linda. 1976. *Woman's Body, Woman's Right: Birth Control in America.* New York: Penguin Books.

Granberg, Donald. 1978. "Pro-Life or Reflection of Conservative Ideology? An Analysis of Opposition to Legalized Abortion." *Sociology and Social Research* 62:414–429.

Granberg, Donald, and Beth Wellman Granberg. 1980. "Abortion Attitudes, 1965–1980: Trends and Determinants." *Family Planning Perspectives* 12:250–261.

Grasmick, Harold G., Elizabeth Davenport, Mitchell B. Chamlin, and Robert J. Bursik, Jr. 1992. "Protestant Fundamentalism and the Retributive Doctrine of Punishment." *Criminology* 30:21–45.

Grasmick, Harold G., and Anne L. McGill. 1994. "Religion, Attribution Style, and Punitiveness Toward Juvenile Offenders." *Criminology* 32:23–46.

Greeley, Andrew M. 1989. *Religious Change in America.* Cambridge, Mass.: Harvard University Press.

Gregg, Richard B. 1994. "Rhetorical Strategies for a Culture War: Abortion in the 1992 Campaign." *Communication Quarterly* 42:229–243.

Greven, Philip. 1990. *Spare the Child: The Religious Roots of Punishment and the Psychological Impact of Physical Abuse.* New York: Alfred A. Knopf.

Gross, Samuel R. 1993. "The Romance of Revenge: Capital Punishment in America." *Law, Politics and Society* 13:71–104.

Gross, Samuel R., and Robert Mauro. 1989. *Death and Discrimination: Racial Disparities in Capital Sentencing.* Boston: Northeastern University Press.

Haas, Kenneth C. 1994. "The Triumph of Vengeance over Retribution: The United States Supreme Court and the Death Penalty." *Crime, Law and Social Change* 21:127–154.

Hamilton, Lawrence C. 1990. *Modern Data Analysis: A First Course in Applied Statistics.* Pacific Grove, Calif.: Brooks/Cole.

———. 1992. *Regression with Graphics: A Second Course in Applied Statistics.* Pacific Grove, Calif.: Brooks/Cole.

————. 1993. *Statistics with Stata 3.* Belmont, Calif.: Duxbury Press.

Haney, Lynne. 1996. "Homeboys, Babies, Men in Suits: The State and the Reproduction of Male Dominance." *American Sociological Review* 61:759–778.

Heffner, Richard D. 1984. *Democracy in America: Alexis de Tocqueville.* Abridged translation. New York: Mentor Books.

Henshaw, Stanley K. 1990. "Induced Abortion: A World Review, 1990." *Family Planning Perspectives* 22:76–89.

Henshaw, Stanley K., and Kathryn Kost. 1996. "Abortion Patients in 1994–1995: Characteristics and Contraceptive Use." *Family Planning Perspectives* 28:140–158.

Hill, Paul J. 1993. "Should We Defend Born and Unborn Children with Force?" *Defensive Action.* March.

Huff, C. Ronald, and Joseph E. Scott. 1975. "Deviance and Cognitive Consistency: Patterns of Public Attitudes Toward Deviance." *Sociology and Social Research* 59:330–343.

Ignatieff, Michael. 1978. *A Just Measure of Pain: The Penitentiary in the Industrial Revolution 1750–1850.* New York: Penguin Books.

————. 1983. "State, Civil Society and Total Institutions: A Critique of Recent Social Histories of Punishment." In *Social Control and the State,* edited by Stanley Cohen and Andrew Scull. New York: St. Martin's Press.

Jamieson, Kathleen Hall. 1992. *Dirty Politics: Deception, Distraction, and Democracy.* New York: Oxford University Press.

Jelen, Ted G. 1988. "Changes in the Attitudinal Correlations of Opposition to Abortion, 1977–1985." *Journal for the Scientific Study of Religion* 27:211–228.

Johnson, Stephen D., and Joseph B. Tamney. 1988. "Factors Related to Inconsistent Life-Views." *Review of Religious Research* 30:40–46.

Katz, Jack. 1989. *Seductions of Crime: Moral and Sensual Attractions in Doing Evil.* New York: Basic Books.

Katz, Yaacov J., and Mati Ronen. 1986. "A Cross-Cultural Validation of the Conservatism Scale in a Multi-Ethnic Society: The Case of Israel." *Journal of Social Psychology* 126:555–557.

Klein, Lawrence R., Brian Forst, and Victor Filatov. 1978. "The Deterrent Effect of Capital Punishment: An Assessment of the Estimates." In *Deterrence and Incapacitation: Estimating the Effects of Criminal Sanctions on Crime Rates,* edited by Alfred Blumstein, Jacqueline Cohen, and Daniel Nagin. Washington, D.C.: National Academy of Science.

Knox, William E., and Harriet J. Kupferer. 1971. "A Discontinuity in the Socialization of Males in the United States." *Merrill-Palmer Quarterly* 17:251–261.

Kohlberg, Lawrence, and Donald Elfenbein. 1976. "Moral Judgments about Capital Punishment: A Developmental Psychological View." In *Capital Punishment in the United States,* edited by Hugo Adam Bedau and Chester M. Pierce. New York: AMS Press.

Lake, Randall A. 1986. "The Metaethical Framework of Anti-Abortion Rhetoric." *Signs: Journal of Women in Culture and Society* 11:478–499.

Lambert, William W., Leigh M. Triandis, and Margery Wolf. 1959. "Some Correlates of Beliefs in the Malevolence and Benevolence of Supernatural Beings: A Cross-Societal Study." *Journal of Abnormal and Social Psychology* 48:162–169.

Luker, Kristin. 1984. *Abortion and the Politics of Motherhood.* Berkeley: University of California Press.

————. 1991. "Dubious Conceptions: The Controversy over Teen Pregnancy." *American Prospect* 5:73–83.

McCullough, Gary. 1993. "Griffin Is a Hero!" *Life Advocate.* May: 44.

McCutcheon, Allan L. 1987. "Sexual Morality, Pro-Life Values, and Attitudes Toward Abortion: A Simultaneous Latent Structure Analysis for 1978–1983." *Sociological Methods and Research* 16:256–275.

McGarrell, Edmund F. and Marla Sandys. 1996. "The Misperception of Public Opinion Toward Capital Punishment." *American Behavioral Scientist* 39:500–513.

McIntosh, William Alex, and Jon P. Alston. 1977. "Review of the Polls: Acceptance of Abortion among White Catholics and Protestants, 1962–1975." *Journal for the Scientific Study of Religion* 16:295–303.

McKeegan, Michelle. 1992. *Abortion Politics: Mutiny in the Ranks of the Right.* New York: Free Press.

MacKinnon, Catharine A. 1989. *Toward a Feminist Theory of the State.* Cambridge, Mass.: Harvard University Press.

Maloy, Kate, and Maggie J. Patterson. 1992. *Birth or Abortion? Private Struggles in a Political World.* New York: Plenum Press.

Marquart, James W., Sheldon Ekland-Olson, and Jonathon R. Sorensen. 1994. *The Rope, the Chair and the Needle: Capital Punishment in Texas, 1923–1990.* Austin: University of Texas Press.

Marty, Martin E., and R. Scott Appleby. 1991. *Fundamentalisms Observed.* Chicago: University of Chicago Press.

Mead, George Herbert. 1918. "The Psychology of Punitive Justice." *American Journal of Sociology* 23:577–602.

Mello, Michael. 1991. "On Metaphors, Mirrors and Murders: Theodore Bundy and the Rule of Law." *New York University Review of Law and Social Change* 18:887–938.

———. 1996. *Against the Death Penalty: The Relentless Dissents of Justices Brennan and Marshall.* Boston: Northeastern University Press.

Messerschmidt, James. 1987. "Feminism, Criminology and the Rise of the Female Sex 'Delinquent,' 1880–1930." *Contemporary Crises* 11:243–263.

———. 1993. *Masculinities and Crime: Critique and Reconceptualization of Theory.* Lanham, Md.: Rowman and Littlefield.

Milovanovic, Dragan. 1988. *A Primer in the Sociology of Law.* Albany: Harrow and Heston.

Nakell, Barry. 1982. "The Cost of the Death Penalty." In *The Death Penalty in America,* 3d. ed., edited by Hugo Adam Bedau. New York: Oxford University Press.

Nelsen, Hart M., Neil H. Cheek, Jr., and Paul Au. 1985. "Gender Differences in Images of God." *Journal for the Scientific Study of Religion* 24:396–402.

Nielsen, Joyce M. 1990. *Sex and Gender in Society: Perspectives on Stratification.* Second Edition. Prospect Heights, IL: Waveland Press.

Oakley, Ann. 1981. "Interviewing Women: A Contradiction in Terms." In *Doing Feminist Research,* edited by Helen Roberts. Boston: Routledge & Kegan Paul.

Page, Ann L., and Donald A. Clelland. 1978. "The Kanawha County Textbook Controversy: A Study of the Politics of Lifestyle Concern." *Social Forces* 57:265–281.

Passell, Peter. 1976. "The Deterrent Effect of the Death Penalty: A Statistical Test." In *Capital Punishment in the United States,* edited by Hugo Adam Bedau and Chester M. Pierce. New York: AMS Press.

Passell, Peter, and J. B. Taylor. 1975. "The Deterrence Controversy: A Reconsideration of the Time-Series Evidence." *Stanford Law Review* 28:61–80.

Patton, Michael Q. 1990. *Qualitative Evaluation and Research Methods.* 2d ed. Newbury Park, Calif.: Sage.

Pelikan, Jaroslav. 1988. *The Melody of Theology: A Philosophical Dictionary.* Cambridge, Mass.: Harvard University Press.

Penning, James M. 1994. "Pat Robertson and the GOP: 1988 and Beyond." *Sociology of Religion* 55:327–344.

Petchesky, Rosalind P. 1990. *Abortion and Woman's Choice: The State, Sexuality, and Reproductive Freedom.* Revised ed. Boston: Northeastern University Press.

Peterson, Ruth D., and William C. Bailey. 1991. "Felony Murder and Capital Punishment: An Examination of the Deterrence Question." *Criminology* 29:367–395.

Pierce, Glenn L., and Michael L. Radelet. 1991. "The Role and Consequences of the Death Penalty in American Politics." *New York University Review of Law and Social Change* 18:711–728.

Potts, Malcolm. 1985. "The Intellectual History of Abortion." In *Perspectives on Abortion,* edited by Paul Sachdev. Metuchen, N.J.: Scarecrow Press.

Polgar, Steven, and Ellen S. Fried. 1976. "The Bad Old Days: Clandestine Abortion among the Poor in New York City before Liberalization of the Abortion Law." *Family Planning Perspectives* 8:125–127.

Powell, Graham E., and Robert A. Stewart. 1978. "The Relationship of Age, Sex and Personality to Social Attitudes in Children Aged 8–15 Years." *British Journal of Social and Clinical Psychology* 17:307–317.

Purdum, Elizabeth D., and J. Anthony Paredes. 1989. "Capital Punishment and Human Sacrifice." In *Facing the Death Penalty: Essays on a Cruel and Unusual Punishment,* edited by Michael L. Radelet. Philadelphia: Temple University Press.

Quicker, John C. 1973. "A Consideration of the Relationship of 'Punitiveness' to Delinquency as Developed in Opportunity Theory." *The Journal of Criminal Law and Criminology* 64:333–338.

Radelet, Michael L. 1981. "Racial Characteristics and the Imposition of the Death Penalty." *American Sociological Review* 46:918–927.

———. 1989. *Facing the Death Penalty: Essays on a Cruel and Unusual Punishment.* Philadelphia: Temple University Press.

Radelet, Michael L., Hugo Adam Bedau, and Constance Putnam. 1992. *In Spite of Innocence: The Ordeal of 400 Americans Wrongly Convicted of Crimes Punishable by Death.* Boston: Northeastern University Press.

Radelet, Michael L., and Margaret Vandiver. 1988. *Capital Punishment in America: An Annotated Bibliography.* New York: Garland Press.

Raden, David. 1981. "Authoritarianism Revisited: Evidence for an Aggression Factor." *Social Behavior and Personality* 9:147–153.

Rankin, Joseph. 1979. "Changing Attitudes Toward Capital Punishment." *Social Forces* 58: 194–211.

Ranulf, Svend. 1938. *Moral Indignation and Middle Class Psychology.* New York: Schocken Books.

Rapoport, Elizabeth. 1991. "The Death Penalty and Gender Discrimination." *Law and Society Review* 25:367–383.

Ray, John J. 1985. "The Punitive Personality." *Journal of Social Psychology* 125:329–333.

Ray, J. J., and J. A. B. Ray. 1982. "Some Apparent Advantages of Subclinical Psychopathy." *Journal of Social Psychology* 117:135–142.

Reinharz, Shulamit. 1992. *Feminist Methods in Social Research.* New York: Oxford University Press.

Reuter, Peter. 1992. "Hawks Ascendant: The Punitive Trend of American Drug Policy." *Daedalus* 121:15–52.

Rhode, Deborah L. 1989. *Justice and Gender.* Cambridge, Mass.: Harvard University Press.

Richardson, James T., and Sandie Wightman Fox. 1972. "Religious Affiliation as a Predictor of Voting Behavior in Abortion Reform Legislation." *Journal for the Scientific Study of Religion* 11:347–359.

Rothman, Barbara Katz. 1989. *Recreating Motherhood: Ideology and Technology in a Patriarchal Society.* New York: W. W. Norton.

Rothman, David. 1995. "More of the Same: American Criminal Justice Policies in the 1990s." In *Punishment and Social Control: Essays in Honor of Sheldon L. Messenger,* edited by Thomas G. Blomberg and Stanley Cohen. New York: Walter de Gruyter.

Samaha, Joel. 1997. *Criminal Justice.* 4th ed. St. Paul, Minn.: West Publishing Co.

Scott, Jacqueline. 1989. "Conflicting Beliefs about Abortion: Legal Approval and Moral Doubts." *Social Psychology Quarterly* 52:319–326.

Scott, Jacqueline, and Howard Schuman. 1988. "Attitude Strength and Social Action in the Abortion Dispute." *American Sociological Review* 53:758–793.

Sellin, Thorsten. 1959. *The Death Penalty.* Philadelphia: American Law Institute.

Sheingold, Stuart, Toska Olson, and Jana Pershing. 1994. "Sexual Violence, Victim Advocacy, and Republican Criminology: Washington State's Community Protection Act." *Law and Society Review* 28:729–763.

Sidanius, Jim, Rose M. Brewer, Elliot Banks, and Bo Ekehammar. 1987. "Ideological Constraint, Political Interest and Gender: A Swedish-American Comparison." *European Journal of Political Research* 15:471–492.

Sidanius, Jim, Bo Ekehammar, and Jeffrey Lukowsky. 1983. "Social Status and Sociopolitical Ideology among Swedish Youth." *Youth and Society* 14:395–415.

Skolnick, Arlene S. 1987. *The Intimate Environment: Exploring Marriage and the Family.* 4th ed. Glenview, Ill.: Scott, Foresman.

Smith, Tom W. 1981. "Qualifications to Generalized Absolutes: 'Approval of Hitting' Questions on the GSS." *Public Opinion Quarterly* 45:224–230.

Solinger, Rickie. 1992. *Wake Up Little Susie: Single Pregnancy and Race before* Roe v. Wade. New York: Routledge.

Stanko, Elizabeth. 1985. *Intimate Intrusions: Women's Experience of Male Violence.* Boston: Routledge and Kegan Paul.

Straus, Murray A. 1991. "Discipline and Deviance: Physical Punishment of Children and Violence and Other Crime in Adulthood." *Social Problems* 38:133–154.

———. 1992. "Ten Myths about Spanking Children." Unpublished manuscript. Durham, N.H.: Family Research Laboratory.

———. 1994. *Beating the Devil Out of Them: Corporal Punishment by Parents and Its Effect on Children.* Boston: Lexington/Macmillan.

Straus, Murray A., Richard J. Gelles, and Suzanne K. Steinmetz. 1980. *Behind Closed Doors.* New York: Doubleday Books.

Sullivan, John L., George E. Marcus, and Daniel R. Minns. 1975. "The Development of Political Ideology: Some Empirical Findings." *Youth and Society* 7:148–170.

Sutherland, Edwin H. 1925. "Murder and the Death Penalty." *Journal of Criminal Law and Criminology* 15:522–536.

Tamney, Joseph B., Stepen D. Johnson, and Ronald Burton. 1992. "The Abortion Controversy: Conflicting Beliefs and Values in American Society." *Journal for the Scientific Study of Religion* 31:32–46.

Thomas, Charles W., and Samuel C. Foster. 1975. "A Sociological Perspective on Public Support for Capital Punishment." *American Journal of Orthopsychiatry* 45:641–657.

Tocqueville, Alexis de. 1899. *Democracy in America.* Volume II. Translated by Henry Reeve. New York: Colonial Press.

Tyler, Tom R., and Renee Weber. 1982. "Support for the Death Penalty: Instrumental Response to Crime, or Symbolic Attitude?" *Law and Society Review* 17:21–45.

Van den Haag, Ernest. 1982. "In Defense of the Death Penalty: A Practical and Moral Analysis." In *The Death Penalty in America,* 3d ed., edited by Hugo Adam Bedau. New York: Oxford University Press.

Vidmar, Neil, and Phoebe C. Ellsworth. 1976. "Public Opinion on the Death Penalty." In *Capital Punishment in the United States,* edited by Hugo Adam Bedau and Chester Pierce. New York: AMS Press.

———. 1982. "Research on Attitudes Toward Capital Punishment." In *The Death Penalty in America,* 3d ed., edited by Hugo Adam Bedau. New York: Oxford University Press.

Vidmar, Neil, and Dale T. Miller. 1980. "Social Psychological Processes Underlying Attitudes Toward Legal Punishment." *Law and Society Review* 14:565–602.

Von Drehle, David. 1995. *Among the Lowest of the Dead: The Culture of Death Row.* New York: Times Books.

von Hirsch, Andrew. 1986. *Doing Justice: The Choice of Punishments (Report to the Committee for the Study of Incarceration, 1976).* Boston: Northeastern University Press.

———. 1995. "The Future of Proportionate Sentencing." In *Punishment and Social Control: Essays in Honor of Sheldon L. Messenger,* edited by Thomas Blomberg and Stanley Cohen. New York: Walter de Gruyter.

Wald, Kenneth D., Dennis E. Owen, and Samuel S. Hill, Jr. 1988. "Churches as Political Communities." *American Political Science Review* 82:531–548.

———. 1990. "Political Cohesion in Churches." *Journal of Politics* 52:197–215.

Wanner, Richard A., and T. C. Caputo. 1987. "Punitiveness, Fear of Crime, and Perceptions of Violence." *Canadian Journal of Sociology* 12:331–344.

Warr, Mark, and Mark Stafford. 1984. "Public Goals of Punishment and Support for the Death Penalty." *Journal of Research on Crime and Delinquency* 21:95–111.

Wilcox, Clyde. 1990. "Race Differences in Abortion Attitudes: Some Additional Evidence." *Public Opinion Quarterly* 54:248–255.

Wilson, Glenn D., and Anthony H. Brazendale. 1973. "Social Attitude Correlates of Eysenck's Personality Dimensions." *Social Behavior and Personality* 1:115–118.

Young, Robert L. 1992. "Religious Orientation, Race and Support for the Death Penalty." *Journal for the Scientific Study of Religion* 31:76–87.

Zeisel, Hans, and Alec M. Gallup. 1989. "Death Penalty Sentiment in the United States." *Journal of Quantitative Criminology* 5:285–296.

Index

punitiveness, 182, 186, 199–203
socially disadvantaged, 91
solutions, 93–95, 120–122, 143–145,
183–185
Cook, Elizabeth A., 11, 54, 55, 56, 57, 58, 99
Cook, Kimberly J., 20, 65, 66
Cooper, David D., 23
Cozin, C., 199
Cuomo, Mario, 32, 42

Dahmer, Jeffrey, 50, 88, 114, 115
D'Anjou, L. M., 199
Davis, James A., 3, 55
Davis, Nanette, 12, 13
Davis, Richard Allen, 50–51, 116–117
de Parrie, Paul, 20
death penalty, 1, 10, 26, 29
aggravating circumstances, 9
brutality, 2, 24
cost of, 62, 63, 119, 176, 180
deterrence of, 1, 23, 24, 27, 37
executions, 2, 10, 23, 28
in Florida, 23, 71
in Georgia, 23
in Louisiana, 23
mitigating circumstances, 9
race and, 10, 27, 39
as retribution, 1
in Texas, 23
in Virginia, 23
and women, 29
death penalty opinions, 59–65, 66–68,
175–181
and age, 60
as barbaric, 86, 191
as deterrent, 176, 178
and drunk driving, 115
and education, 60
evolving standards of decency, 59
eye for an eye, 115, 138, 179, 200, 203. *See
also* Bible, Exodus
and gender, 60
and income, 60
innocents condemned, concern for, 87,
118–119, 140–141, 176, 179–180,
192–193
Marshall Hypothesis, 191

and race, 60–61
and region, 60, 61
and religion, 60, 61
retribution, 190–191, 192, 200
serial murders, 87, 114
symbolic explanations, 63–65
trends in, 59
typical supporter, 61
utilitarian explanations, 62–63
as vengeance, 191, 192, 193
Democratic Party, 31, 32, 33–35, 71
candidates, 33
conventions, (1988) 34, (1992) 42, (1996) 47
New Democrat, 31
platform, 1996, 47
primaries, 1992, 39–40
pro-life stance, 31
Southern Democrats, 35, 38
Doe v. Bolton, 13
Dole, Robert, 32, 33, 45–53, 169
and Christian Coalition, 48
in presidential debates, 51
Dorman, James E., 199
Dukakis, Michael, 33–39, 178
on abortion, 37–38
and anti-abortion protesters, 35
on death penalty, 34, 35, 37
1988 presidential campaign, 34, 36
Duke, David, 80, 210n2
Durham, Alexis, 59

Ebaugh, Helen Rose F., 54, 55
Ekehammar, Bo, 199
Ekland-Olson, Sheldon, 28
Elfenbein, Donald, 60
Ellis, Godfrey J., 197
Ellison, Christopher G., 197, 199
Ellsworth, Phoebe C., 28, 59, 60, 62, 63,
190–191
Elrod, H. Preston, 59
Epstein, Lee, 12, 13, 14, 15, 33, 38, 59, 60
Erikson, Kai T., 195
Erlich, Isaac, 24
Espy, Watt, 23
Estrich, Susan, 36
euthanasia, 91
Eysenck, 198–199